THE ART OF Bi
CARRIE MCKENZIE

LONG EARED OWL IN RED

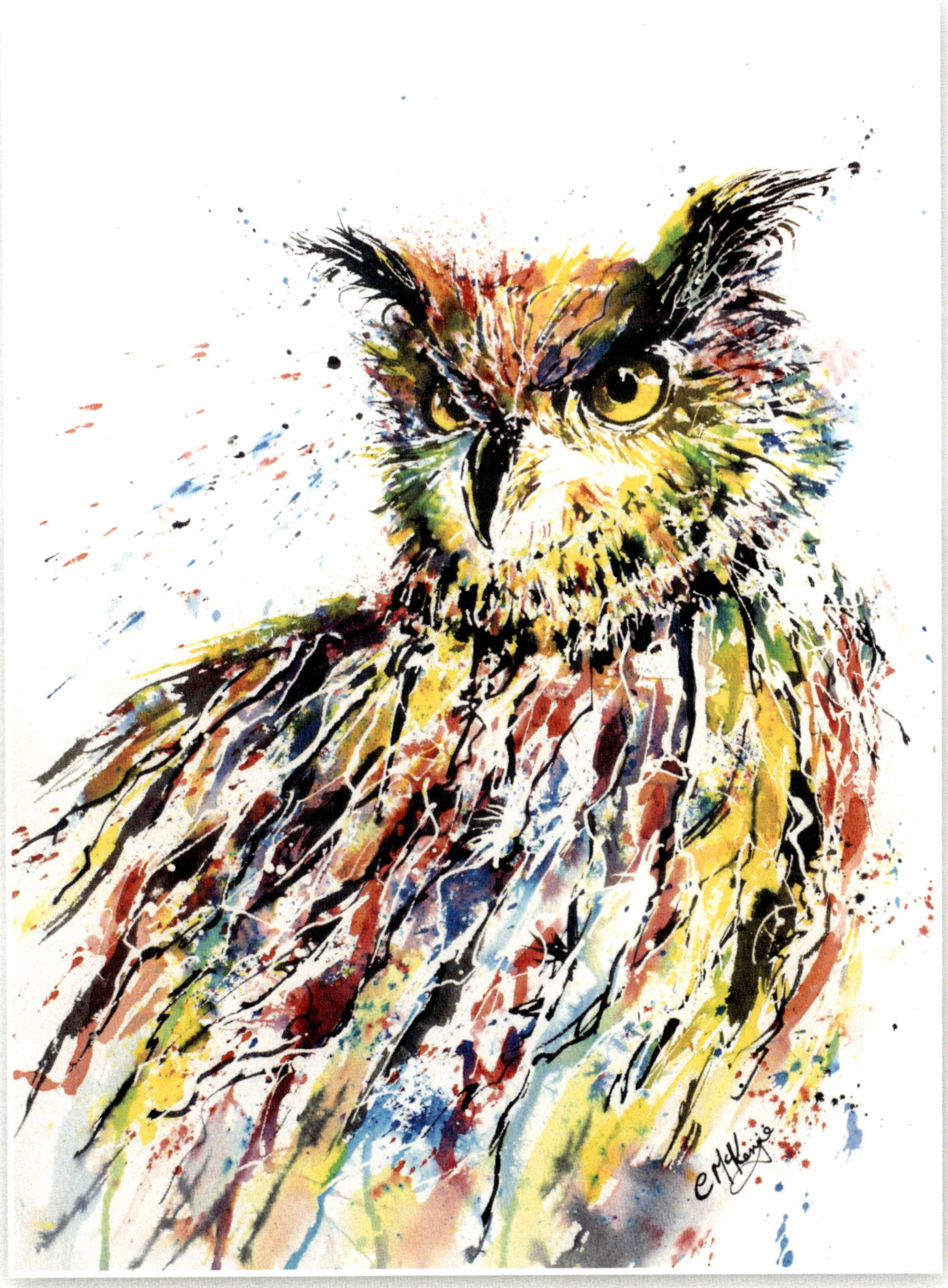

THE ART OF BRUSHO®

A guide to beautiful paintings

Discover the unique and delightful effects of
PAINTING WITH BRUSHO®
with

Carrie McKenzie

ISBN-13: 978-1999714109 (Roseforth Publishing)

ISBN-10: 1999714105

Roseforth Publishing
Halifax
England
roseforthpublishing@outlook.com

ACKNOWLEDGMENTS

Thanks to the many artists and tutors who have inspired me over the years and helped me to find my own painting style, especially those who enthused me to try out different mediums such as Brusho. Thanks also to my friends and family who have supported my journey in art and always been ready to advise or help.

DEDICATION

I dedicate this book to my children, for their wholehearted love and belief in me. Their unwavering support and encouragement have helped to make my creative dreams possible.

CONTENTS

THE ART OF BRUSHO®

INTRODUCTION

Welcome to my book The Art of Brusho. I want to share my own Brusho learning journey with you so that you can become more familiar with this wonderful art medium, and create your own striking painting using my tried and tested tips and techniques.

Although I paint in oils, acrylics, and pen and ink, I do love the magical effects of watercolour; it's such a thrill when paint and water mingle on the paper to shape the image in exquisite ways. So you can imagine how excited I was, to discover another water-based pigment, Brusho, and intrigued to find out how it compared with my much-loved watercolour.

I have discovered that, although there are similarities, Brusho has its own quirky and delightful properties. I can well understand why it has been described as 'little pots of magic'. Brilliant, bold and colourful, Brusho is great for creating contemporary striking artwork. Fun, expressive and unpredictable, Brusho is colour-rich, exciting and ideal for creating loose impressionistic paintings.

In fact, because it is so loose and expressive, many people find it easier to handle than traditional watercolour painting. It's an excellent medium for complete beginners, because you can achieve some fabulous effects relatively quickly. It's also useful for practising artists, particularly watercolourists, who want to loosen up a bit and develop a more spontaneous style.

Sometimes, it 's just great fun to try something a bit random and impulsive, experiment al little and get your creative juices flowing!

Another advantage of Brusho is that it is relatively inexpensive compared to watercolours and other painting mediums. A little goes a long, long way. Your Brusho paints should last you for many months, or even years! This should encourage you even more to free up your creative juices and not worry about 'wasting' paint.

Although I have covered some basic painting theory in this book, much of my painting style is based on emotion and expression. Whilst it is useful to know the 'golden rules' (such as good composition and perspective) an artist should never be afraid to challenge them – breaking the rule can often be what makes a successful and innovative painting.

Part of the journey is learning to lose a bit of control and let the paint do its own thing. The very nature of Brusho's unpredictability means that you get lots of 'happy accidents' along the way. I have provided step-by-step demonstrations that are designed to introduce you to different techniques and opportunities. Your versions will inevitably look somewhat different to mine because Brusho performs differently on every occasion in its special and random way. So be prepared for Brusho to introduce freedom into your work, and create your own distinctive paintings using these exercises and projects as guidelines rather than exact copies.

Above all, be ready to celebrate and enjoy the individuality of what you create with a magical explosion of colour with Beautiful Brilliant Brusho!

Carrie

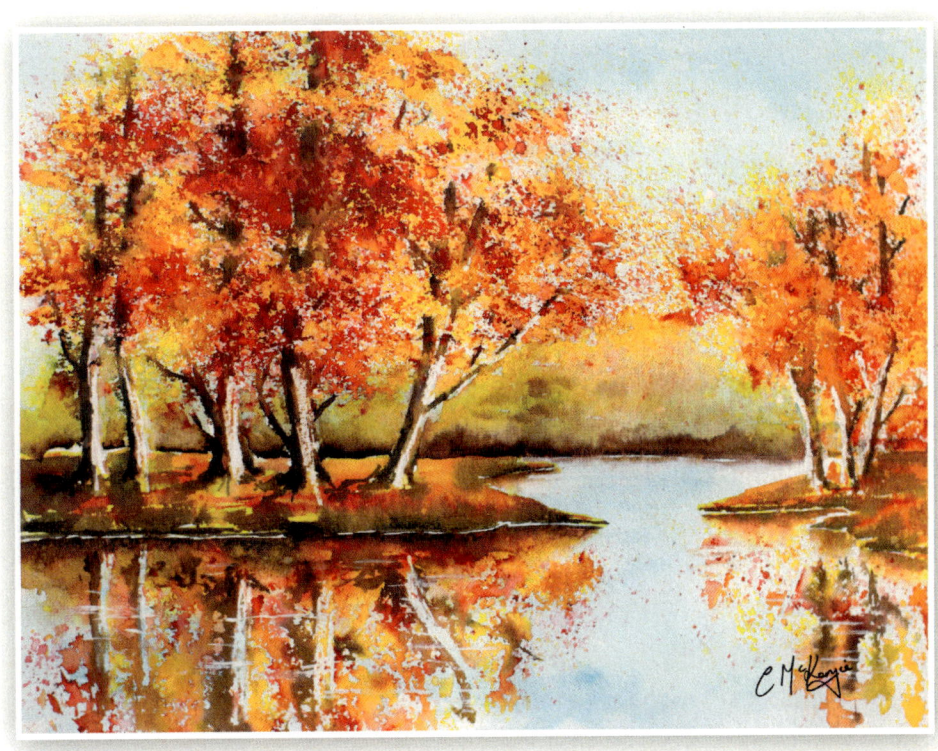

1 : BRUSHO ESSENTIALS

Because Brusho is a water-soluble pigment, you can use many of the same techniques as for watercolour. Even if you are a skilled watercolourist, it's worth following and practising the same techniques with Brusho in order to become familiar with the way this very distinctive pigment performs.

As you work through this book, you will learn some of the techniques that work beautifully with Brusho pigments, and also develop an understanding of its key advantages and disadvantages.

This first chapter covers the following essentials:

The basic materials and equipment you need to start creating your own Brusho art.

The basic elements that work together to create a successful painting: Composition, Tonal Values and Colour (scale and perspective are also important). Although you can follow the step-by-step exercises and projects without reading about these first, it will help you immensely to understand some of the underpinning theory before you put it into practice. This will prove invaluable when you compose your own paintings.

ESSENTIAL MATERIALS & EQUIPMENT

Brusho® Paint

Let's start with the most exciting material – Brusho paint itself! Brusho is a very intense paint powder that dilutes with water to give glorious bursts of colour.

Manufactured by Colourcraft Ltd, Sheffield, England, Brusho® comes in 34 highly concentrated colours, which the company advise is completely safe and non-toxic (in fact it is often used in schools); and is as lightfast as watercolour.

It is also extremely economical; a starter set of 12 Brusho paints costs little more than a single 14ml tube of artist watercolour paint. Because the pigment is so intense you don't need much of it, so a little goes a long way. Your Brusho paint should last you for many years. Because it mixes with water, you don't need to mix it with any other expensive mediums, allowing you to experiment and practise your painting skills to your heart's content.

The starter pack of 12 colours in 15g pots, usually sufficient for most people to begin with, consists of:

Black, Dark Brown, Ultramarine, Turquoise, Emerald Green, Leaf Green, Purple, Brilliant Red, Scarlet, Orange, Yellow and Lemon

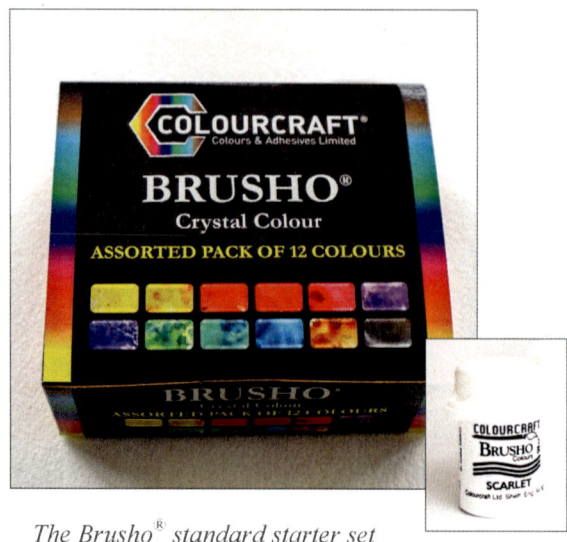
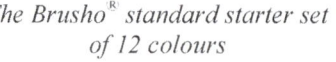

The Brusho® standard starter set of 12 colours

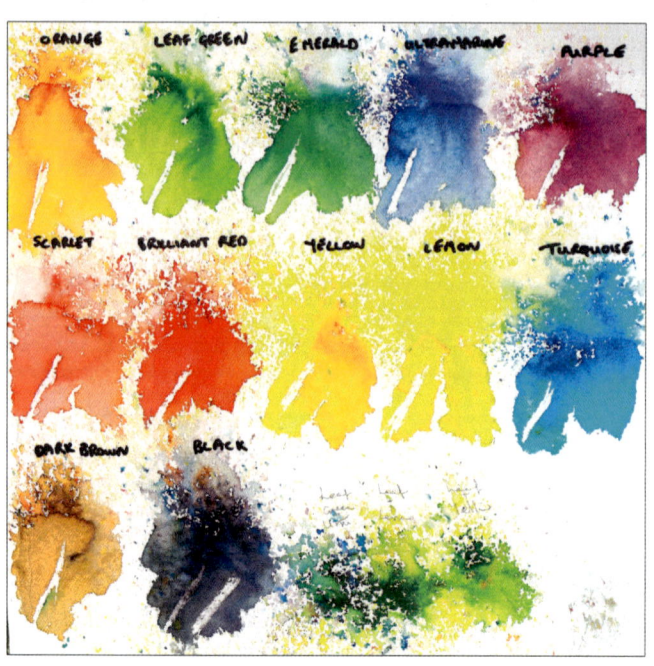

Using the paint

- Brusho paint comes in small plastic pots with the colour name labelled on the side of them.

- It's a great temptation when you get your first set of Brusho to want to use every colour in the box in every painting. However, as with most painting mediums, I find a limited palette works best.

- If too many colours mingle on the paper it is likely to result in the dreaded mud! Too many colours also result in confusion and lack of harmony in the painting.

- Brusho paints are inter-mixable, allowing you to create a countless number of different colours. For example, mixing Ultramarine with Yellow will give you an earthier green suitable for foliage.

- When mixing Brusho crystals in your palette, try to keep the colours as pure and uncontaminated as possible – the powdered grains are very fine and just a few stray speckles of Purple will ruin a Lemon wash. For this reason, I usually use separate palettes for my light and dark colours.

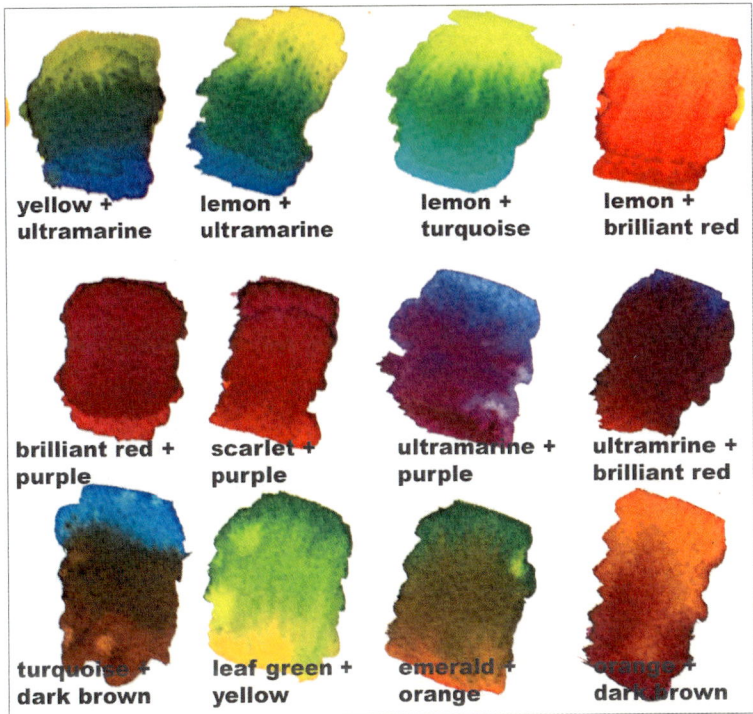

A few colour mix examples

STUDIO TIP

- *Resist the urge to take the lid off the top of the pots as the tiny speckles fly everywhere. Instead, make a couple of tiny holes in the lid by piercing it with a cocktail stick, pencil or bradawl, so you can use it like a saltshaker. Although this means you have to store the pots upright afterwards it does prevent over-using and wasting the pigment, as well as cross-contamination with other colours. Alternatively, you can just pierce a single hole in the small indentation in the middle of the lid and keep covered with a notice-board pin.*

- *Write the name of the colour on the top of the pots in waterproof pen so that you don't have to keep lifting them up when you are working to find the right colour – you will be amazed how much time this saves you later, and also avoids picking up the wrong colour by mistake. If you have some coloured waterproof pens you can also mark the top of the pot with the appropriate colour.*

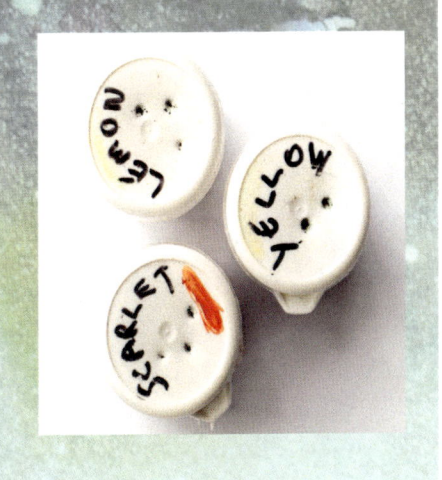

Brusho's quirky crystals

One of the reasons Brusho is so unpredictable is because small speckles of other colours often appear in a main colour.

This is particularly evident with the Black pigment, which delightfully includes stray speckles of red, blue and yellow. Artists often make their own black using these three primary colours, so in a way it makes perfect sense for the colours to be nestling in the black powder. However, you rarely come across the splits so obviously in other art pigments.

You have to learn to live with this characteristic and embrace it in your paintings. In fact for this very reason, Black is one of my favourite Brusho colours. You will soon gain confidence to accept and marvel at the unforeseen reactions that you tend to get with Brusho crystals.

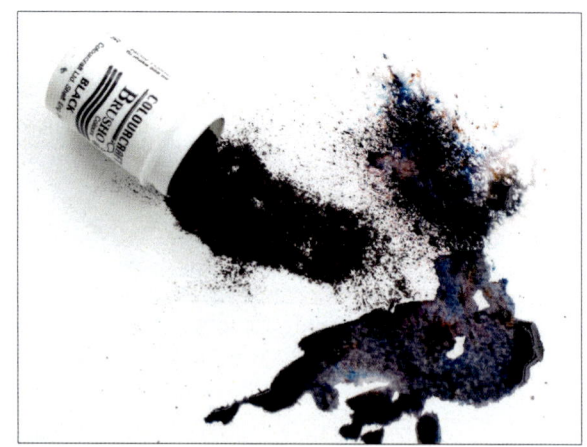

Brushes

You will need a selection of watercolour brushes in various sizes. Although you can use your best quality watercolour brushes, I prefer to keep the brushes that I use for Brusho completely separate. You don't need to buy expensive brushes, there are some very good synthetic-fibre brushes available nowadays that are a good alternative to sable. They are less costly but still quite springy and responsive. As a minimum, I would recommend round brushes in sizes 12, 6 and 2 and a rigger brush for fine lines and details.

I also have a couple of Chinese-style brushes similar to those used by calligraphers because they hold a lot of paint but come to a fine point. If I'm painting large sky areas I will also use a 1.5" or 2" hake.

It is important to ensure that your brushes are kept scrupulously clean in between mixing, or painting, different colours in order to keep them pure and fresh. To avoid having to stop and clean the brush each time I change colour – which means having to stop and interrupt the painting process – I do use a lot more brushes. When I change colour I simply use a different brush.

At the end of a painting session, keep your brushes in good condition by cleaning them thoroughly in warm soapy water, then rinse and dry with some absorbent paper towel. (Save old brushes to use with masking fluid.)

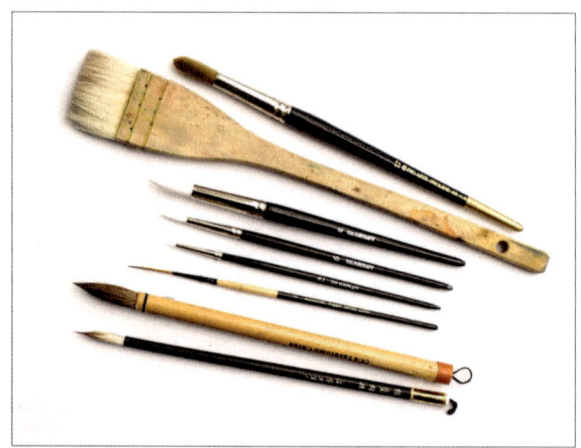

Paper

The majority of the projects in this book are carried out on watercolour paper. I believe choosing a good quality paper is one of the most important aspects to consider.

For Brusho, I usually use Bockingford or Saunders Waterford NOT 425gsm (200lb). I don't stretch my paper, as I like to be able to lift the paper and move it around to get the paint flowing, so I find this slightly heavier medium weight more suitable. But the standard 140lb would also work for most paintings.

STUDIO TIPS

Try to use a large brush for most of your work. If you use a small brush, your work will be tight and fiddly. So reserve the small brush for adding small details. Using a large brush with a good point will help to make your work loose, free and spontaneous.

To avoid having to stop and clean the brush each time I change colour – which means having to stop and interrupt the painting process – I do use a lot more brushes. When I change colour I simply use a different brush.

Beware of cheap lightweight paper as it tends to cockle when applying water and the results are usually disappointing.

Miscellaneous equipment

- *a clean palette with separate wells* for mixing the colours with water – a cheap white plastic one will do. I do use several palettes in order to keep the lighter coloured paints away from the darker ones, but this is not essential.
- *two large water containers* so that you can keep one for clean water and one for mixing – old jam jars or large yoghurt pots will suffice – I use two large plastic measuring jugs that I picked up in a bargain store for £1 each.
- *a water sprayer/atomiser* – a cheap plant sprayer or old kitchen cleaner spray will do. I have a few different types as I find they tend to spray in slightly different ways giving different results – some sprinkle, some spritz and some spray, you just need to experiment and adjust the nozzles to become familiar with the effects.
- *paper kitchen towel* – this is vital for mopping up excess water either from the painting or your brush, or for lifting paint by dabbing it directly on the paint. You can also use it to mask areas of the painting you want to protect whilst spritzing or spraying other areas with Brusho.
- *an old hand towel* to mop up excess water when you are spraying large areas of paper and moving it around.
- *pencil and putty rubber* or plastic eraser
- *black waterproof ink pen* - these come in different sizes but just a 0.5 will suffice
- *drawing board* – to rest your work on or a piece of hardboard will do
- *masking tape* – use to tape your paper to the board (although I rarely do this) or to use as a mask on the paper for painting a straight line, eg a horizon level
- *masking fluid* – use to preserve white paper when applying a coloured wash on top. It comes in various colours.
- *Brusho® wax resist stick* or chunk of candle wax from an old candle – use to preserve white paper
- *an apron* to protect your clothes – Brusho is a an intense pigment and although it washes out with water, it could spoil your best white top!
- *plastic covering or old newspaper* to protect the table
- *disposable gloves* if you want to protect your hands – although brusho does wash off, it can leave some temporary staining.
- *ruler* – for drawing straight lines – I use a clear plastic one
- *pipette* – useful for adding clean water to mix paint in the palette as it avoids dirtying the water by repeatedly dipping a colour-loaded brush in it
- *hairdryer* – useful for speeding up the drying time – but use with caution as the paint needs time to mix and spread and do its own thing
- *household salt* – you can also use coarse sea or rock salt if you have it
- *acrylic inks* – sepia and black, to add additional vibrancy and interest to brusho paintings
- *granulation medium* – to create mottled granular patterns in the brusho paint; works beautifully when also used in conjunction with acrylic inks.

(don't be put off by the long list, they're all reasonably cheap or even cheerfully free!)

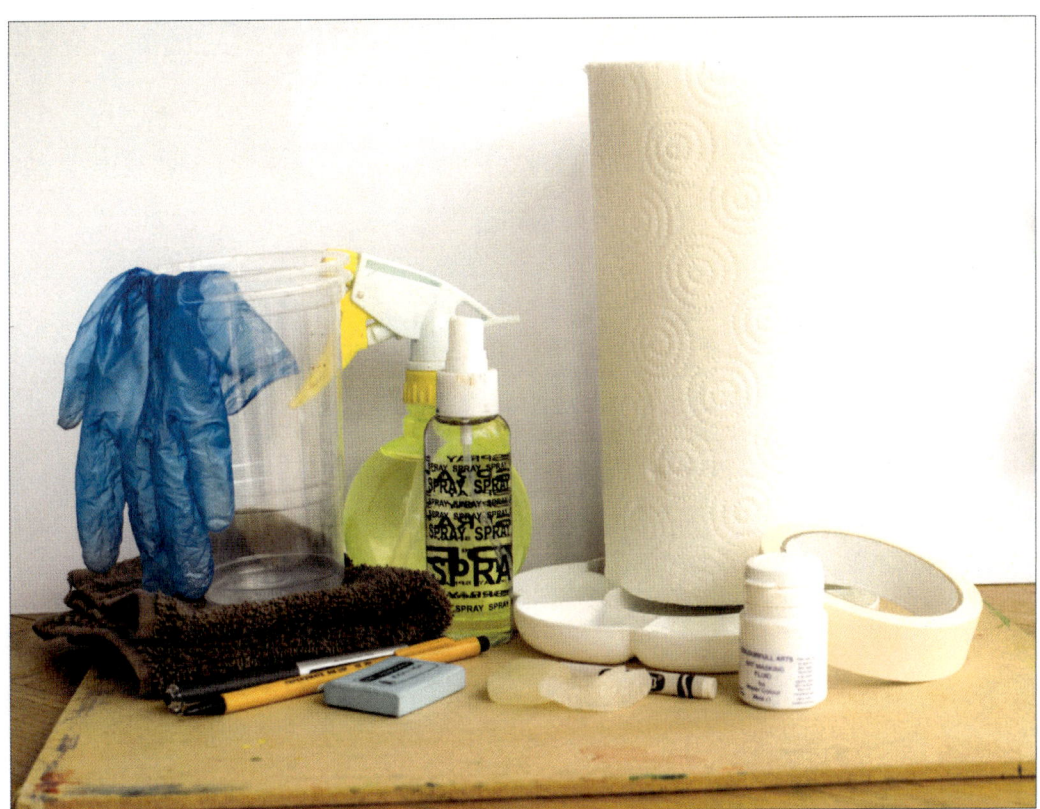

ESSENTIAL ELEMENTS OF A PAINTING

Composition and design

True to the old adage that a picture speaks a thousand words, art is "a visual language". Verbal language is made up of letters, words and sentences to convey complex meanings, ie the language we speak. Similarly, visual language is made up of various visual elements and principles that give structure to a painting.

Composition is the way that these visual elements are planned and put together to create meaningful art, express ideas and convey mood. There are certain "rules" to composition, although I prefer to think of them as guidelines because sometimes pushing the boundaries can give a painting a certain edge. However, deciding to break a rule can be part of the composing process, so it's useful to understand some of the basics even if it's just to change them! Here are a few pointers on composition and design

Use a viewfinder: Use two L-shaped pieces of card like a frame to isolate the interesting part of a busy scene. Move around the scene, make it bigger or smaller, and try different crops for the most attractive composition. You could even try slanting it for an unusual, eye-catching viewpoint.

Focal point: After choosing what you want to paint, consider what is the most important bit of the painting that you want the viewer's eye to rest on, ie main focal point or centre of interest. You can emphasise the focal point in the composition through the arrangement of shapes, tone, colour, hard lines, contrast, etc.

The rule of thirds: One of the most popular methods for positioning the focal point is to divide your painting into nine equal parts by drawing two equally spaced vertical lines and two equally spaced horizontal lines. Then choose one of the four intersecting points on the grid to position the focal point.

Making one area of the painting more dominant creates imbalance, tension and consequently more interest. You could divide into fifths, sevenths or even tenths, as long as you create this imbalance. Another method is to use an "S" or "Z' shape; often used in landscape paintings, it draws the eye into the painting using natural lines.

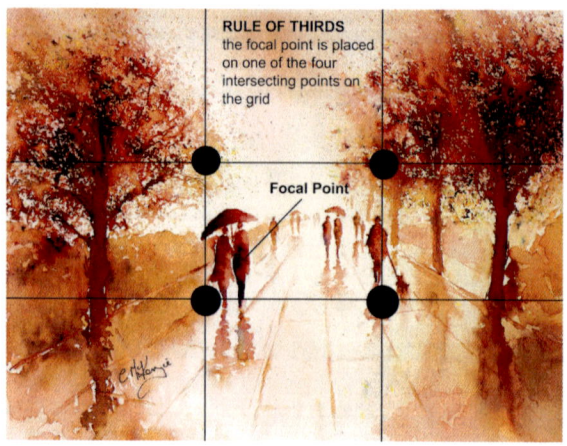

RULE OF THIRDS
the focal point is placed on one of the four intersecting points on the grid

Focal Point

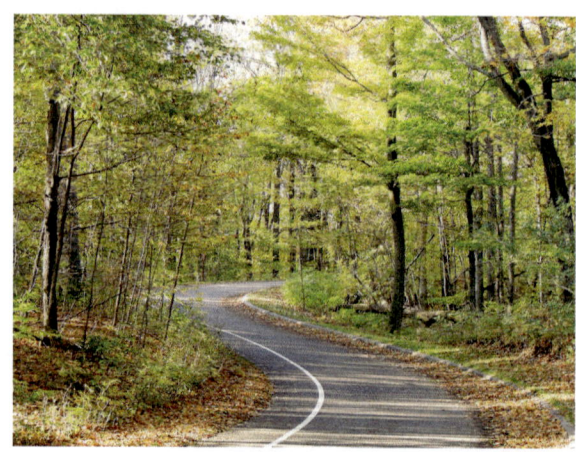

The rule of odds: Having an odd number of items stops your eye and brain from grouping or pairing them up, and keeps your eye moving around the composition. If you do depict a pair, alter their size and position.

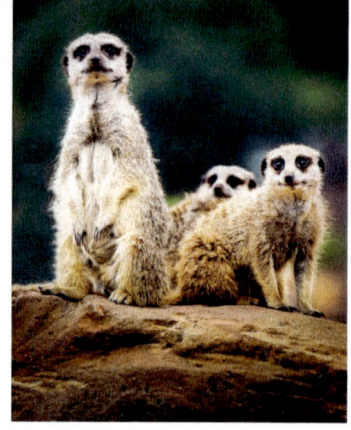

The addition of the third meerkat peeping out from the back of the photograph provides the rule of odds balance as well as giving the image more depth

Unity, variety and imbalance: There should be unity within the overall composition with nothing sticking awkwardly out of place or looking like it doesn't belong. However, too much unity is static and boring. It is important to include variety within the unity for a strong composition that keeps the viewer interested.

Make sure that tonal values (lights, darks and mid-tones) are in different amounts. Include a mix of hard and soft edges in the painting, using the harder edges where you want to draw attention.

Vary the space between the elements in your composition, the angles they lie at, and their sizes to make your painting more interesting.

Even a portrait can be positioned so the face or figure is slightly off-centre.

Contrast: Using black and white right next to each other creates the most powerful contrast in tone.

Strong differences between dark and light colours will draw the viewer's attention to a particular spot very easily. Too much contrast, however, can become chaotic.

Movement, rhythm and pattern: Create movement with real or implied lines – for example, the position of figures, the waves of the sea.

Repetition of any of the painting elements in a consistent way creates pattern, and in a varied way creates rhythm. Patterns and repetition are visually appealing, and enliven a picture, but should not be too obvious.

More interest is obtained when the pattern is interrupted. The more curves or diagonals you have the more movement you will put into your painting.

Suggested lines our eyes have a natural attraction to lines so it can be useful to use natural lines (real or implied) to lead the viewer's eye into the painting.

Examples could be the lines of a person's arm, a shaft of light, or the branch of a tree, which are strategically placed to point towards the main subject. Linear elements such as trees, roads, and rivers should not point towards the edge or run out of the picture.

Avoid roads, paths and rivers having straight lines, use an s-movement or curve instead.

Depth: This is the illusion of distance.

Depth creates a three dimensional effect, making objects feel closer, or further away. Good use of perspective encourages the eye to move from foreground to background.

Elements such as paths, walls, or groups of people, receding into the distance will create the impression of depth.

Things get bluer and lighter as they recede – distant hills can look completely blue. Add more detail in the foreground, less in the background.

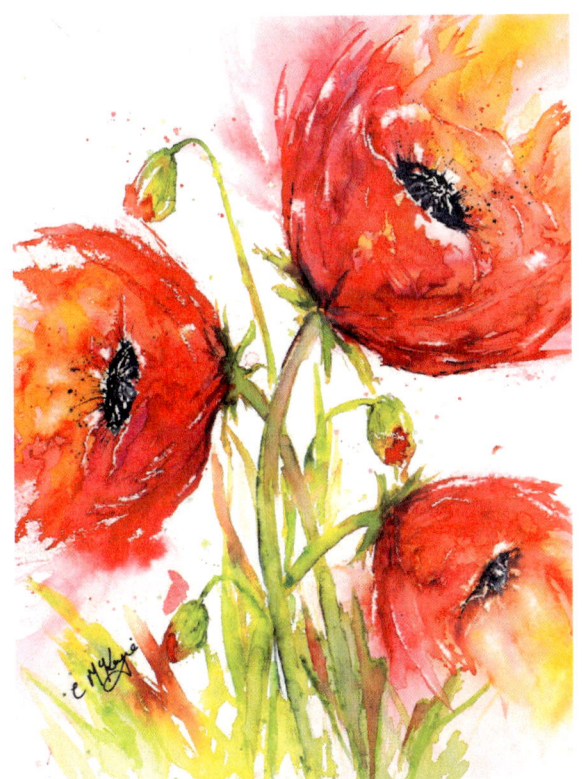

There is variety of shape, size, angle and tone in the poppy heads and the leaves. The strongest contrast is in the dark black centres, which move the viewer's attention around the painting.

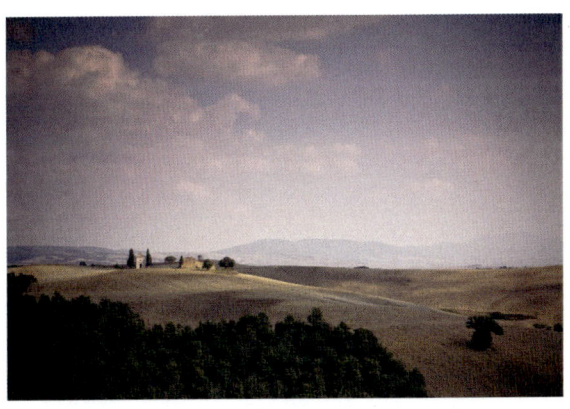

Notice how blue, and light in tone the distant hills appear to be in this photograph. The slightly curved line of the track leads the eye towards the cluster of buildings that is the centre of interest.

Tonal values

By adding different amounts of water to the Brusho pigment, a wide range of tones can be produced from a single colour, and still more from mixed colours.

Along with shape and composition, tonal value is one of the most important elements of a painting. Tone simply refers to the lightness or darkness of a colour. Despite the simplicity of the definition, tone can often be confused with colour and quite difficult to assess. If you strip out the colour of an image by converting it to black and white, the different shades of grey would be the range of tones. A good balance of lights, darks, and mid-tones can turn a flat lifeless painting into an exciting, dynamic work of art. Not all colours will yield the same range of tones. Yellow, for instance, will not give as wide a range of tones as Ultramarine, because it is not a 'dark' colour to start with.

Areas of light and dark also convey a 3-dimensional illusion to the subject matter, giving it form, as demonstrated in the grey scale image of an apple. Our eyes are drawn to a light element against a dark element, which is why many artists place their lightest light next to their darkest dark, right where they want to draw attention to the focal point of interest.

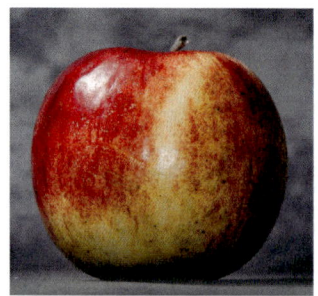

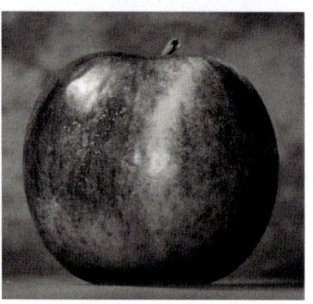

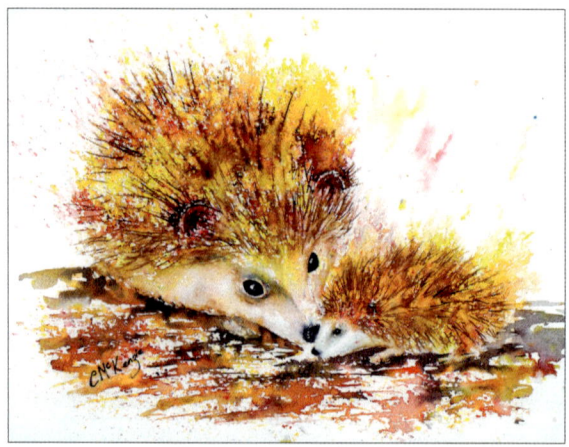

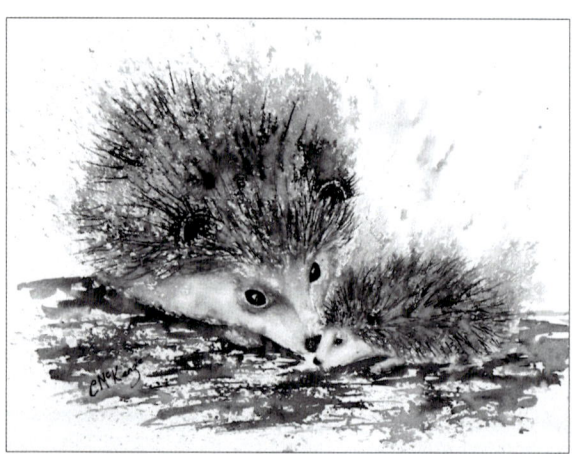

The grey scale image of the hedgehogs shows the full range of tones in the painting. The centre of interest is the mother's eyes keeping watch over her offspring – the darkest darks are her pupils, and placed right next to them are the lightest lights of catch lights in her eye.

What you perceive to be a dark colour may, in fact, have a light tonal value, because tones can appear darker or lighter depending on what is going on around them. For this reason, a successful painting doesn't always need a wide tonal range; by using relative tone effectively. a limited range of tones can work beautifully.

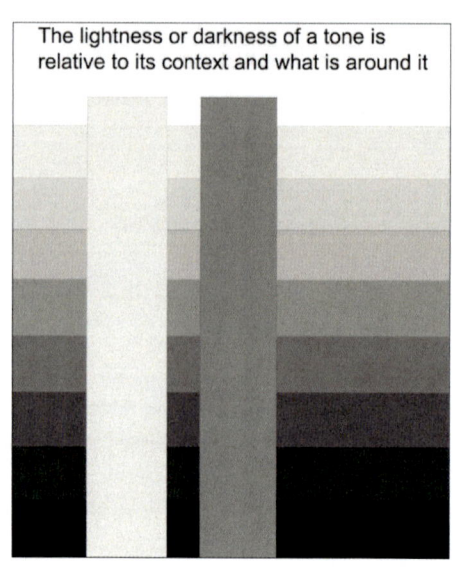

The lightness or darkness of a tone is relative to its context and what is around it

Here are a few techniques to help you see your painting in monochrome as it progresses so that you can make tonal adjustments where needed along the way:

- Make a **black and white thumbnail sketch** to plan and assess where the tonal values need to be. Remember to include the background tones – it's part of the overall tonal structure and will affect everything else in the painting (even experienced artists can struggle with planning the background)

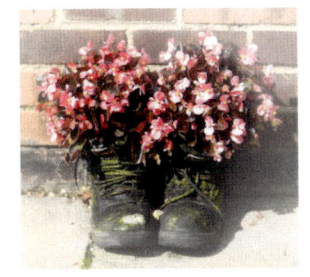 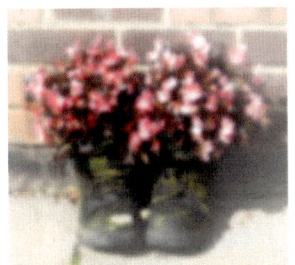

- **Squinting** at the painting reduces the mid-tones, leaving only the darks and lights. This is a useful and quick method although it doesn't always identify the subtleties of the mid-tones and it's still easy to be distracted by colour.

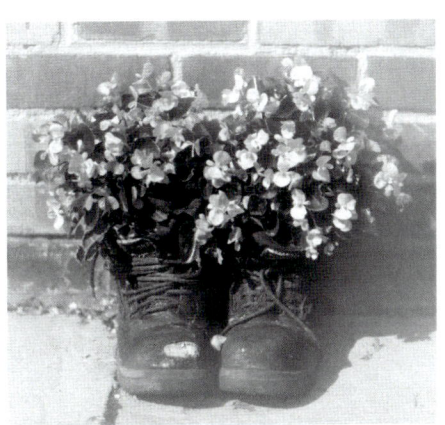

- **Convert the image to black and white (greyscale)** via a digital camera that has an option to view an image in black and white before actually taking a photograph of it, value.

    Or, convert a colour photograph to a black and white one using photo editing software (or a photocopier) and study the tones on a printed image or on screen.

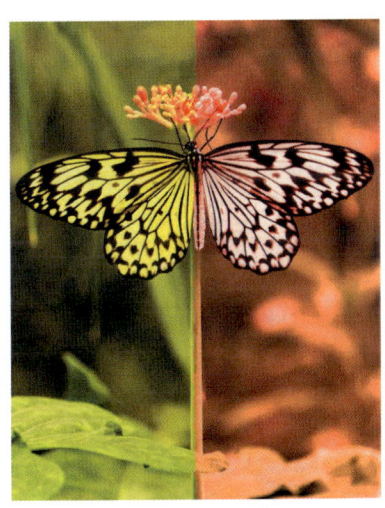

- Another quick method is to **put a red filter over your image**. The red dominates all other colours and just relays the tonal values back to your eye. Note how much paler in tone the butterfly wing appears under the red filter. I've used the red filter in Photoshop, but you can use a piece of red Plexiglas or even some red plastic from an office file.

STUDIO TIP

Always do a final check on a finished painting to make sure you haven't lost your darkest darks and lightest lights. If it looks bland and lifeless, it's not finished and you need to do more work on the tones.

BASIC COLOUR THEORY & THE COLOUR WHEEL

As with any other painting medium, knowing how Brusho colours behave and influence each other is fascinating and worth spending time on. As well as understanding why some colour mixes work better than others, it's also important to consider the emotional effect of different colours in your painting.

You can choose colours that match reality, or take advantage of artistic licence and use them to create mood and feelings, or to portray your own artistic vision. Whole books have been written on colour theory, and there are many different versions of the colour wheel. For the purposes of this book I will attempt to keep it simple and relate it, where possible, to the Brusho starter pack of 12 colours.

Primary colours

Red, Blue and Yellow are the triad of primary colours from which all other colours can be made. But you can't mix a primary colour from other colours.

You can complete a whole painting with just the three primaries, as mixing them in different strengths creates many secondary colours.

There are many different shades of primary colours (ie different reds, blues and yellows) in the Brusho paint range. For instance, Brilliant Red is a more bluey-red than Scarlet, which is a more orangey-red.

Secondary colours

Mixing 2 primary colours together produces the secondary colours. You can use your Brusho primary colours in different proportions to mix countless different secondary colours.

- blue + red = violet or purple
- red + yellow = orange
- yellow + blue = green.

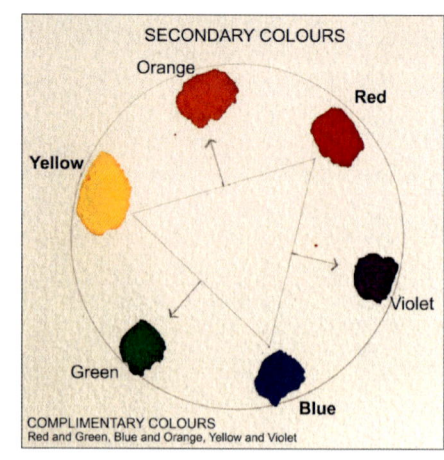

PRIMARY COLOURS TRIAD

Yellow   Red   Blue

SECONDARY COLOURS

Orange   Red   Yellow   Violet   Green   Blue

COMPLIMENTARY COLOURS
Red and Green, Blue and Orange, Yellow and Violet

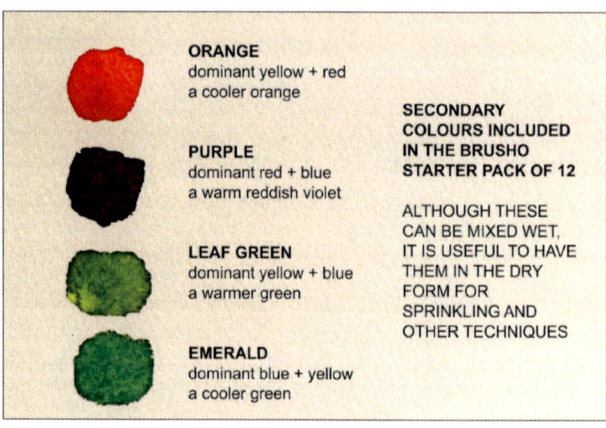

ORANGE
dominant yellow + red
a cooler orange

PURPLE
dominant red + blue
a warm reddish violet

LEAF GREEN
dominant yellow + blue
a warmer green

EMERALD
dominant blue + yellow
a cooler green

SECONDARY COLOURS INCLUDED IN THE BRUSHO STARTER PACK OF 12

ALTHOUGH THESE CAN BE MIXED WET, IT IS USEFUL TO HAVE THEM IN THE DRY FORM FOR SPRINKLING AND OTHER TECHNIQUES

These secondary colours become the complementary colours of the primaries, which is explained more fully further on. The Brusho® starter pack of 12 includes some pots of ready mixed secondary colours. This is useful because although you can mix them in your palette from primaries, there are times when you will want to use secondary colours in their dry powder form for the sprinkling techniques that you will learn later in this book.

Tertiary colours

Mixing a primary colour with a secondary colour produces the tertiary colours (ie there are now 3 colours in the mix).

The proportion of primary and secondary colour in the mix, plus the amount of water added, will affect the quality and intensity of the tertiary colours. For example, mixing a primary colour yellow with a secondary colour orange will give you an orangey-yellow

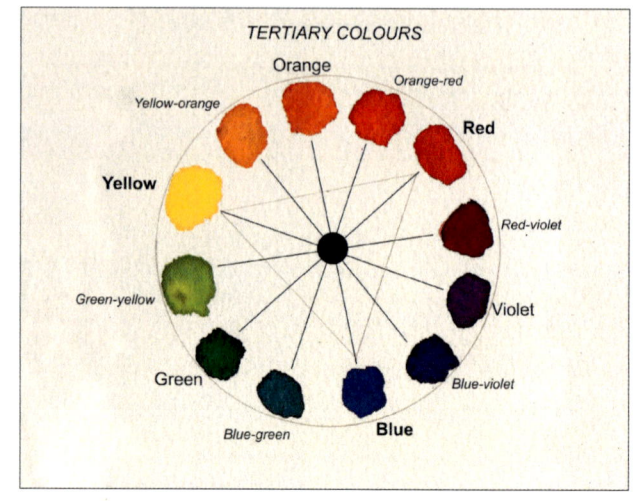

TERTIARY COLOURS

Orange   Orange-red   Yellow-orange   Red   Yellow   Red-violet   Green-yellow   Violet   Green   Blue-violet   Blue-green   Blue

Colour temperature

This can be a confusing topic because people often have different perceptions about what colours they feel to be warm or cool. The basic principles are that:

- warm colours are considered to be red, orange and yellow.
- cool colours are considered to be blue, green and violet/purple.
- within each colour group there are warm and cool versions. For example, although blue is said to be a cool colour, ultramarine is a warm blue because it leans towards red. Cobalt blue is a cool blue because it leans away from red

Colours can also be considered as being warmer or cooler depending on which colour they sit closest to on the colour wheel. For example:

- a warm yellow will be nearer to orange whereas a cool yellow will be nearer to green.
- a warm red will be nearer to orange, whereas a cool red will be nearer to violet.
- a warm blue will be nearer to red, whereas a cool blue will be nearer to green.

The Brusho starter pack of 12 colours comes with a triad of cool primary colours and a triad of warm primary colours. It is useful to have both a 'warm' and 'cool' version of each primary colour in order to obtain the appropriate colour temperature for a painting.

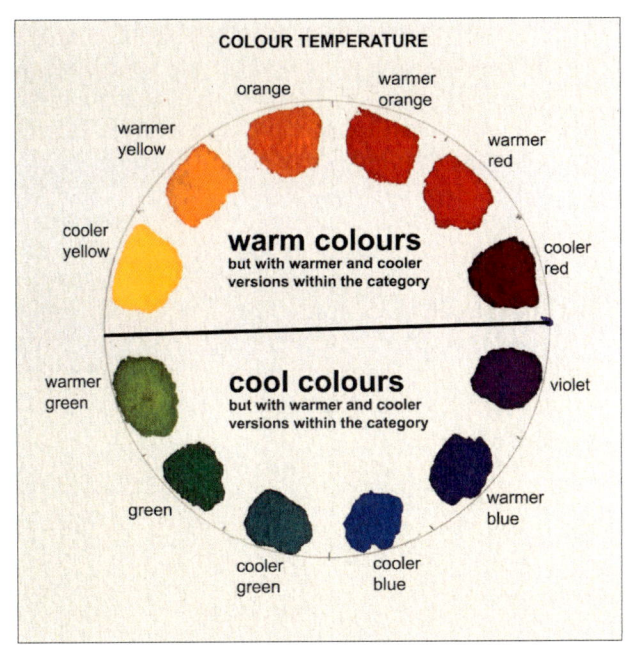

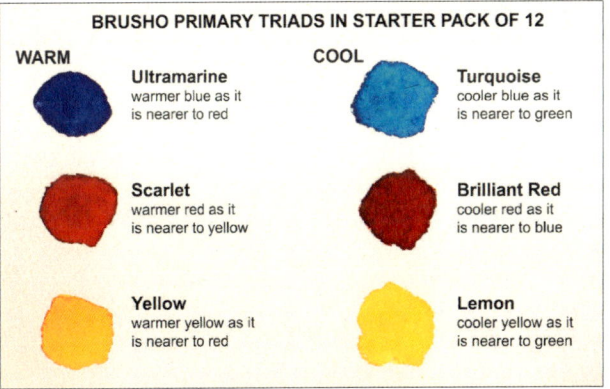

The guiding principle of colour temperature is that warm colours visually come forward whereas cool colours recede and take your eye into the distance.

If you put a warm colour, such as Scarlet, in the distance, the viewer's eye will jump across and miss the main subject. Generally, distant objects are bluer, greyer and lighter.

It's important to balance the colour temperature in your painting so that it is neither 100% cool nor 100% warm. Avoid a perfectly equal split, one temperature needs to dominate - a 75% : 25% ratio works well. Remember that if you mix warm primary colours, you will get warm secondary colours, and vice versa.

Even if you create a totally yellow painting you can include warm and cool passages within it by including a variety of cool and warm yellows. The overall mood (colour temperature) of the painting will be warm because you are using yellow (which gives the impression of warmth when we look at it). You can make your painting even warmer by adding a touch of red to the yellow, or cooler by adding a touch of blue

Natural light tends to create warm shadows, so use warm colours in the shadows to make them look alive. Anything affected by a blue sky will take on a cooler temperature.

Warm and cool colours help to describe the shadow and light side of shapes, they give them form rather than being flat. Knowledge of how colour temperature affects the mood and emotion of your painting will improve your work immensely.

Complementary colours and neutral Colours

Complementary colours sit diagonally opposite each other on the colour wheel, and provide the most contrast. Green is the complementary colour for red, orange is the complementary colour for blue, and violet is the complementary colour for yellow.

When complementary colours are placed side-by-side they have a powerful effect, the one making the other seem more intense and bright. Introducing a small patch of red in a large area of green foliage will make both the red and the green seem much brighter. This high contrast creates vibrancy especially when used at full saturation. So to make a colour stand out, just put a tiny splash of its complement next to it.

Mixing a primary, such as Brilliant Red, with its complement, Green, will dull or neutralise the colour towards browns and greys. If you mix to all three primary colours (red, blue and yellow) together you will get a non-colour or neutral colour, ie browns, greys or even a black, depending on the ratio of the mixes. By managing the proportions of each colour you can create a splendid range of subtle, neutral tones that depict those of the natural world.

However, it's worth remembering that the more colours are mixed together the less pure the resulting colour will be and you need to be careful not to create the dreaded mud!

The trick with all this is, if you want to produce bright, vibrant colours, don't use red, blue and yellow in the same mix. But if the colour is a little too bright, and you want to dull it down, or neutralise it a little, add a dash of its complementary colour.

Adding grey or black to a bright colour just deadens the colour, whereas adding a little complementary colour neutralises, or subdues it from the original colour.

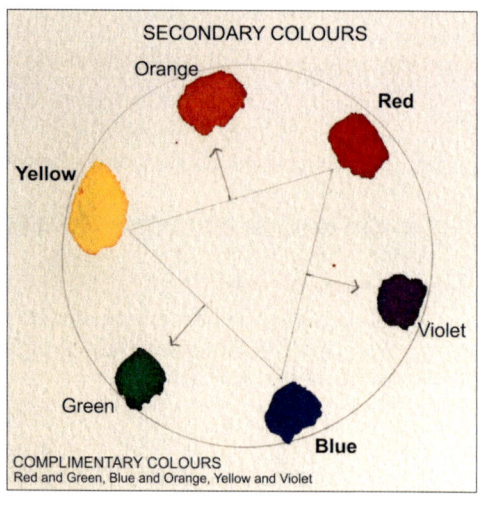

SECONDARY COLOURS

Orange · Red · Yellow · Violet · Green · Blue

COMPLIMENTARY COLOURS
Red and Green, Blue and Orange, Yellow and Violet

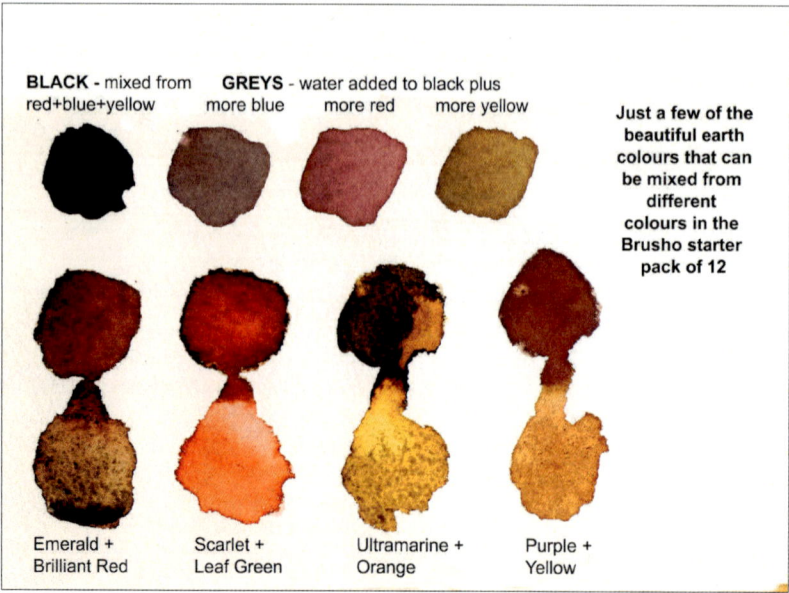

BLACK - mixed from red+blue+yellow

GREYS - water added to black plus
more blue · more red · more yellow

Just a few of the beautiful earth colours that can be mixed from different colours in the Brusho starter pack of 12

Emerald + Brilliant Red

Scarlet + Leaf Green

Ultramarine + Orange

Purple + Yellow

The standard starter pack of 12 colours includes 2 ready-mixed neutral colours, Dark Brown and Black. This is useful when you want to use them in their dry powder form (ie not as a wet paint mix) for the sprinkling or other techniques.

Although there is a Dark Brown, you can mix many additional hues of brown - add a little Ultramarine to Orange for a cool brown, or Brilliant Red and Leaf Green for a warm brown.

For a very dark brown, simply add a little Ultramarine to some Dark Brown straight from the pot. Grey is not included in the Brusho starter pack of 12, but you can mix a lovely warm grey with Yellow and Purple.

Colour harmony (analogous colours)

A useful method of creating a harmonious or serene effect in a painting that is pleasing to the eye is to use analogous colours. These are three, or more, colours that are positioned next to each other on the colour wheel. Start by choosing a main colour, then select two or three colours on either side of it. An example would be to make yellow the main colour, supported by yellow-green and yellow-orange.

Make sure you have enough contrast when choosing this type of scheme. If the overall effect is too bland, the viewer will lose interest through lack of stimulation. If there is insufficient colour harmony and the effect is too chaotic the viewer will switch off through over stimulation. Harmony is a delicate balance.

An example of a painting completed with analogous colours is Warm Rain in Chapter 2.

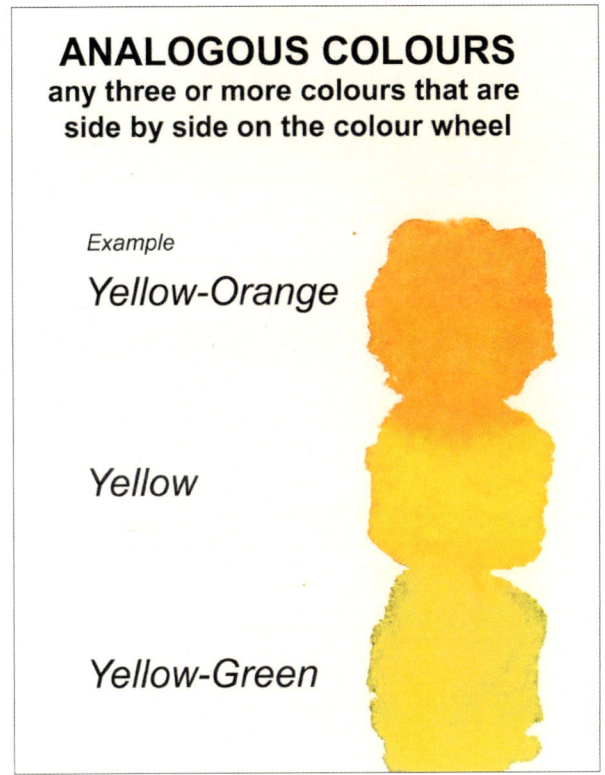

ANALOGOUS COLOURS
any three or more colours that are side by side on the colour wheel

Example
Yellow-Orange

Yellow

Yellow-Green

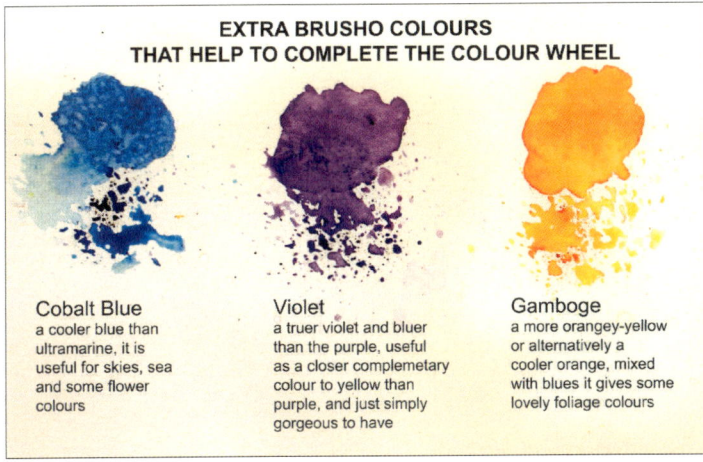

EXTRA BRUSHO COLOURS
THAT HELP TO COMPLETE THE COLOUR WHEEL

Cobalt Blue
a cooler blue than ultramarine, it is useful for skies, sea and some flower colours

Violet
a truer violet and bluer than the purple, useful as a closer complemetary colour to yellow than purple, and just simply gorgeous to have

Gamboge
a more orangey-yellow or alternatively a cooler orange, mixed with blues it gives some lovely foliage colours

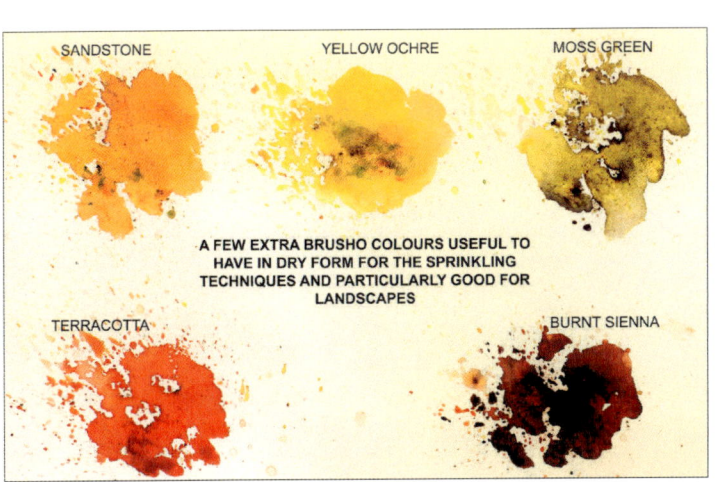

SANDSTONE   YELLOW OCHRE   MOSS GREEN

A FEW EXTRA BRUSHO COLOURS USEFUL TO HAVE IN DRY FORM FOR THE SPRINKLING TECHNIQUES AND PARTICULARLY GOOD FOR LANDSCAPES

TERRACOTTA   BURNT SIENNA

Additional Brusho colours

I have to admit I'm something of a colour junkie! In addition to the standard starter pack of 12 colours, there are currently 22 more Brusho® colours available to dip into. Here are a few more colours that I have come to particularly know and love:

a) *Cobalt Blue, Prussian Blue, Violet* and *Gamboge* are useful colours for completing the colour wheel. Cobalt blue is a cooler blue than Ultramarine, and good for skies, seas and some flower colours. Violet is a truer violet than the reddish Purple in the pack, and thus a truer complementary colour for yellow. It is also quite simply a gorgeous colour that can't be mixed. Gamboge is a more yellowy-orange than the Orange in the pack, so it doubles as a warmer yellow or cooler orange. It is also combines well with the blues to make lovely foliage colours. *Prussian Blue* is a greener, duller blue than Ultramarine

b) *Sandstone, Yellow Ochre, Moss Green, Terracotta* and *Burnt Sienna*. These are all beautiful, earthy landscape colours and useful to have in dry powder form for the sprinkling techniques on landscape foregrounds.

I have included a few paintings completed with some of these additional colours in the gallery sections later in this book so that you can see how they look in a finished painting.

A final word on colour

Colour can be as much about how you feel as what you actually see. We frequently use expressions like feeling blue, being green with envy or red with rage. Picasso wrote, "Colours are like facial features, they follow the changes of the emotions".

As an artist, you don't have to copy nature's exact colours; you can exaggerate them or even change them completely to convey the right mood or atmosphere. Getting the shapes and tonal values right gives you the scope to be adventurous with colour.

Don't be afraid to push colour boundaries and use your imagination. Vincent Van Gogh painted his famous yellow sunflowers in a yellow vase on a yellow table against a yellow wall to create an energetic image that exudes hope and joy.

Looking back at the colour wheel theory, we know that brown is actually made up of reds, blues and yellows – so instead of painting some rocks a dull brown, why not push the colours and use some hot reddish-orange tints that make them zing or some cool blue, violet hues for a tranquil look.

Look closely at the trunks and branches of trees and you will see purples, greens and reds weaving in and out of the grey-brown bark.

Brusho's colour-rich properties make it an ideal medium for experimenting, and having fun, with colour.

GALLERY

SHELLBY

People often think of tortoises being a browny-grey colour, but they are such funny little characters, why not liven them up a little with some hot colours!

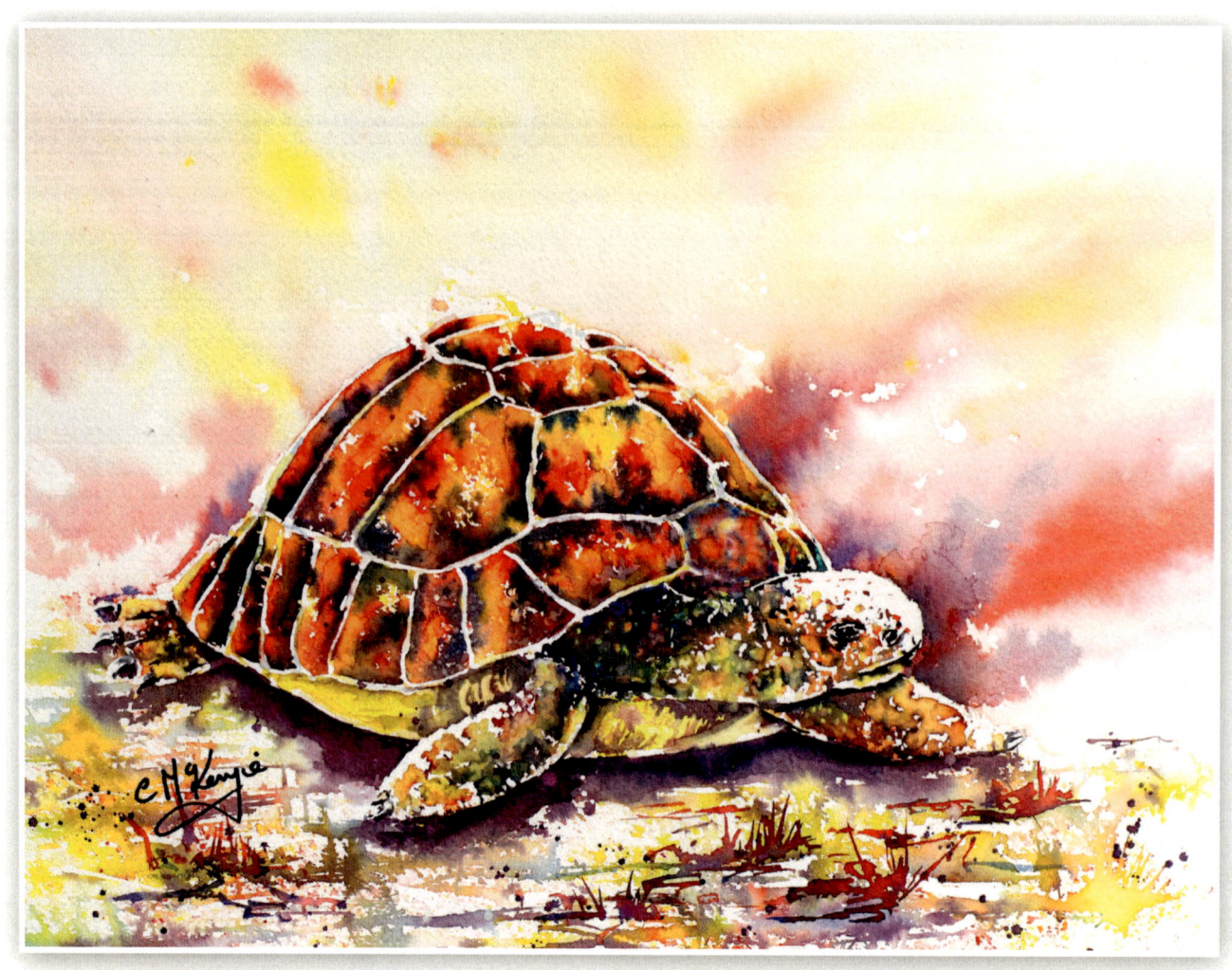

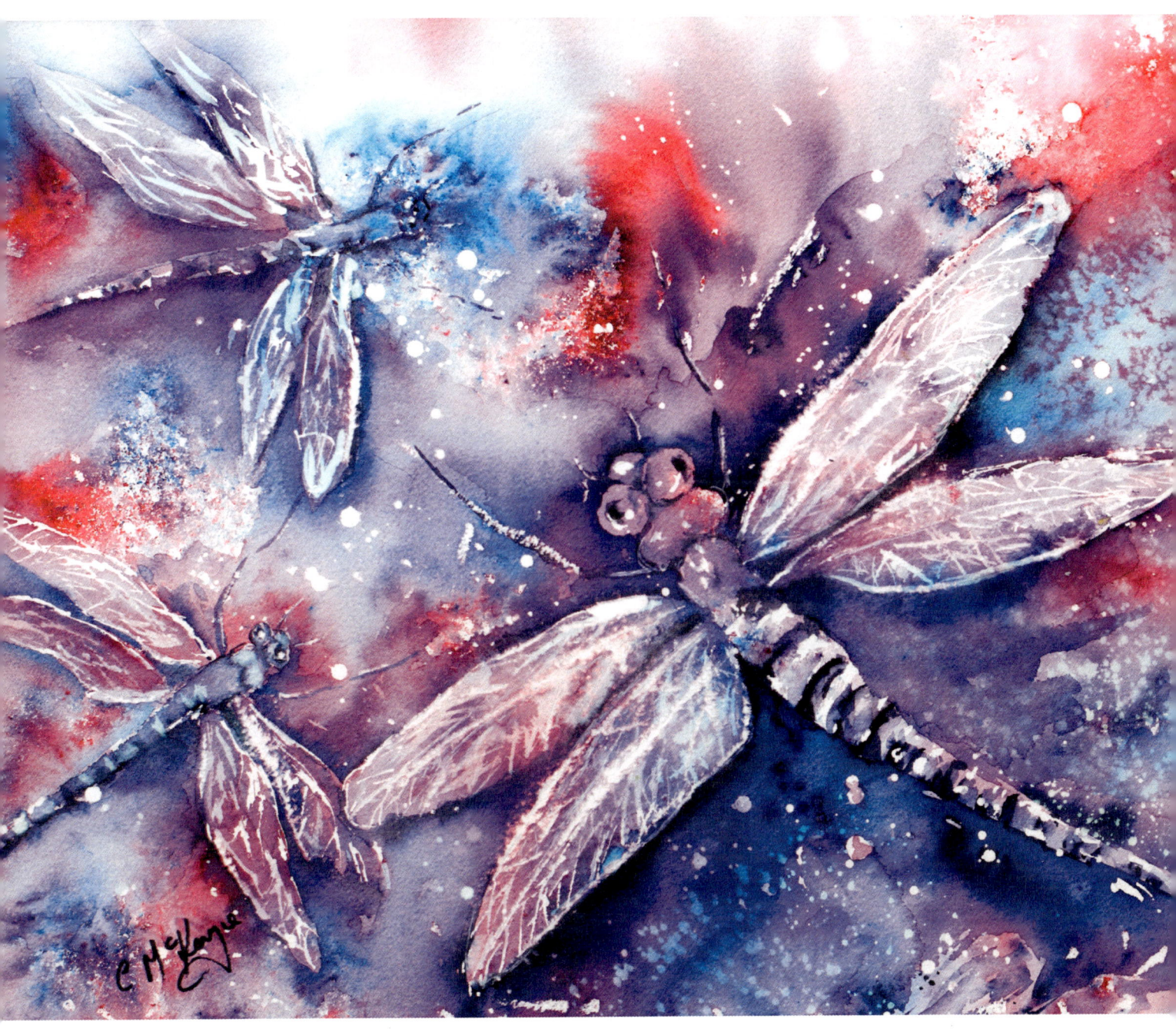

DRAGONFLIES DANCE

I've deliberately used colours in pinky-reds, blues and purples, to convey a harmonious, dreamy, ethereal, dancing mood.

2 : BRUSHO BASICS

Brusho is a strong pigment, so you only need a small amount to obtain rich colour. Just mix a few grains of powder with water to start with and add more if you need to until you get used to the strength. Different colours behave differently — for instance, Ultramarine is a much stronger pigment than Lemon so you need less of it. The amount of water you add to the powder also determines the strength of colour.

There are a number of different methods and techniques that you can use with Brusho. To help you to become familiar with how the pigment behaves, here are a few simple, but fun, exercises to get you started. Understanding the nature of the medium, and its applications, will greatly increase your future success with it.

When doing a full painting, you can choose just one, or a combination, of the different methods to achieve the overall look. Some of the techniques are similar to watercolour, but Brusho pigments don't always react in quite the same way, so even if you are familiar with them it's still worth trying the exercises with Brusho and comparing results.

Technique 1 – Apply wet paint to wet paper (wet-on-wet)

➤ Applying wet colour to wet paper gives a lovely, diffused effect with soft edges. You can control the spread of paint to a certain degree by judging the wetness of the paper when you apply the wet paint. Some Brusho colours spread more rapidly than others. It will also depend on which paper you are using.

➤ Mix some fairly strong Brilliant Red (about the consistency of double cream) in one of your palette wells. Wet a 6" square of watercolour paper with clean water. Immediately, paint a vertical red line at the left-hand side of the square. The paint will flood into the wet paper and continue to spread for some time.

➤ Leave the paper to dry for a minute or two. Paint another line to the right side of the first one. Notice the difference in how far the paint travels on the paper now that it is a little drier. Repeat this process several times, leaving the paper to dry a little in between, until the paper is nearly dry.

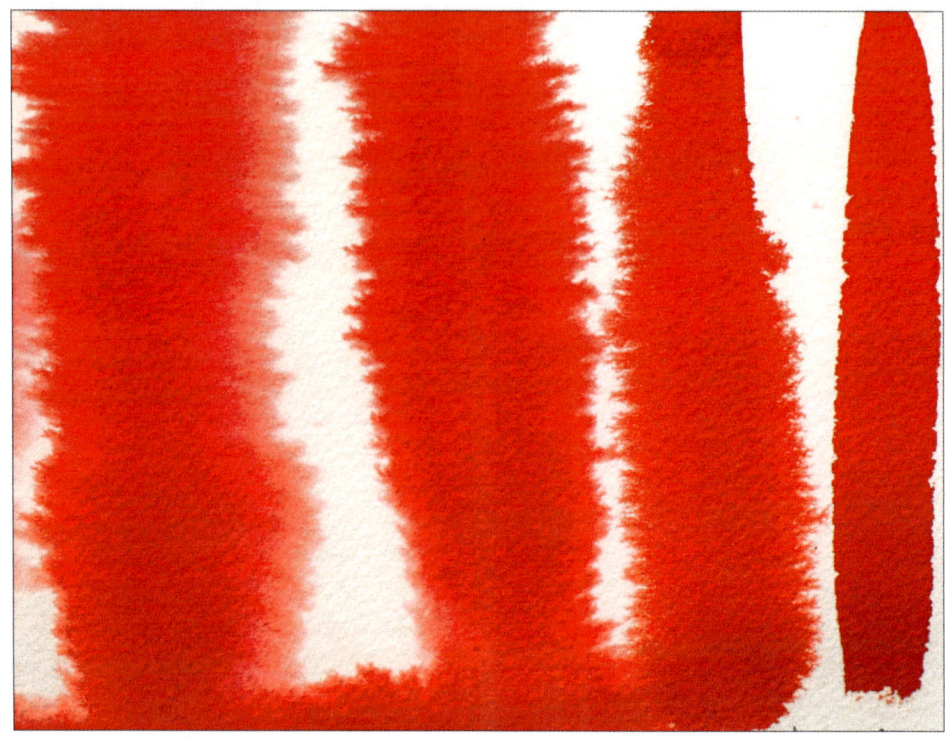

Technique 2 – Apply wet paint to dry paper (wet-on-dry)

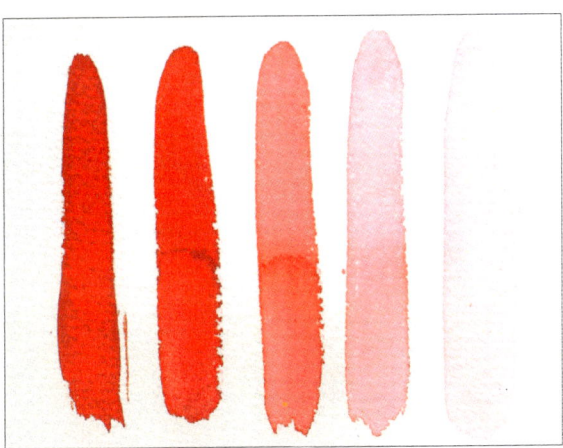

➢ Applying wet colour to dry paper gives you more control than wet-on-wet. The paint stays exactly where you put it with hard edges.
➢ Mix a small amount of Brilliant Red in your palette. Add just enough water to make a thin paste so that paint is almost neat. Paint a thin line at the left side of some dry watercolour paper. See how the paint stays exactly where you put it. This will represent the darkest tonal value of that particular colour.
➢ Add a few more drops of water to the paint then paint another line next to the first one. Note how the addition of water lightens the tone of the colour. Repeat this process several times, ending with a very pale almost white colour, which will be the lightest tonal value of that particular colour.
➢ Remember, tonal values and contrast are key to a successful painting. You need a good mix of light, dark and medium tones to balance the composition.
➢ Try this exercise again, using different colours to see what their tonal range is like. You could produce a tonal value scale for every colour in your pack.

Technique 3 – Blending and softening, lost and found

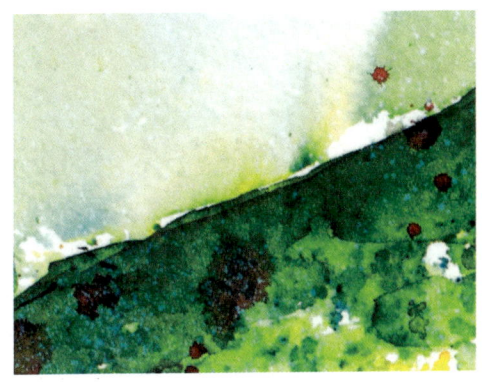

➢ This technique starts with the wet-on-dry approach but then softens some of the hard edges..
➢ Paint a red line about half-an-inch wide at the left side of some dry paper.
➢ While the paint is still wet, take a clean, damp brush and gently stroke the right side of the line to soften and draw the colour away until it blends and disappears into the background.
➢ Try blending just sections of the line with a damp brush. This is referred to as 'lost and found', meaning that you lose the hard edge and then find it again. Instead of blending and softening the entire line, you move the damp brush away from the line then go back to it.
➢ Try not to space out your lost edges too evenly; a random effect looks more natural.

You will find as you work through this book that I use the blending and softening technique in nearly all my paintings, so it's worth spending a little extra time learning how to soften hard edges this way.

Detail from Waiting for a Kiss, showing "lost and found" blending and softening technique

Demonstration
BANANAS VERSION 1

MATERIALS
Yellow
Leaf Green
Dark Brown
Purple

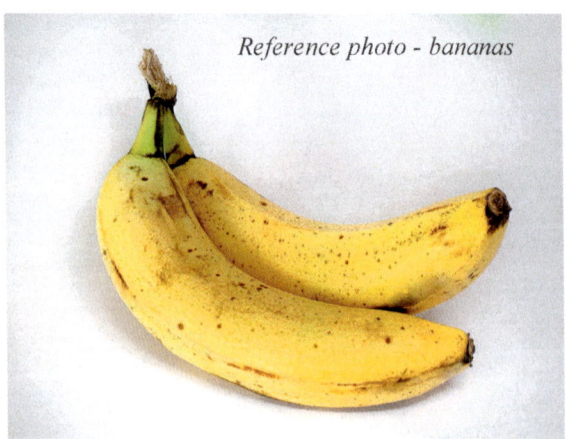

Reference photo - bananas

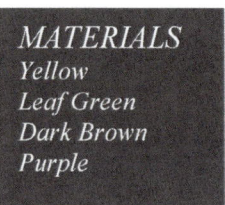

1 Let's start by painting some simple bananas. Draw the outline of the bananas. If you are not confident with drawing straight onto watercolour paper, draw on a piece of cartridge paper first then trace onto watercolour paper.

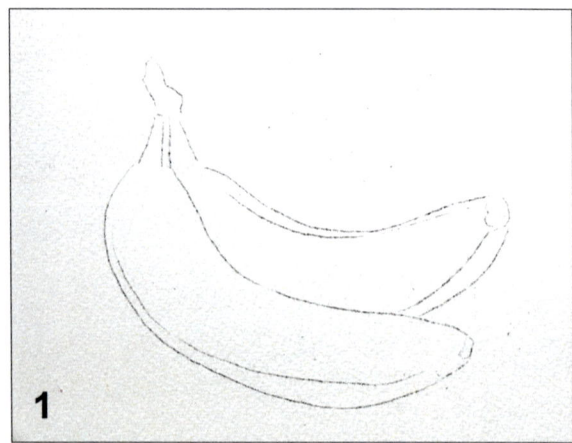

2 Mix some Yellow and Leaf Green in your palette. Paint the bananas with Yellow, varying the dilution so that some parts are lighter in tone than others. Let it dry for a minute, but while it is still fairly damp, drop in a very weak dilution of Leaf Green at the top and bottom of each banana - let it mingle with the yellow.

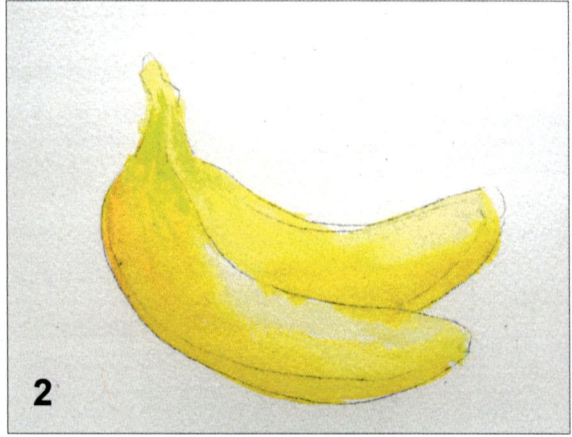

3 Whilst the paint is still damp, use the pointed tip of your brush to paint a few Dark Brown flecks to the body of the bananas. These should blend a little into the damp yellow paint. Vary the dilution of Brown pigment so that some flecks are lighter in tone and less defined than others. Leave to dry.

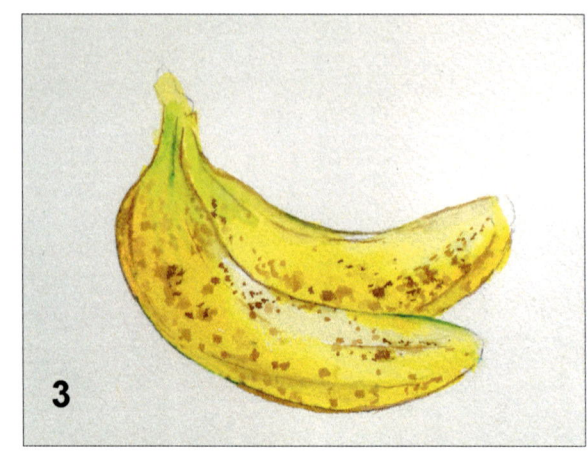

4 Using a rigger brush, draw several broken lines in Dark Brown and Green following the contours across the length of the bananas to define their shape. Use the lost and found technique to gently smooth and blend sections of the lines with a damp brush so they don't look like railway tracks! Next, paint the brown stalk at the tip of the bananas, leaving a hard edge on the top of the stalk but blending where it joins the bananas. Repeat at the opposite end of each banana. Leave to dry.

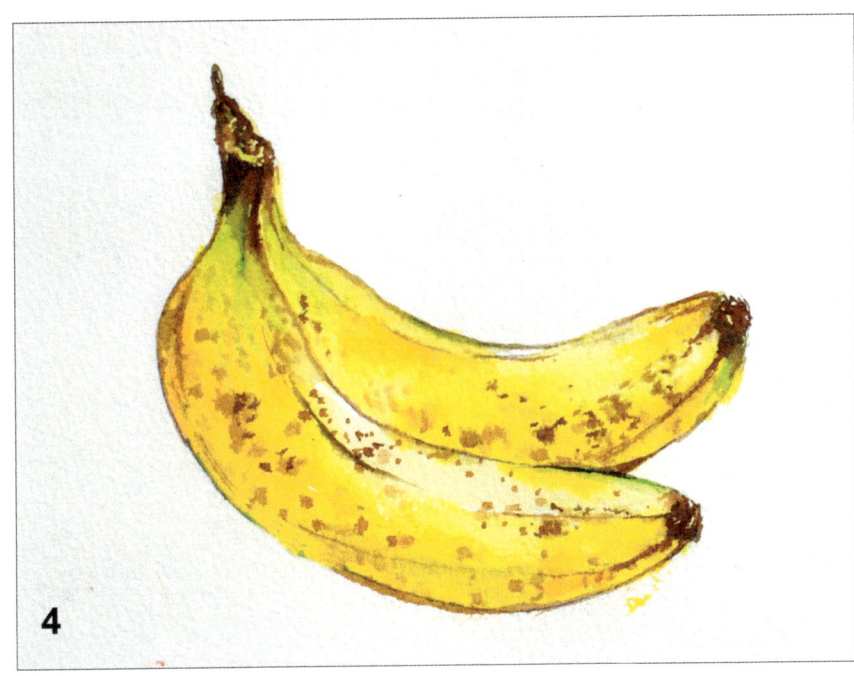

5 Add some dilute Purple shadow to the bottom of the banana at the back, softening the Purple into the Yellow so there is no hard edge, as shown in the illustration below. Paint a stronger Purple shadow underneath the front banana – use the blending technique to soften the shadows at the outer edges

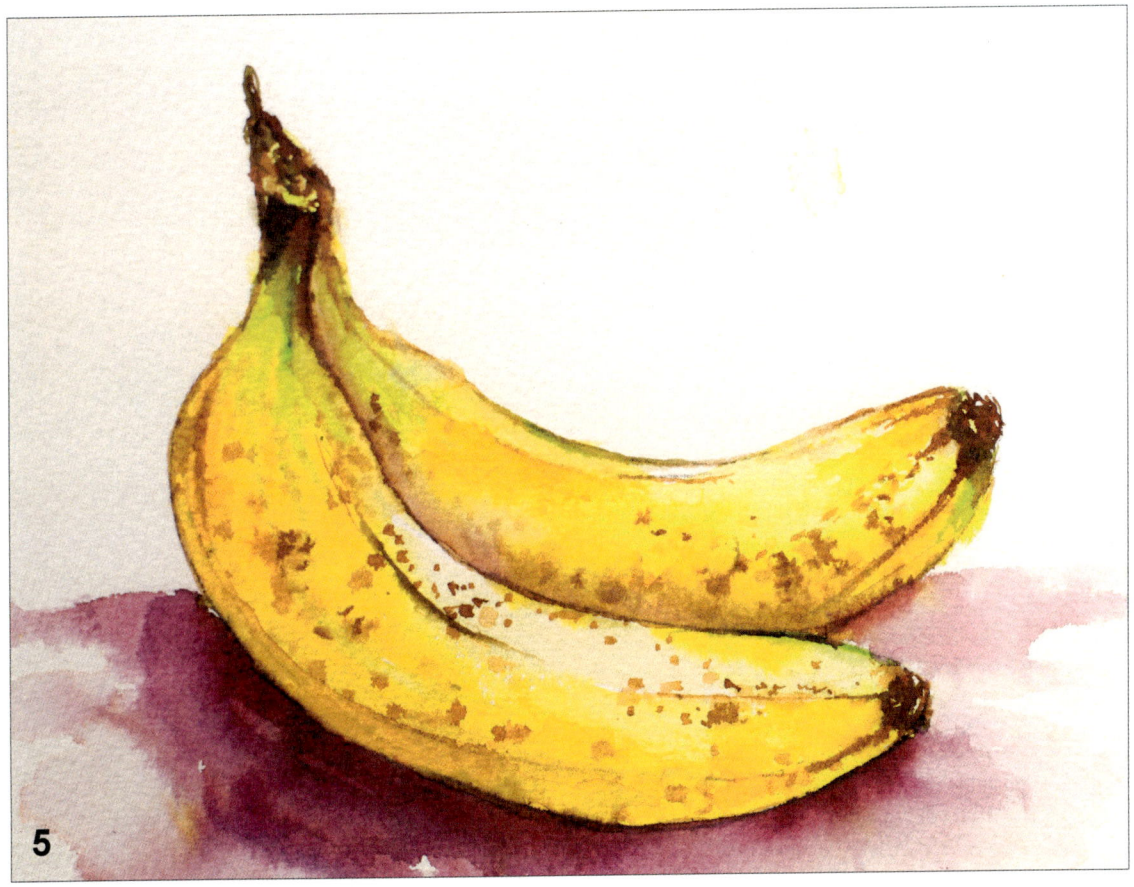

Technique 4 – Spritz on dry paper to create texture

➢ This technique produces a pixelated effect, which is very useful for creating texture such as grasses. It is one of Brusho's most exciting and unique qualities. I use the term *spritz* to mean squirting the water sprayer in a quick, short burst, to turn the Brusho grains into tiny wet bobbles of colour.

➢ Did you remember to pierce a couple of small holes in the top of your Brusho pots so they resemble a saltshaker or pepper pot? If not, do it now.

➢ Lay your watercolour paper flat on the drawing board. Turning the Brusho pots upside down, sprinkle a few grains each of Leaf Green, Lemon, and Turquoise in 3 separate places on some dry watercolour paper. Notice from my example how few grains I have used. You don't need much to make an impact, so be careful not to over-sprinkle.

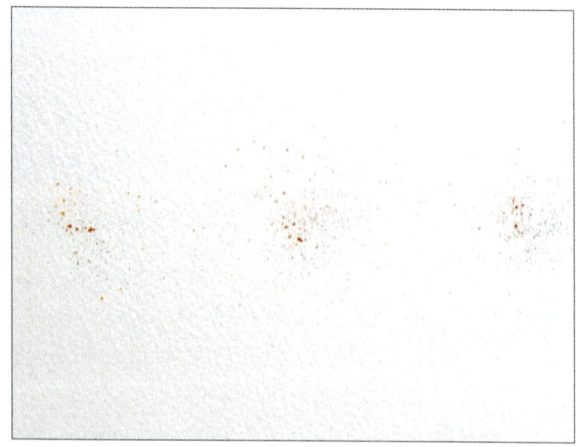

➢ Check your water sprayer by spraying into your water pot until you get the right effect - you want a fine spray rather than a strong jet. Then, holding your water-sprayer about 6" above the paper, lightly 'spritz' the first group of Brusho grains – just spritz a quick, short burst *once* only.

➢ Repeat this exercise for the second group, but this time spritz TWICE. Repeat again with the third group but spritz THREE times.

➢ Look at the difference in distance the grains in each group have travelled and mingled into the water with each spritzing application. One of the biggest problems beginners incur is over-spritzing and ending up with a watery puddle that has no texture.

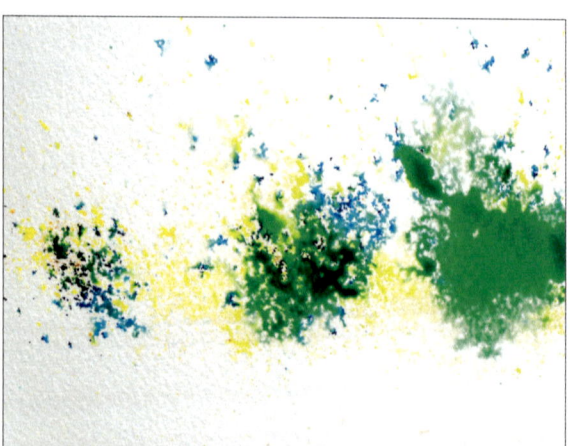

➢ Leave this exercise to one side for an hour or so then check how much further still the colours have travelled in the wet paper. In my example it's particularly noticeable in groups 2 and 3. Be careful not to over-spritz if you want to retain texture, because the pigment carries on moving on the damp paper until it is completely dry.

➢ Unlike some mediums, which cannot be reactivated after they have dried, you can go back and spritz again to re-activate Brusho. To see this work in practice, try spritzing the groups of grains again and note the difference it makes.

➢ You could repeat this exercise again, but hold your water-sprayer at varying heights above the paper to see how the grains behave under different water pressure.

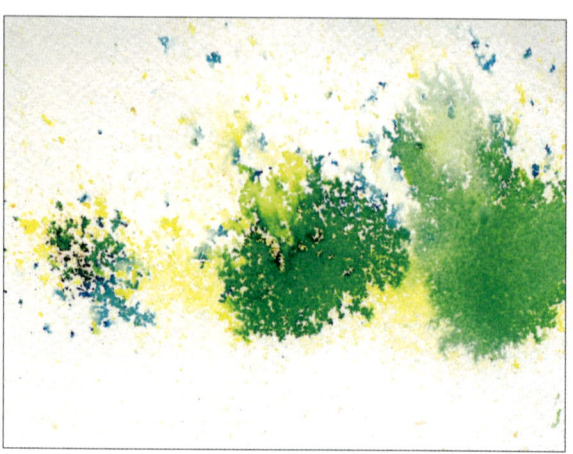

Technique 5 – Spritz & blend paint on dry paper

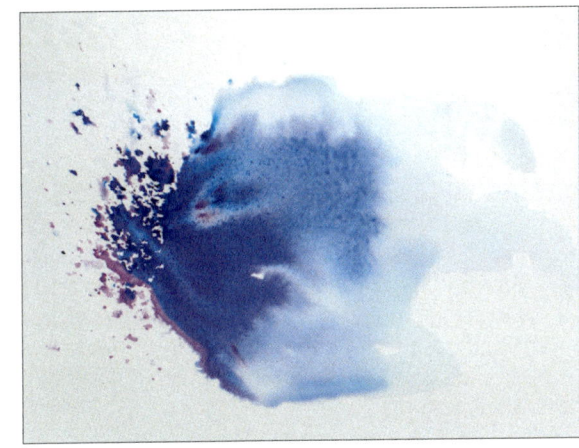

➤ As well as mixing paint in the palette you can also mix it directly on the paper. Sprinkle a few grains of Ultramarine onto dry paper and spritz it lightly as you did previously in Technique 4.
➤ Then use a wet brush to paint into the watery speckles, pushing the paint around with your brush, to get a more solid effect.
➤ You can decide where to leave some texture and where to smooth it out.

Technique 6 – Spritz & flick on dry paper

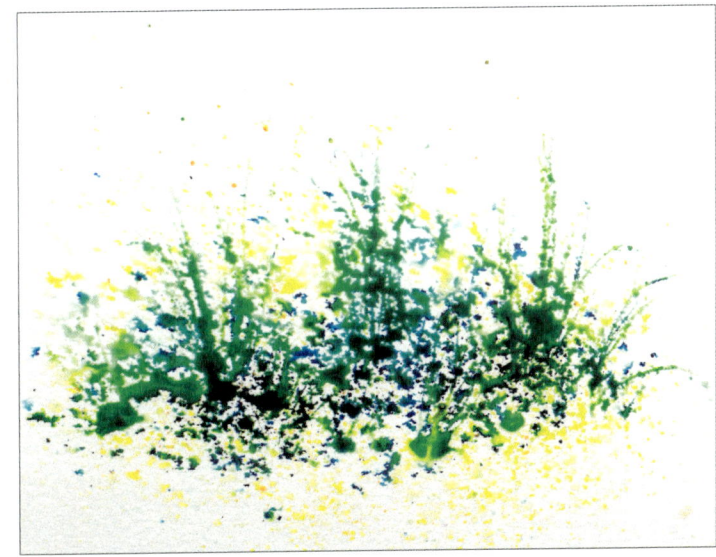

➤ Sprinkle Lemon, Leaf Green and Turquoise on dry watercolour paper.
➤ Spritz lightly to create texture.
➤ While the paint is still wet, take a clean damp Rigger brush and flick some of the watery grains upwards to create grasses.
➤ Vary the direction and bend of the grasses to they don't look static and regimental

Technique 7 – Sprinkle on wet paper

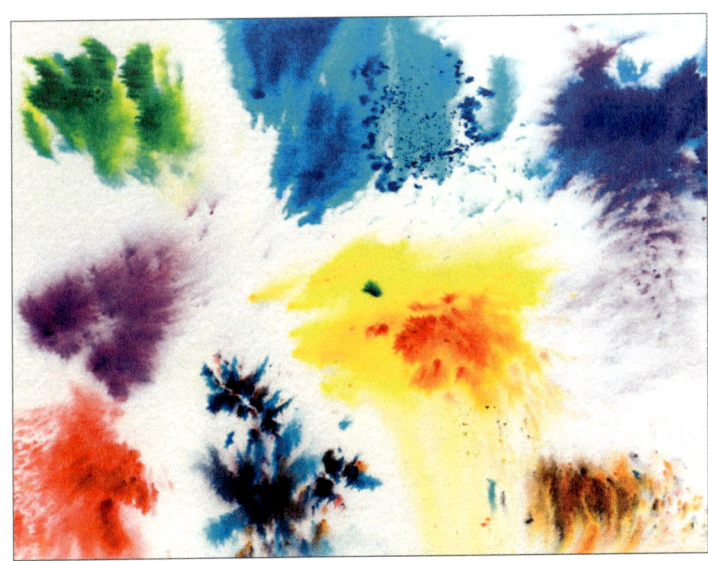

➤ Wet a piece of watercolour paper thoroughly all over
➤ Sprinkle different colours on the paper and watch how the pigments flow into the water creating beautiful patterns.
➤ Note the way that the different colours behave – some colours 'pop' and disperse more than others.
➤ The crystals will carry on moving until the paper has completely dried, so wait a while to see the full effects.

Demonstration
BANANAS VERSION 2

MATERIALS
Yellow
Leaf Green
Dark Brown
Purple

1 Repeat Steps 1-3 of the Bananas Version 1 exercise again.

2 When you get to Step 4, instead of painting the brown flecks on with a brush, sprinkle just a few Dark Brown grains on to the bananas and let them blend slightly into the damp yellow wash below. If the paper turns out to be too dry when you sprinkle on the grains, give them a quick spritz.

3 Complete Steps 5-6 as before.

4 Sprinkle and spritz a few of the same colours around the bananas to create a harmonious background.

5 This method creates more texture than the previous banana painting, demonstrating two very different ways of applying Brusho paint. Compare the two versions – which do you prefer?

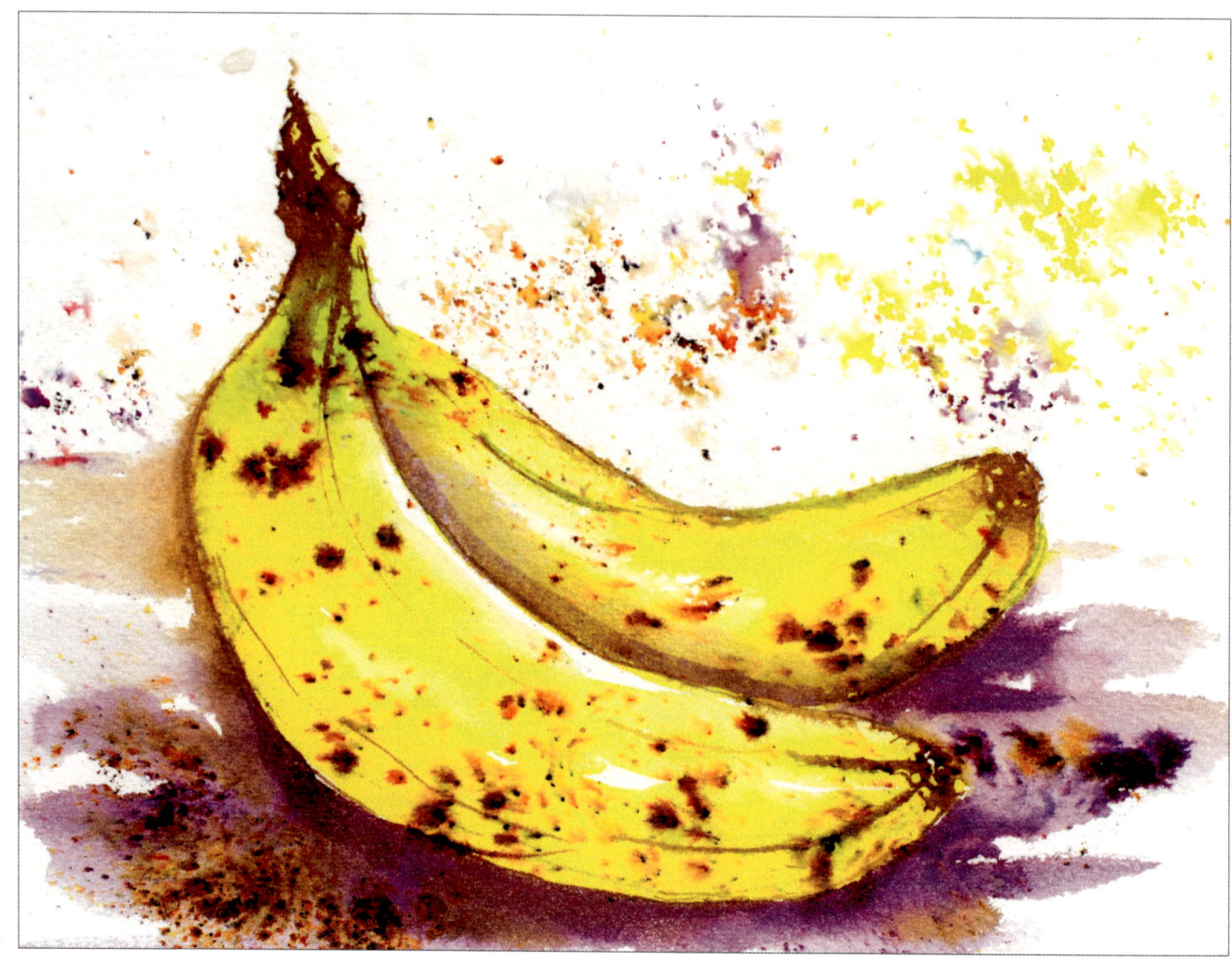

Demonstration
TREES AND GRASSES

MATERIALS
Lemon
Leaf Green
Dark Brown
Ultramarine
Turquoise
Brilliant Red

1 Draw the loose outline of an imaginary group of three trees on a piece of watercolour paper. Make the trees a little different in shape, and vary the distance between them, to add interest. Remember that trees are wider at the bottom than they are at the top.

2 Mix some Dark Brown in your palette and paint in the tree trunks and a few branches. Mix some Ultramarine and drop it on the right side of each tree, and some of the branches, to give them form.

3 Sprinkle Lemon, Leaf Green and a little Turquoise and Brilliant Red around the top of the tree trunks to form the canopy of leaves. Leaves are usually lighter at the top of the tree; so use more Lemon at the top of the canopy of leaves and a little Ultramarine at the bottom to darken the underside. Spritz lightly - remember how much the tiny grains continue to travel on wet paper so don't overdo the spritzing – wait a while until the paper dries to see the result - you can always spritz again if you need to.

4 Sprinkle the same colours at the base of the trees to form the grasses. Spritz lightly, then use your rigger brush to flick some of the watery bobbles upwards to resemble grasses. Paint in a few more branches and twigs with Dark Brown. Add a few extra touches such as random fence posts, or a little animal, to complete your painting.

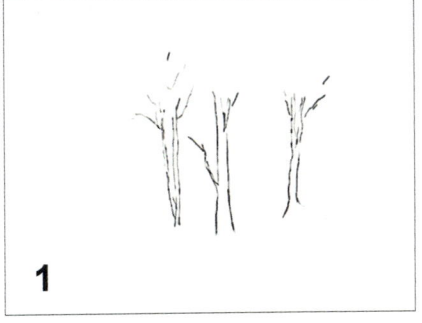

1

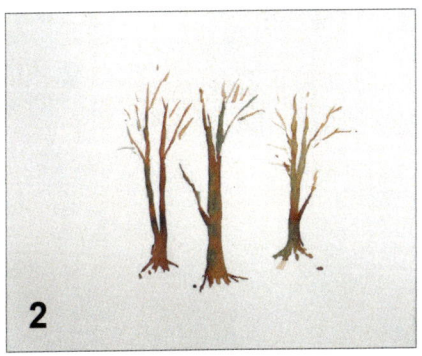

2

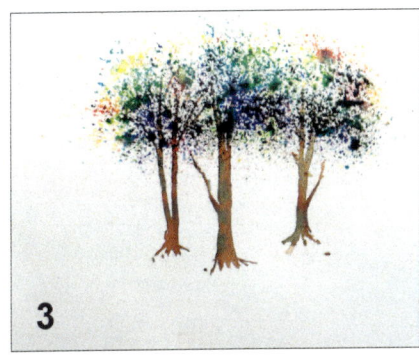

3

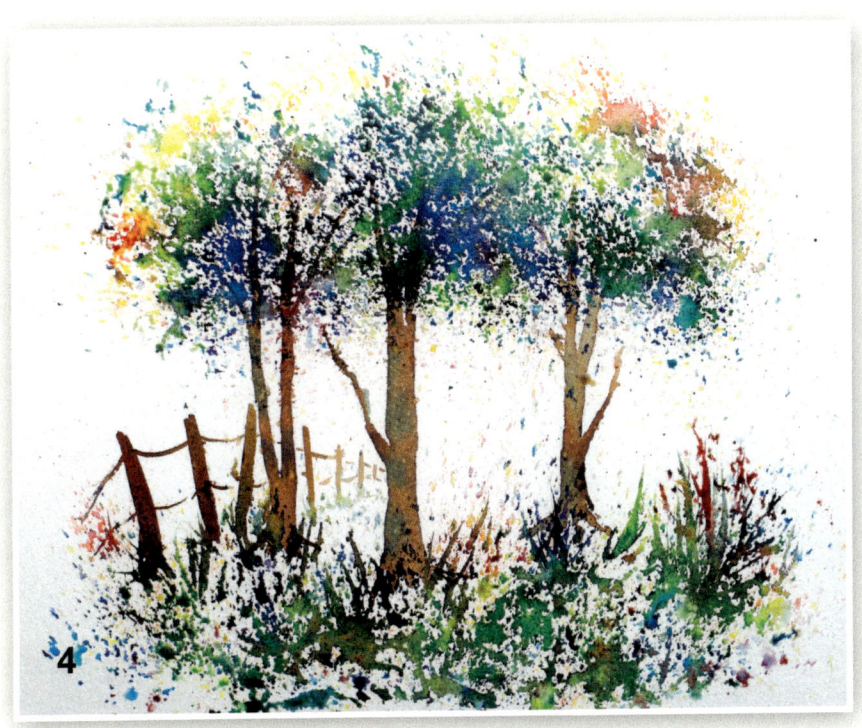

4

27

Technique 8 – Spray to create large washes

There are times when you don't want texture, for instance when painting a sky or a background wash. I find that Brusho pigment tends to stain the paper faster and more easily than watercolour so be prepared to work fairly quickly when creating a large wash, particularly if it's a sky.

It can be useful to set a time limit of say 5-10 minutes and then stop. Go with whatever you have got at this point - going back into a large wash can easily over-work and muddy it.

Earlier, we used the term *spritz* for squirting the water sprayer in one or two quick short bursts to retain texture. Now we are going to use the term *spray* for using the water sprayer in longer, sweeping spray movements to get a smoother, blended effect.

Spray on dry paper – method 1

➢ First, mix Turquoise and Lemon in separate wells of your palette. Then paint them directly onto the top of the dry watercolour paper, overlapping the colours in some places, but not all.

➢ Then, while the paint is still wet, lift the paper up at the top end and use the water-sprayer to spray the paint in a downward and diagonal movement, bringing the colour down/across the paper. Wiggle the paper about a little to encourage the flow and help the blending process. Place an old towel underneath to catch the excess water and paint runs.

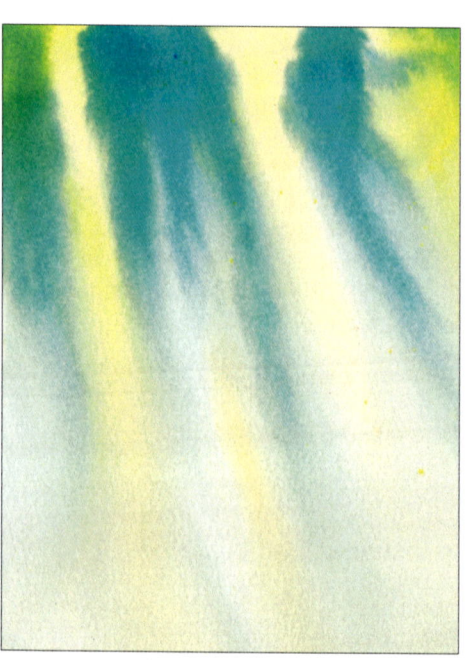

Spray on dry paper – method 2

➢ This time, instead of first mixing it in the palette, sprinkle Brilliant Red and Yellow directly onto the top of a new piece of dry watercolour paper.

➢ Then, lifting the paper up off the drawing board at the top end, use the water-sprayer to spray in a downward and diagonal movement to bring the colour down and across the paper.

➢ This method tends to leave more texture than the previous one, which can be useful for certain effects

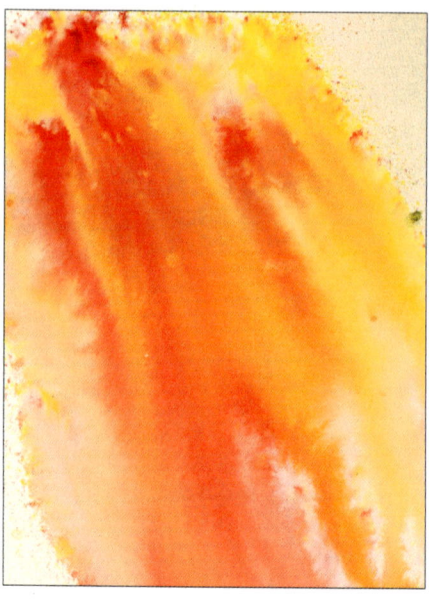

Spray on wet paper

➤ Mix Lemon, Scarlet and Dark Brown in separate wells of your palette. Then wet a piece of watercolour paper all over with your large brush and some clean water.

➤ Load your brush with colour and drop it onto the top of the wet paper, overlapping the colours in some places, but not all. Lift the paper up off the drawing board at one end and use the water-sprayer to spray the colours in a downward and diagonal movement, bringing the colour down/across the paper.

➤ Wiggle the paper about a little to help the blending process. Remember to place your towel underneath to catch the drips. Notice that you get a much softer and paler blend when spraying wet paint onto wet paper rather than wet onto dry.

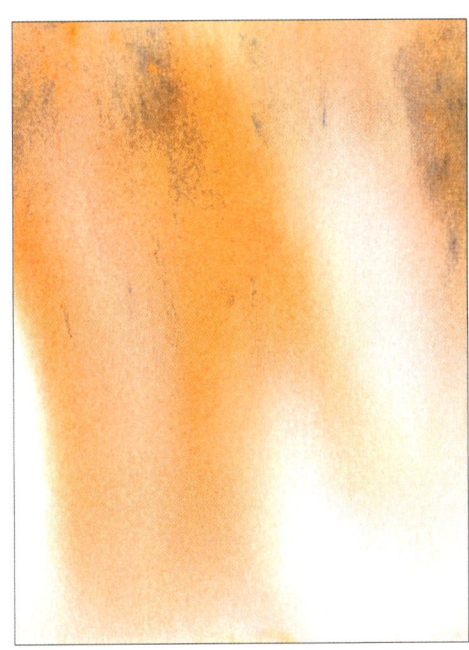

Spray on wet paper for a soft, vignette effect

➤ This time, you are going to repeat the last exercise and add extra colour to the bottom of the paper to create a vignette effect, keeping the central area light in tone.

➤ Mix some Lemon, Scarlet and Orange in your palette.

➤ Wet the paper all over with clean water.

➤ Drop the colours along the top of the wet paper, then lift the paper up at the top end and spray the colours downwards until the central and bottom areas of the paper are very pale in tone.

➤ Wiggle and bend your paper to help the blending process.

➤ Turn your paper upside down, then, drop some of the same colour along the bottom of the paper, particularly in the corners. Lift the paper up at the bottom end this time, and let the colour run and blend in the wet paper until it is about one-third of the way down.

➤ The middle area of the paper should be fairly pale in tone. If not, you can always blot it with some paper towel, but be careful not to leave hard edges.

➤ Lay the paper flat to dry.

Demonstration
WARM RAIN

MATERIALS
Lemon
Yellow
Dark Brown
Ultramarine
Scarlet

To conclude this chapter, you are going to consolidate some of the techniques you have learned into a full Brusho painting. Have a look at the final image - it's really just a few simple figures walking in the rain on a wet pavement with some trees at either side. You will find it easier to use a piece of watercolour paper at least quarter imperial in size for this project. Note that the drawing is done *after* the first washes of paint are laid.

1 Start by using Technique 8 – spraying to create large washes on wet paper - for the sky and pavement areas. Mix some Lemon, Yellow, Scarlet and a little Dark Brown in separate wells of your palette. Wet the paper thoroughly all over with a large brush. Drop the different colours onto the top of the paper and spray downwards aiming to create warm rain cloud shapes at the top of the paper. Spray the colours enough to make the central and bottom areas very pale in tone.

Turn the paper upside down and drop some more colours at the bottom of the paper to represent the rain cloud reflections in the pavement area. Lift your paper up from the bottom and wiggle it around a little to get the pigment to blend, but avoid it colouring the central area as you want to keep this pale by laying it flat. (Blot the central area with a paper towel if it has too much colour.) Leave to dry.

When dry, pencil a few simple figure shapes walking in the rain. Keep all the heads on roughly the same level, making the figures smaller as they disappear on the horizon. Add a couple of umbrellas.

2 Use the same colours to paint the figures. Apply stronger pigment for the figures nearest the foreground and weaker, more dilute, colour for the figures furthest away to aid perspective.

Mix a little Dark Brown with Ultramarine and, while the figures are still damp, add a little of this mix to the left sides of the figures to give them form.

Using slightly weaker mixes of the colours you painted the figures in, paint their reflections in the wet pavement, blending the bottom of the reflections away with clean water. Make the reflections stronger in colour for the nearest figures and fainter for the farthest ones

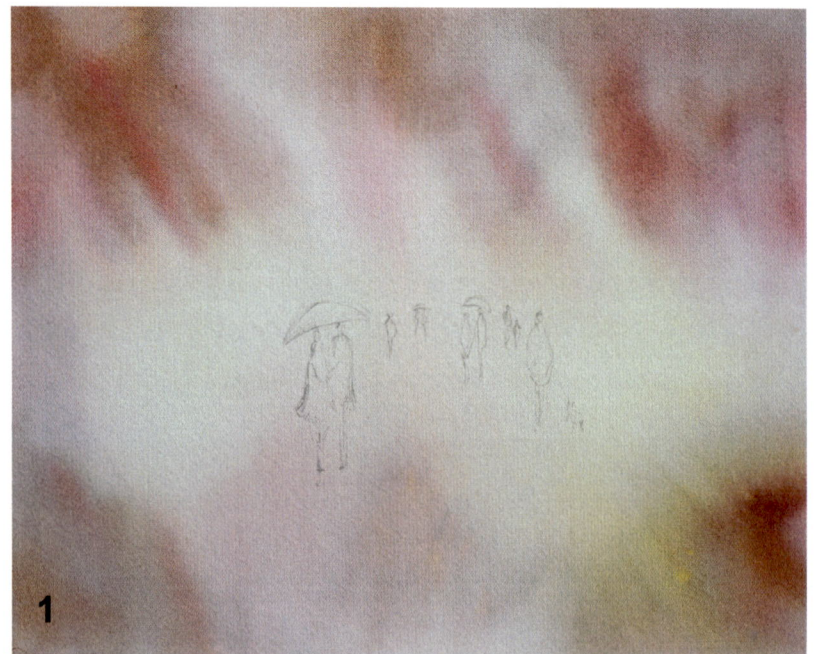

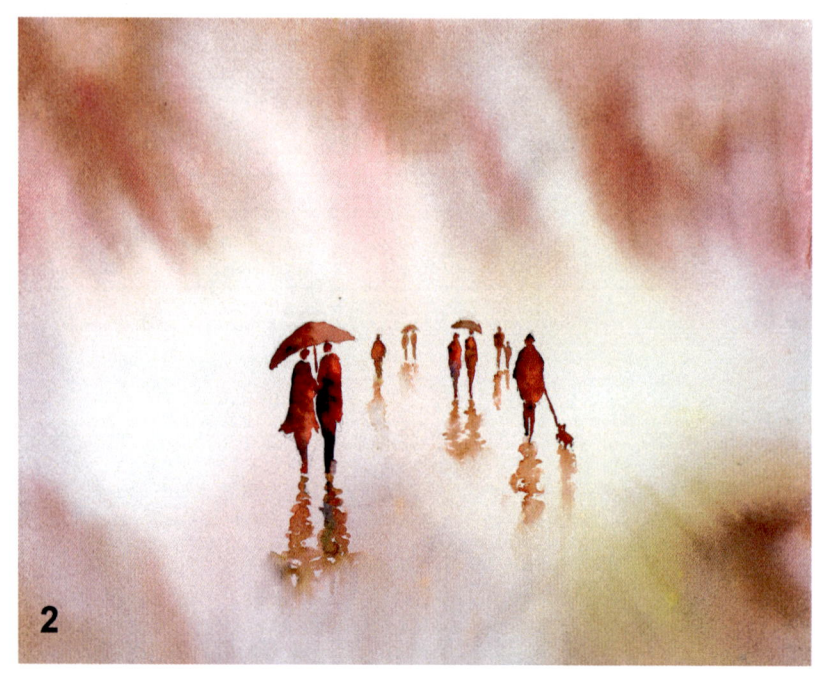

3 Pencil in some tree shapes, making them smaller towards the vanishing point on the horizon. Using the same techniques that you used earlier to create trees, paint in the tree trunks and branches with Dark Brown. Leave to dry. Sprinkle the same colours that you used for the background wash to create the leaf canopies around the top of each tree. Spritz lightly to create a textured canopy of leaves – do not over-spritz or you will lose your lovely leaf texture. Remember, you can always spritz again later to re-activate the Brusho.

Don't worry if a few stray speckles creep into the sky area – they will look like leaves blown about by the rain.

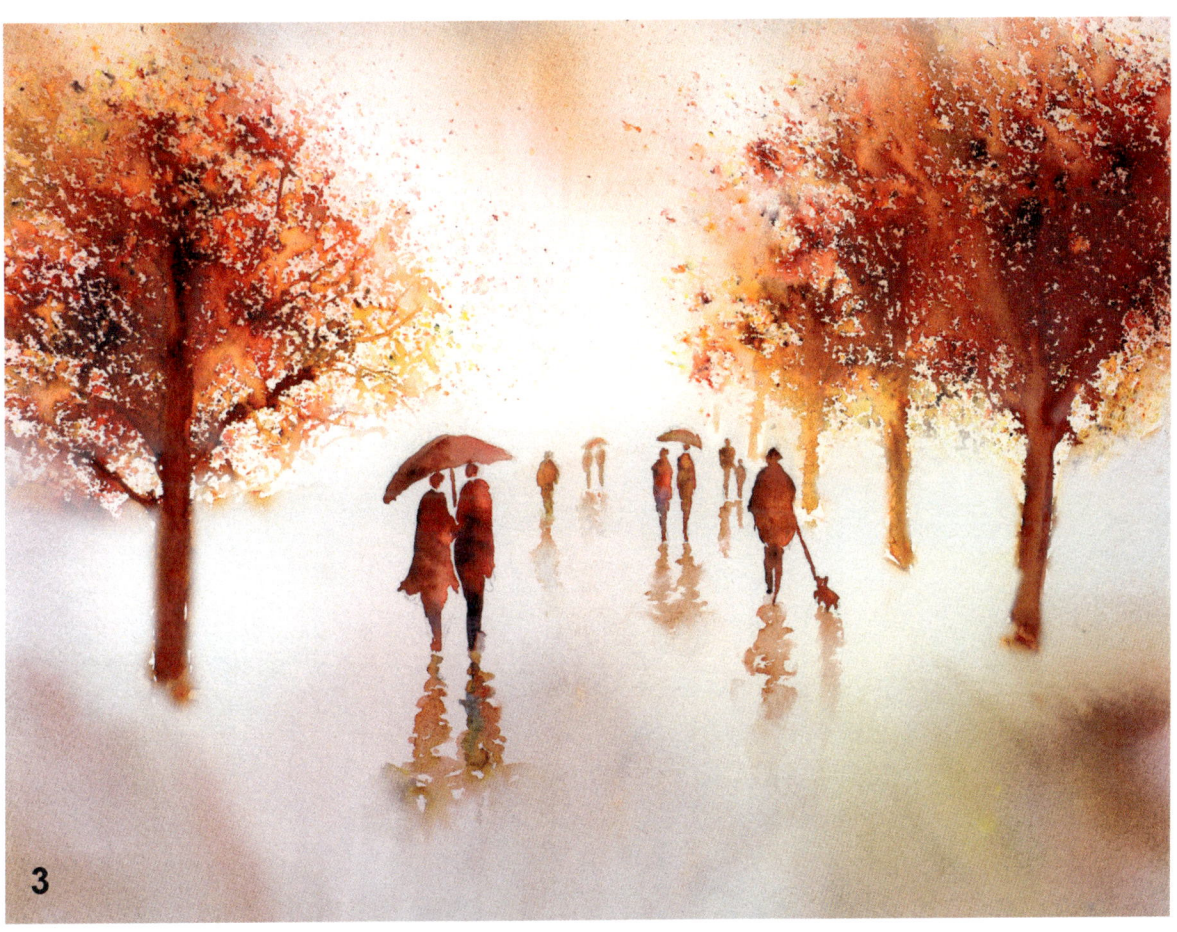

3

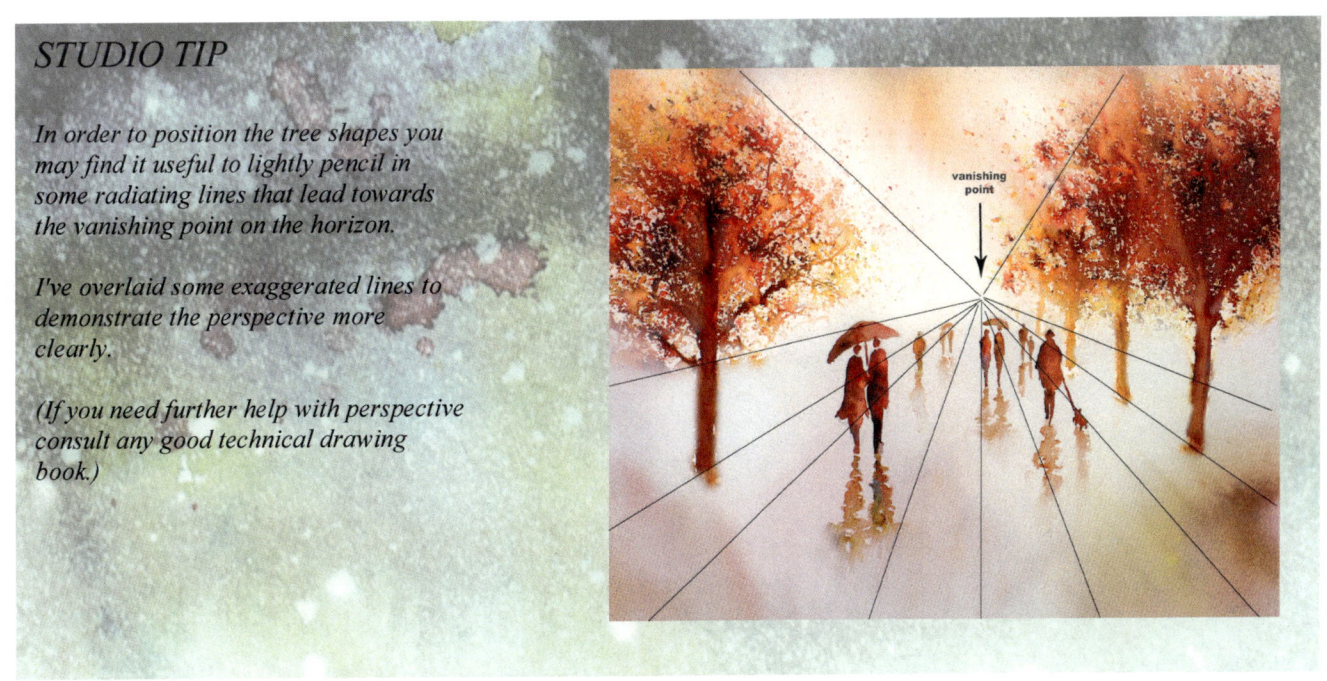

STUDIO TIP

In order to position the tree shapes you may find it useful to lightly pencil in some radiating lines that lead towards the vanishing point on the horizon.

I've overlaid some exaggerated lines to demonstrate the perspective more clearly.

(If you need further help with perspective consult any good technical drawing book.)

4 Use the same colours to paint in some bushes running behind the trees, diluting the colour to make them paler in tone towards the vanishing point.

To paint the reflections of the bushes, use the lost and found blending technique to wet the paper just beneath them and tilt the paper from the top so the paint flows downward. Reflections are darker nearer to their subject and get paler further away, so drop in a little more colour just beneath the bushes to darken the tone of the reflections there. Leave everything to dry completely. Finally, using a rigger, follow your perspective lines and add a few Dark Brown pavement lines here and here - use the lost and found technique to blend the lines into the pavement with a mix of hard and soft edges so they do not sit harshly on top of the pavement like tramlines.

WARM RAIN

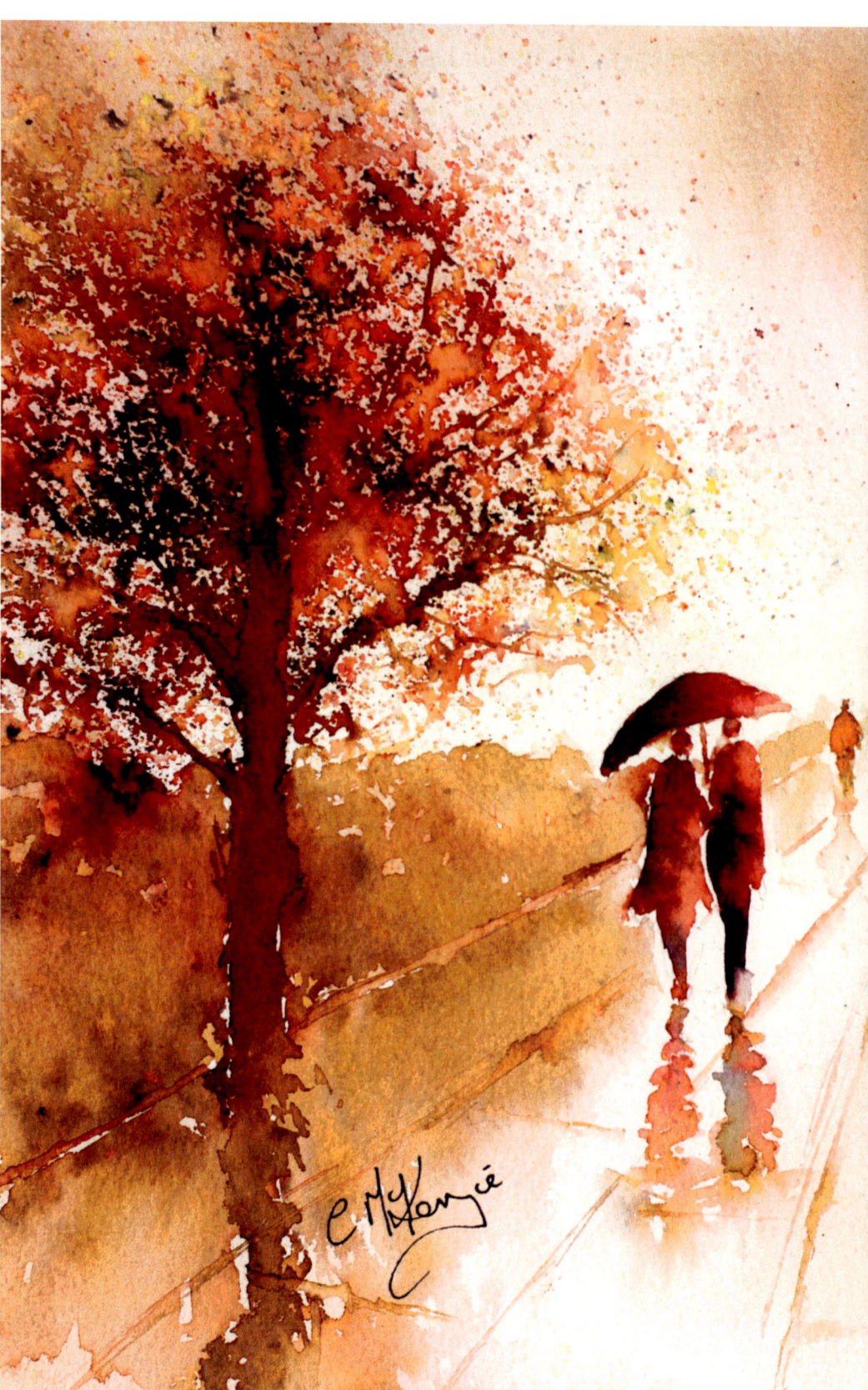

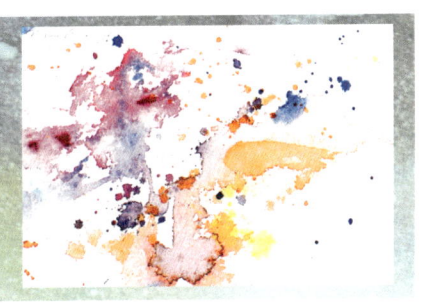

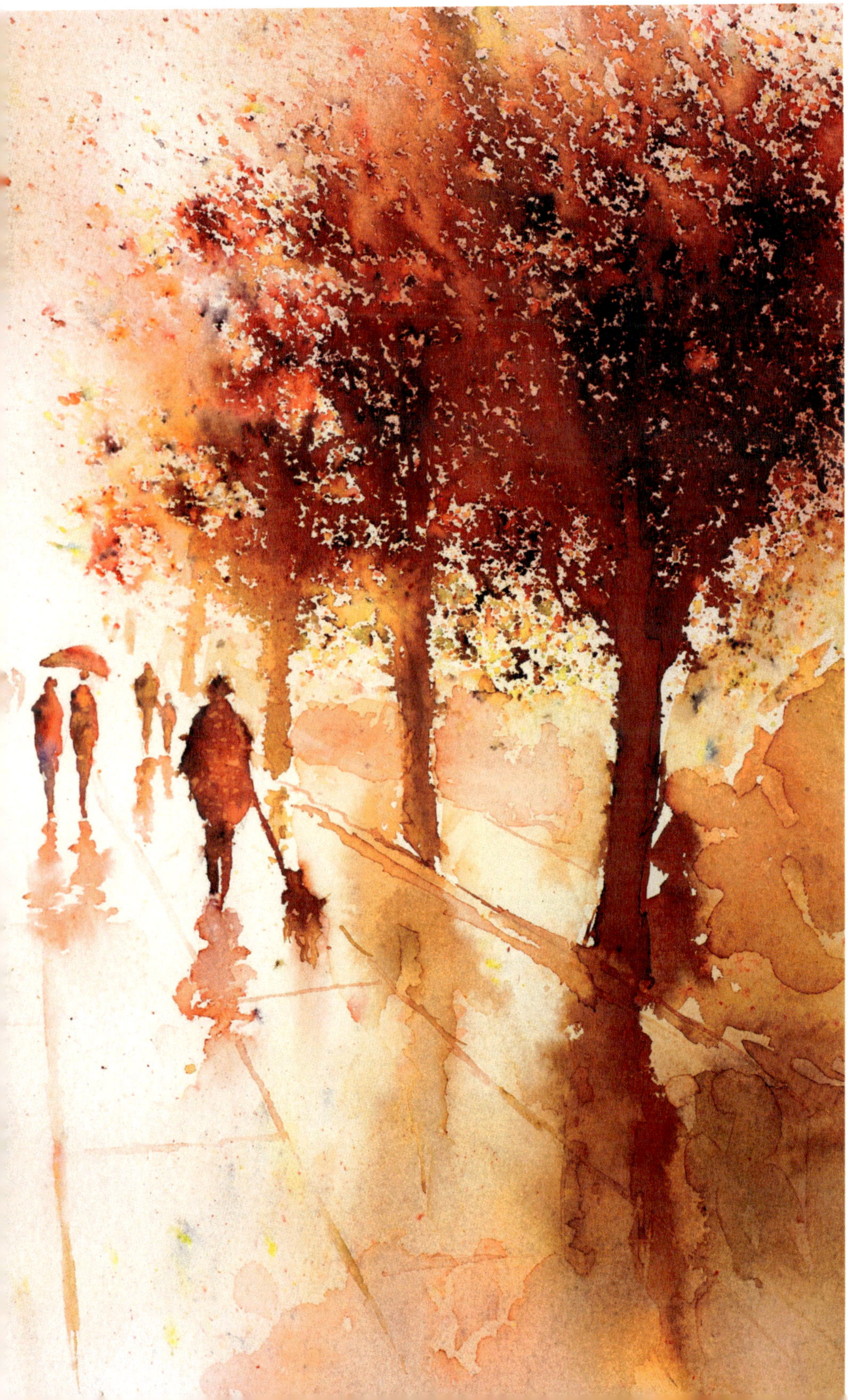

GALLERY

MRS HEDGEHOG AND QUILLIAM

First I sprinkled and spritzed some Yellow, Scarlet and Dark Brown for the hedgehog backs, making sure I didn't over-spritz and lose the texture.

Then, using a rigger, and following the contours of the hedgehog bodies, I flicked some Dark Brown pigment to represent the spikes.

I painted the faces using a more diluted mixture of the same colours.

After protecting the hedgehogs with some paper towel, I sprinkled and spritzed the foreground, then used a damp brush to join some of the speckles with linear marks.

Finally I dropped in some darker shadow colour underneath the hedgehog bodies.

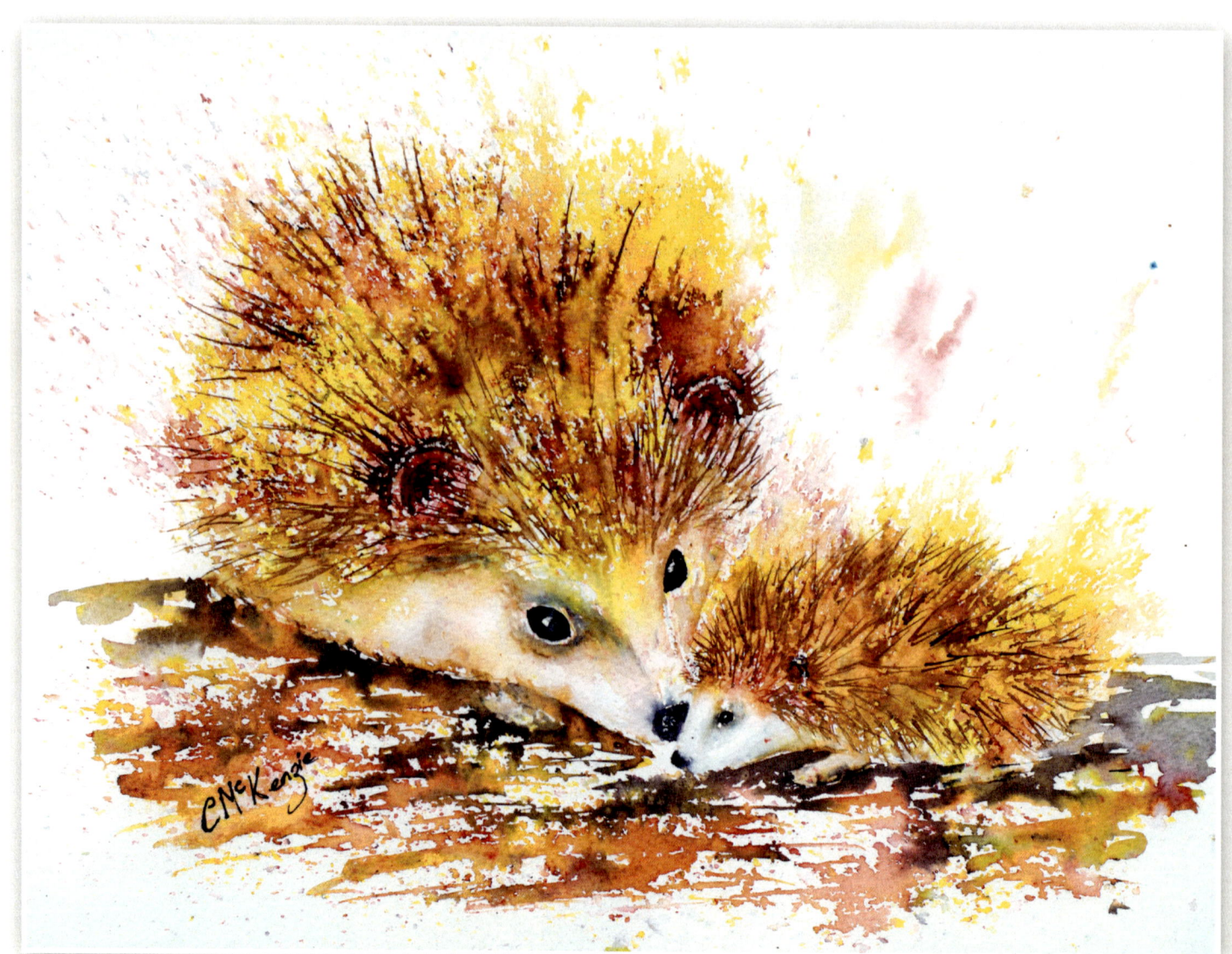

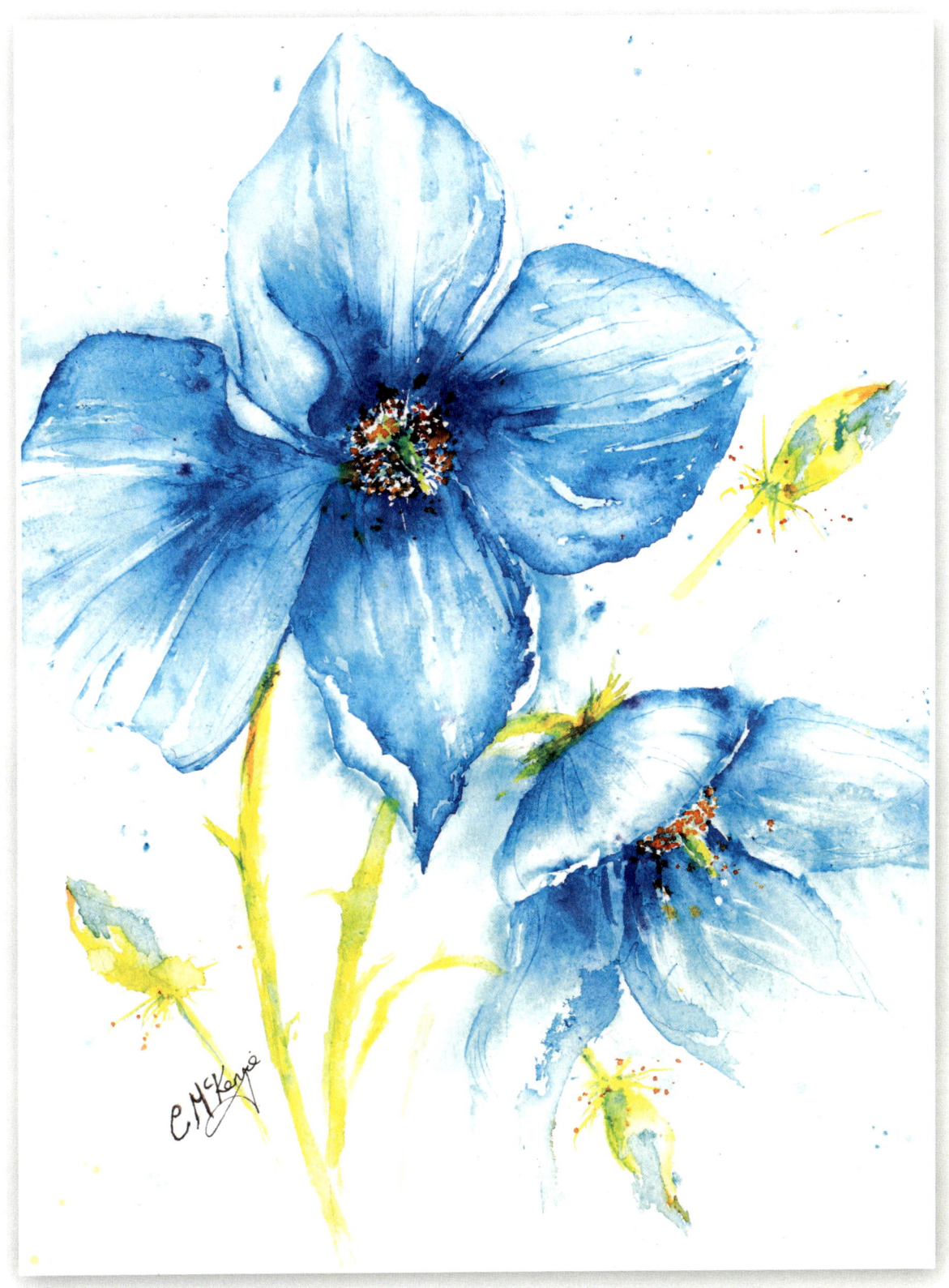

BLUE MECONOPSIS

For this painting, I sprinkled a little Turquoise and Ultramarine within the main flower shapes and then sprayed the colours lightly in the direction of each petal to get a very soft blend and leaving patches of white paper in places.

I used a soft brush to paint the darker details on the petals, the flower stems and the small buds, using the softening and blending and the lost and found techniques

STOODLEY PIKE

Stoodley Pike is a famous landmark not far from where I live, originally constructed in 1814 to commemorate the surrender of Paris to the Allies. The 1,300-foot hill in the south Pennines, topped by the 121-foot Stoodley Pike Monument at its summit, towers over the moors of the upper Calder Valley.

Whenever I've visited it, it has felt quite a brooding place full of mystery and atmosphere, so I wanted to use some of the additional earthier Brusho colours that are available.

The sky was painted using the spray method with Prussian Blue a little Yellow Ochre and Terracotta. I used Yellow Ochre, Terracotta, Moss Green and Purple for the land.

To obtain the darkest colours, I mixed Prussian with Terracotta and a little Purple.

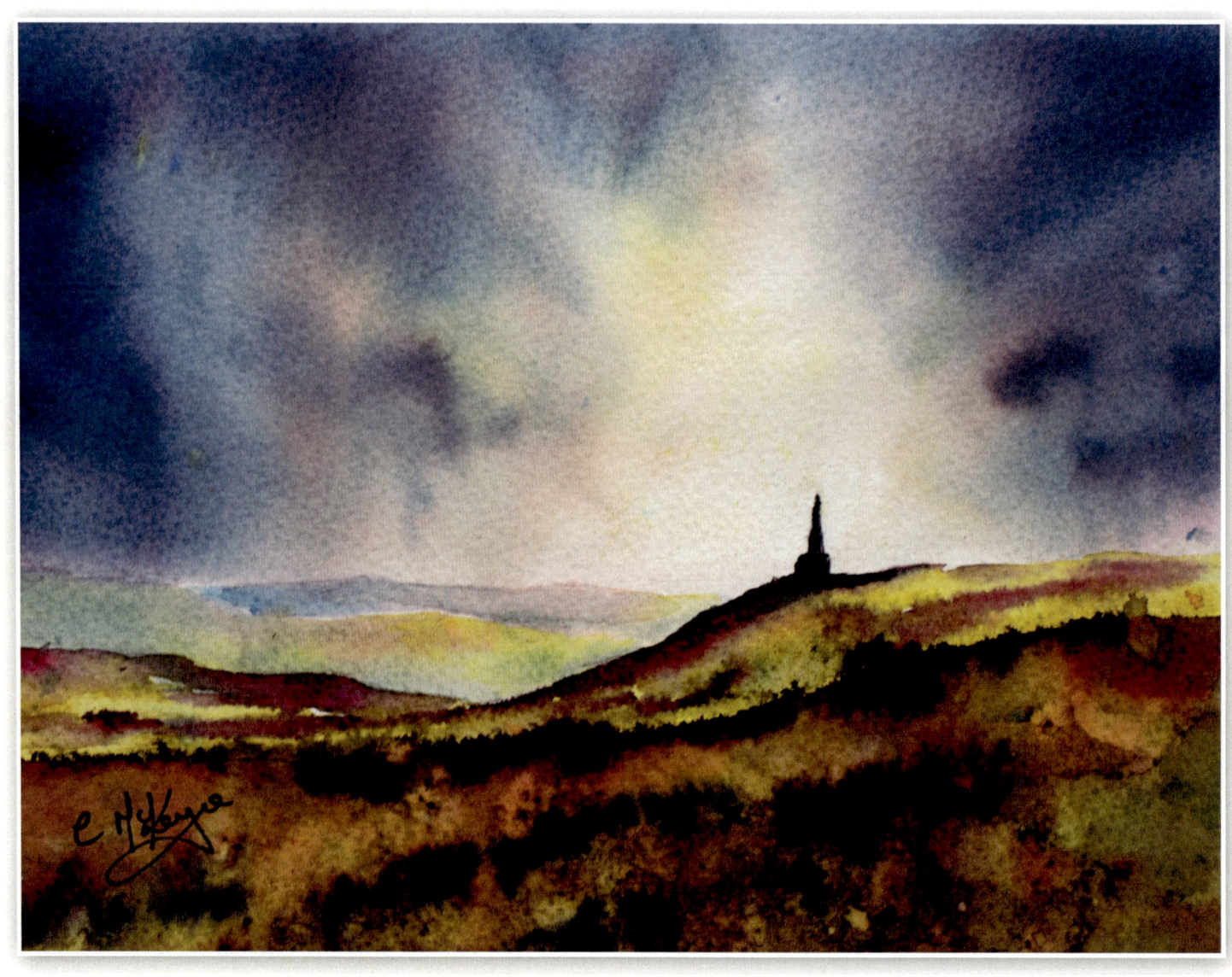

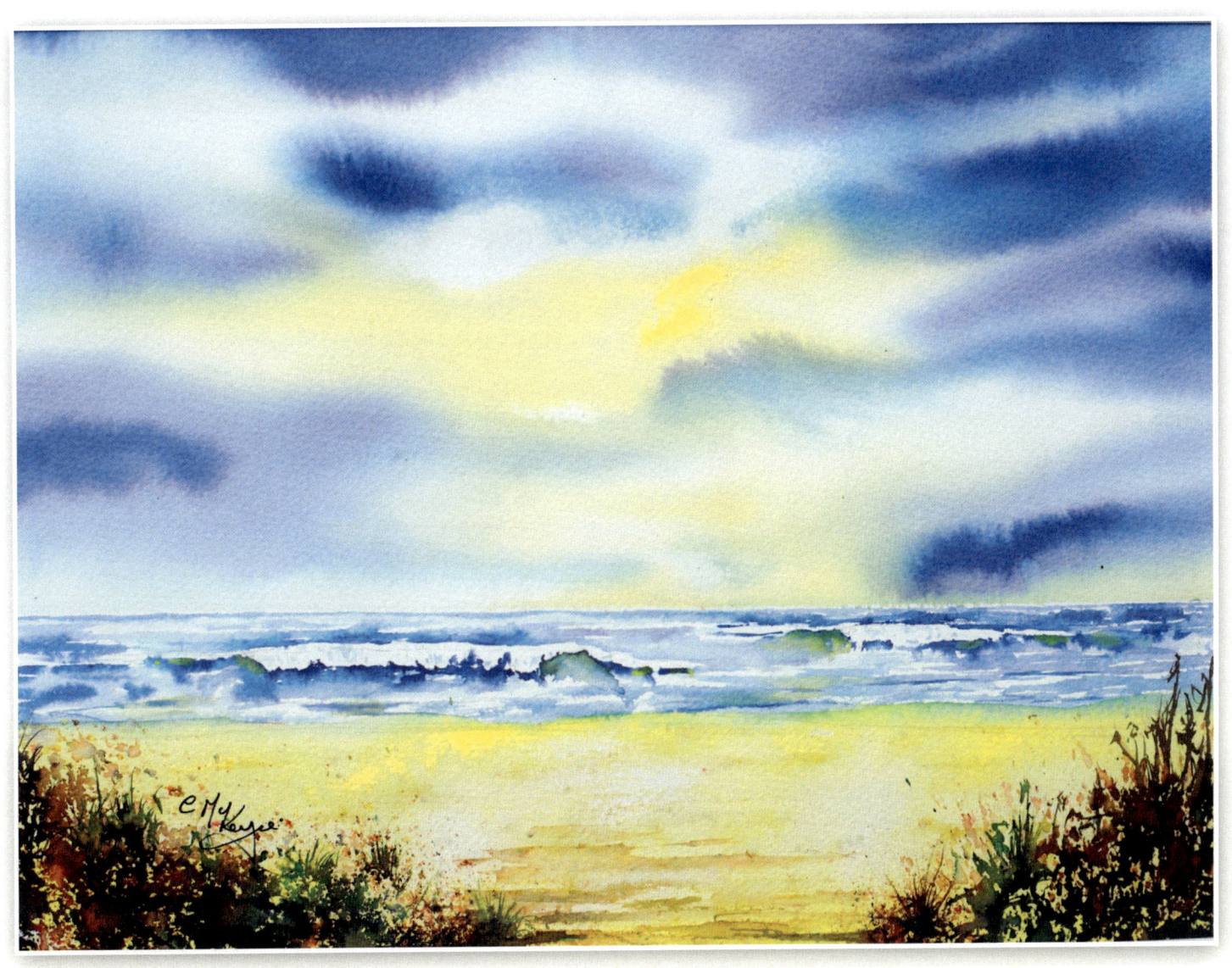

GOLDEN BEACH

For this painting, I used a combination of different Brusho techniques.

The sky and beach areas were completed first using the spray and blend technique, tilting the paper horizontally from side to side to obtain the effect of the clouds drifting across the sky.

I painted the waves with a mix of hard and soft edges using the lost and found technique, leaving patches of white paper for the crests of the waves. When this was dry, I painted the underneath of the waves with darker colour, again softening these into the water below.

When the paint used for the sand was dry, I painted a few light brown random lines to depict the furrows in the sand.

The foreground grasses and bushes were completed using the sprinkle and spritz technique to retain plenty of texture.

3 : WAX, MASKING & SALT

There are different methods and materials that you can use to "resist" the Brusho paint. Which method you choose in a painting will depend on the final result you want to achieve — they each have their different merits.

Technique 9 - Wax resist

The principle of wax resist is that wax and water don't mix. By applying wax to your watercolour paper, any water-based paint that you subsequently apply to those areas will not adhere to the surface. You can apply the wax right at the beginning to preserve the white paper, or at any stage in the painting over existing dry colour washes that you want to preserve.

You can use a chunk of clear wax candle or a white wax crayon. The amount of pressure you apply and the surface of the paper you are using will both affect the way the wax repels the paint.

Wax resist on white paper

➤ Use a chunk of clear wax or a white crayon to make a range of different marks and lines on some dry watercolour paper. Vary the pressure – press down heavily for some marks and skim the wax lightly across the paper for others. Mix some colour in your palette and paint over the paper to reveal the areas of white that have been preserved by the wax. Do all the marks and lines look as you intended? Were you too heavy or too light-handed? Did you leave too much, or too little, white area?

Wax resist on a coloured wash

➤ First paint a Lemon colour wash on a new piece of paper and leave it to dry. Make a variety of marks with the wax as you did previously, then paint over with a Scarlet colour wash. This is a useful technique if you want to retain small areas of light colour in a darker wash without having to paint round them. In my worked example, note that the white wax crayon I used for one of the wiggly lines has not preserved the Lemon wash but instead appears white. This is useful when you want to introduce white highlights into a future layer of colour.

Because the wax stays on the paper, you need to plan where and when you are going to apply it – once it's on, it's on! It's difficult to see it once you've applied it so you don't see the full effect of the wax until after you've applied the paint, by which time it's too late to change it! As you can't see it, one of the easiest mistakes to make is to overdo it. What you intended to be just a small highlight on a petal can easily turn into a gaping white hole left by a hungry caterpillar! So it's worth spending a little time becoming familiar with this medium.

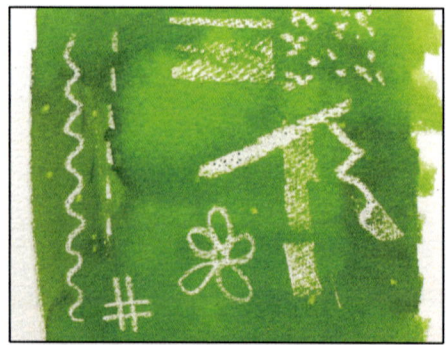

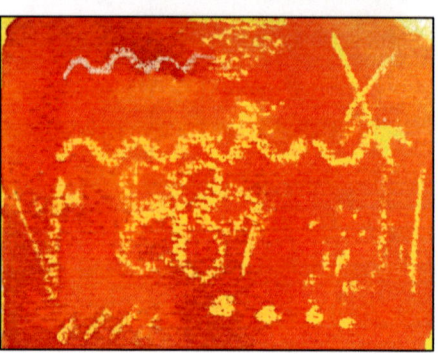

Technique 10 – Masking fluid and masking tape

Like wax, masking tape or fluid is used to protect areas of paper that you want to preserve. Instead of trying to paint around them, you simply apply the tape or fluid over any areas you want to protect, and then paint as if they weren't there. When you've finished, you just remove it.

The other advantage of using masking fluid or tape is that, unlike clear wax, you can see where you've put it. Also, if you don't like the white paper you've preserved you can always paint over it, which is something you can't do with wax.

Masking fluid is useful for blocking out fine details and lines, such as grasses. You can use an old brush to apply the fluid, or specialist rubber-tipped masking tools, a ruling pen, and even cocktail sticks or twigs. If you use a brush, it's important to clean it immediately after use as once the masking fluid dries it is impossible to get off.

You can splatter it on with an old toothbrush or palette knife for subjects such as the white foam of a wave. To remove masking fluid, just rub it gently with a clean finger or putty rubber.

Masking Tape is useful for masking out straight edged shapes like buildings, or separating the sky from the land or sea at the horizon level.

You can cut it to make more intricate shapes if you wish. It is best to use a low-tack variety as it can sometimes damage the surface of the paper when you remove it.

Masking to preserve white paper or a coloured wash

➤ Put a length of masking tape across the middle of a small piece of paper. At either side of the masking tape, apply masking fluid with an old brush or other masking tools, to draw some grasses, flower and other shapes. Also try spattering the masking fluid on with an old toothbrush or palette knife. Leave it to dry.
➤ Paint over the top of the masking tape and masking fluid with Leaf Green and leave it to dry again.
➤ Peel off the masking tape carefully and use your fingers or a putty rubber to gently rub off the masking fluid to reveal the white paper preserved beneath the Leaf Green colour wash.
➤ As with the candle wax technique, you can use exactly the same process to preserve a base colour by applying masking fluid or tape before painting another colour on top.

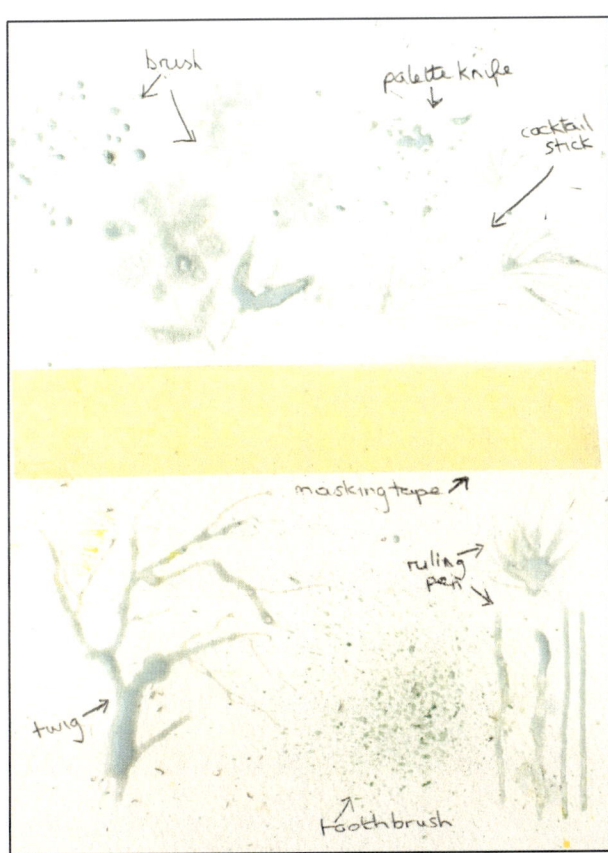

Blue masking fluid applied with different tools

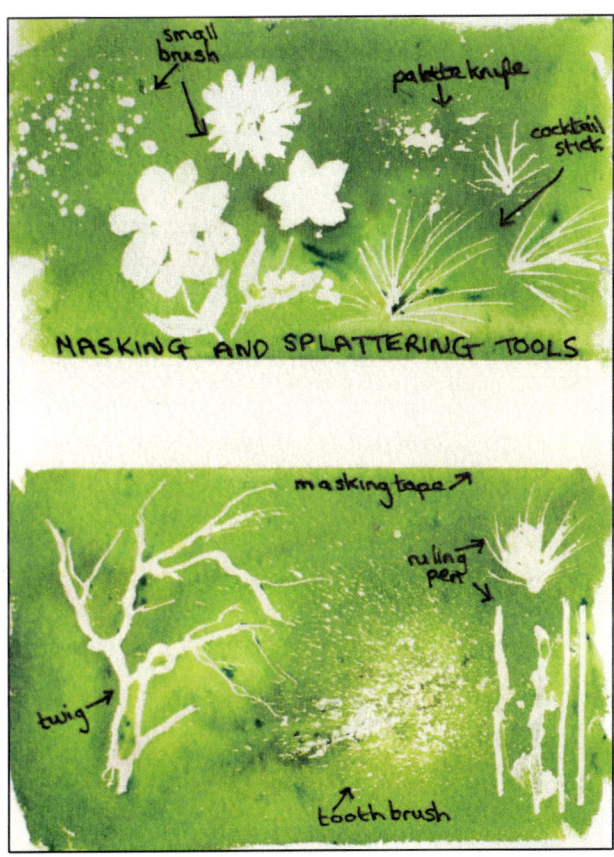

Masking fluid and masking tape removed to reveal white paper

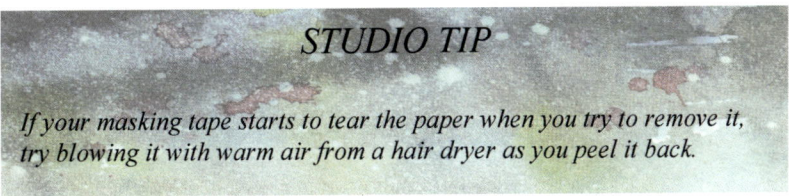

STUDIO TIP

If your masking tape starts to tear the paper when you try to remove it, try blowing it with warm air from a hair dryer as you peel it back.

39

BLUE SHUTTERS

MATERIALS
Yellow
Orange
Dark Brown
Purple
Scarlet
Ultramarine

Clear wax
Masking tape

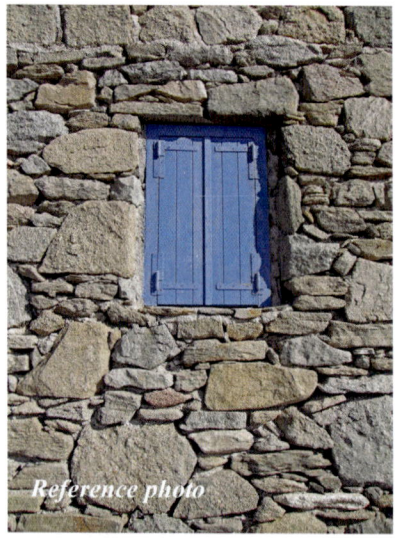

Reference photo

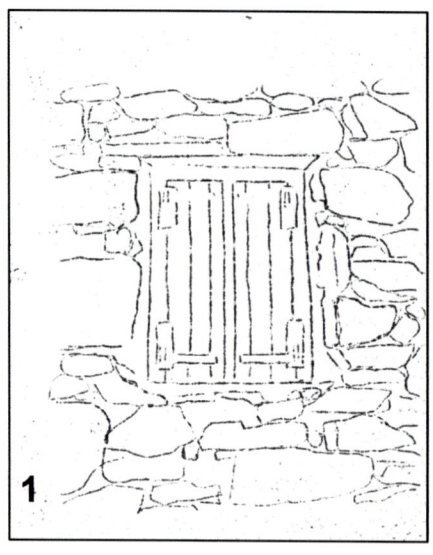

1 Note how colourful the orange, yellow and red stones are in the photo – just right for a Brusho painting. Stones and rocks are also excellent subjects for using the wax resist technique. For our painting, we will make the shutters look a little more aged in keeping with the stonework (you don't have to follow a photograph slavishly). Start by sketching the outline of the blue shutters and surrounding stonework shown in the reference photo.

2 Apply a little wax to a few random parts of the stonework, skimming the surface of the paper to catch the highlights on the stone. Use masking tape cut to size to protect the shutters.

3 Sprinkle some Yellow, and touches of Orange and Scarlet over the stonework. Use the water sprayer to spritz the Brusho just enough to obtain a textured stone effect – don't over-spritz and lose the texture. The white highlights from the wax you applied in step 2 will show up later. Leave to dry.

4 Mix some Dark Brown with a touch of Ultramarine in your palette. Use a rigger or small brush with a fine point, to paint the outlines of the stonework and the gaps in between. Work a section at a time so you can soften some of the lines with the blending technique before they dry. Vary the lines in places and add a little extra dark colour to some of the gaps between the stones. Leave to dry.

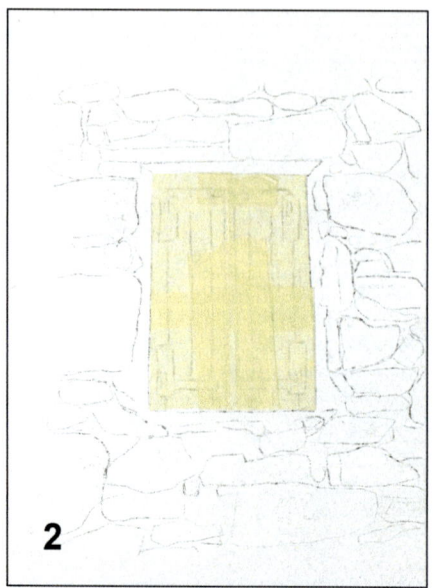

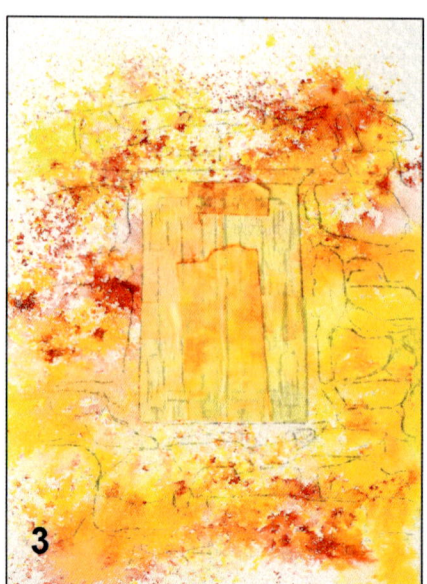

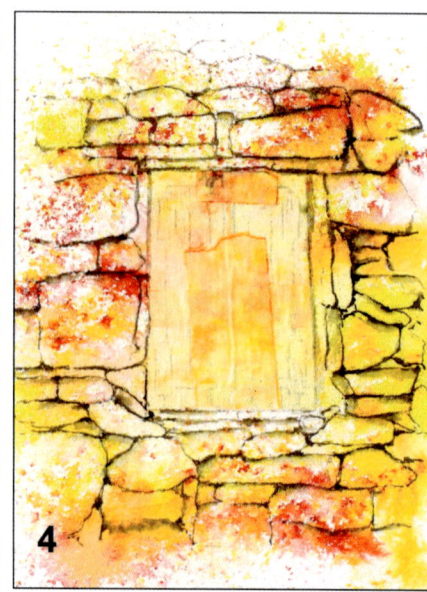

5 Gently remove the masking tape, being careful not to tear the paper underneath.

Apply a watery mix of Ultramarine wash to the shutters – don't worry if it's a bit patchy, it will add to the aged character. Leave to dry.

Then, skim a little wax across the shutters before painting over with a stronger wash of Ultramarine. This will give the effect of worn paintwork

Leave to dry again.

6 Mix a little Dark Brown with the Ultramarine in your palette and use this darker colour to define the hinges and the gaps between the wooden slats, softening and varying the lines in places.

Mix some Purple with a little Ultramarine to paint the shadow areas around the shutters – make the shadow colour darker at the top and right-hand side of the shutters where it is more shaded from the light.

Finally, add a little shadow colour to a few of the stones to complete the painting.

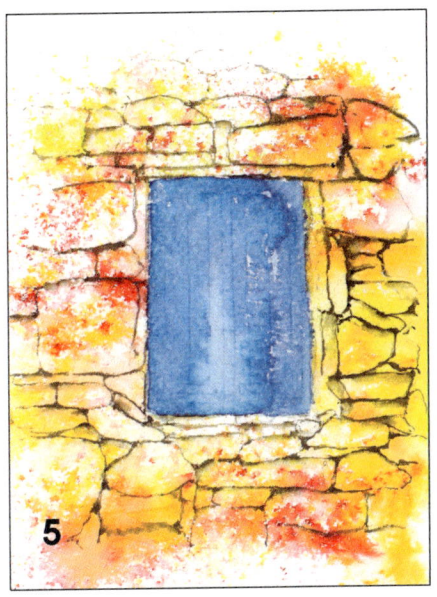

5

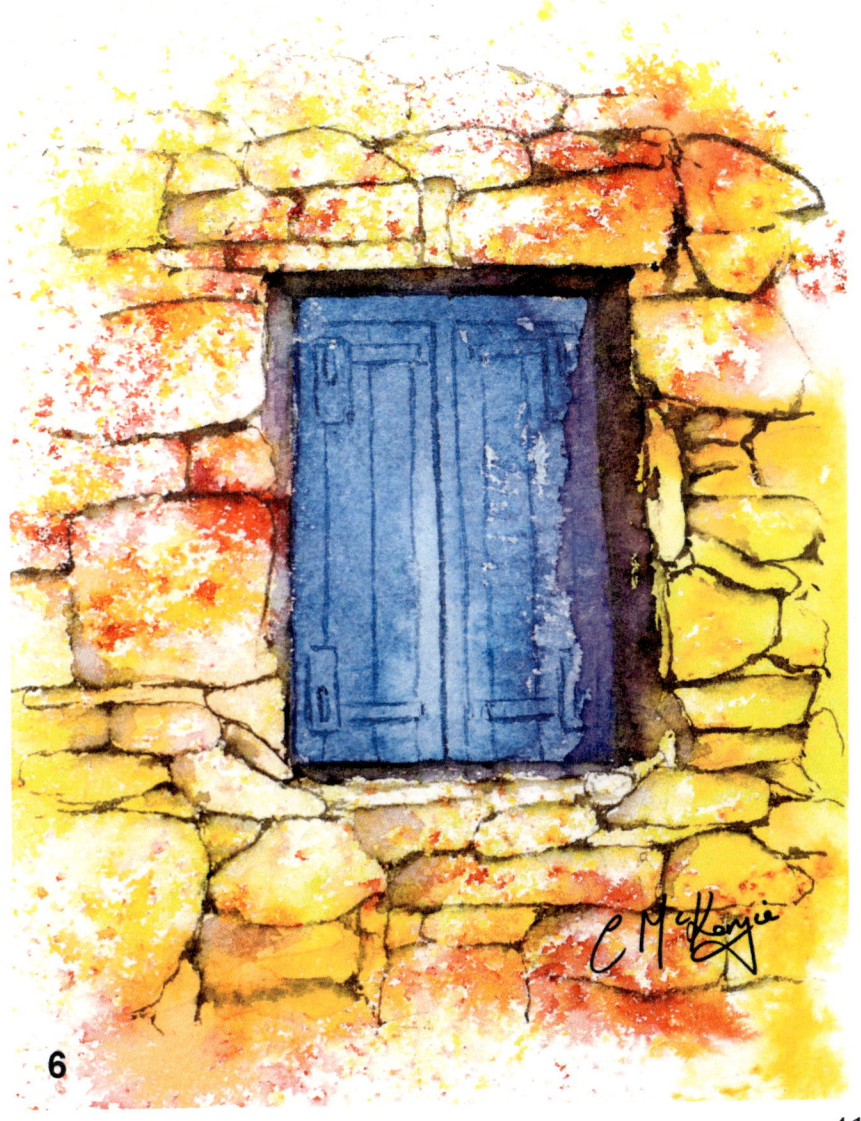

6

41

Technique 11 – Salt crystals

If you sprinkle salt crystals onto a drying wash just as the shine is disappearing, they will absorb the colour from the paint and leave mottled patterns, specks or star shapes. You can use common household salt, rock salt, sea salt, even dishwasher salt – they will all render slightly different patterns. It's a useful technique for creating the appearance of snow, foliage, textured walls, etc., or just to add interest to a background wash. Timing is crucial, it's important to apply the salt when the paper is still wet but not soaking. Alternatively, if the paper is too dry it will not have any effect at all. Try lifting the paper up to your eye level and view it horizontally – you should be able to see the crucial sheen stage.

Salt patterns

➢ Paint a few rectangles in different colours and drop in some salt crystals just as the shine is disappearing from the paper. When it is completely dry, brush off the salt residue to reveal the patterns beneath. Did you get the timing right? Here are some of my worked examples using different salts.

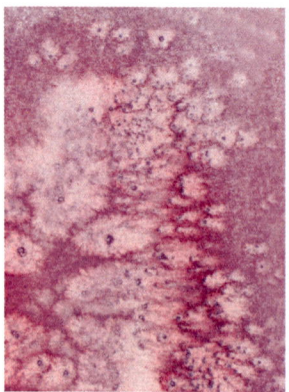
Household salt

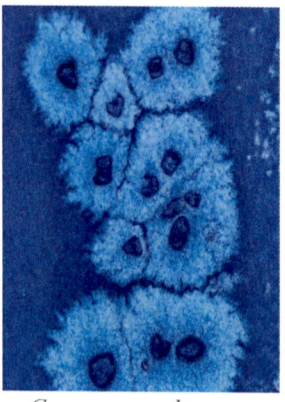
Coarse sea salt

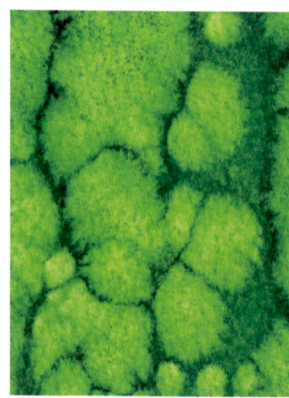
Himalayan salt

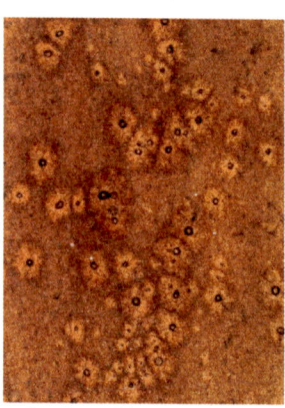
Dishwasher salt

Salt patterns in a background

➢ Draw this little robin redbreast, who visited my garden on an icy, blue winter day. Mix some Yellow, Scarlet, Dark Brown, Yellow, Ultramarine and Black paint in separate wells of your palette.

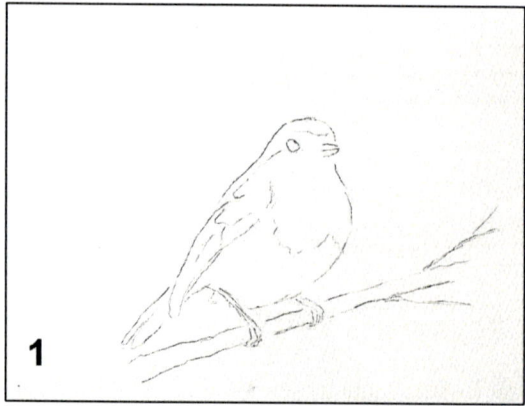

➢ Wet all the sky area, working around the snow on the branches. Then drop in some watery Ultramarine and a few strokes of Purple, let these mingle with the wet wash leaving a few areas for white cloud. Don't make these colours too strong - you are aiming for a pale frosty sky colour. As the sheen starts to disappear from the paper, sprinkle a little salt here and there. Leave to dry, then brush off any salt residue that is left to reveal some lovely delicate frosty salt patterns in the sky.

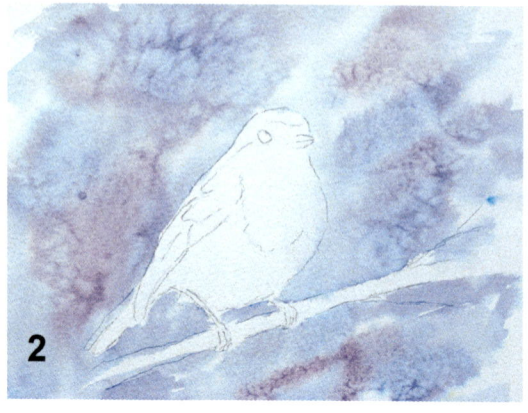

➢ Paint the robin's chest, wing and tail feathers with a weak wash of Yellow.

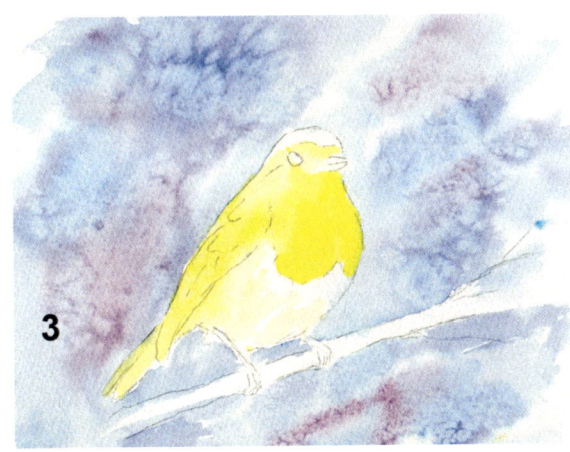

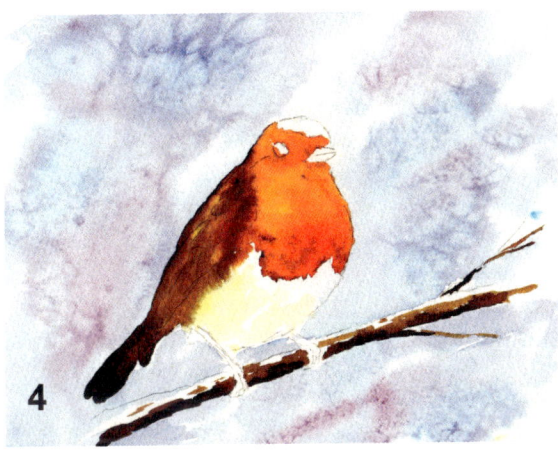

➢ While the Yellow is still damp, drop in some Scarlet in the chest and head areas - let the colours mingle to form an orangey-red. Use Dark Brown to paint the wing and tail feathers. Paint the branch with Dark Brown leaving small areas along the top of the branch unpainted to represent some snow. Leave to dry.

➢ Paint the top of his head and the under-belly area with a very watery Black so it appears light grey. Paint his legs and claws with the same watery grey, adding a stronger mix to define them. Paint the eye and the beak with Black, leaving a small dot of white paper in the eye as a highlight. Leave to dry.

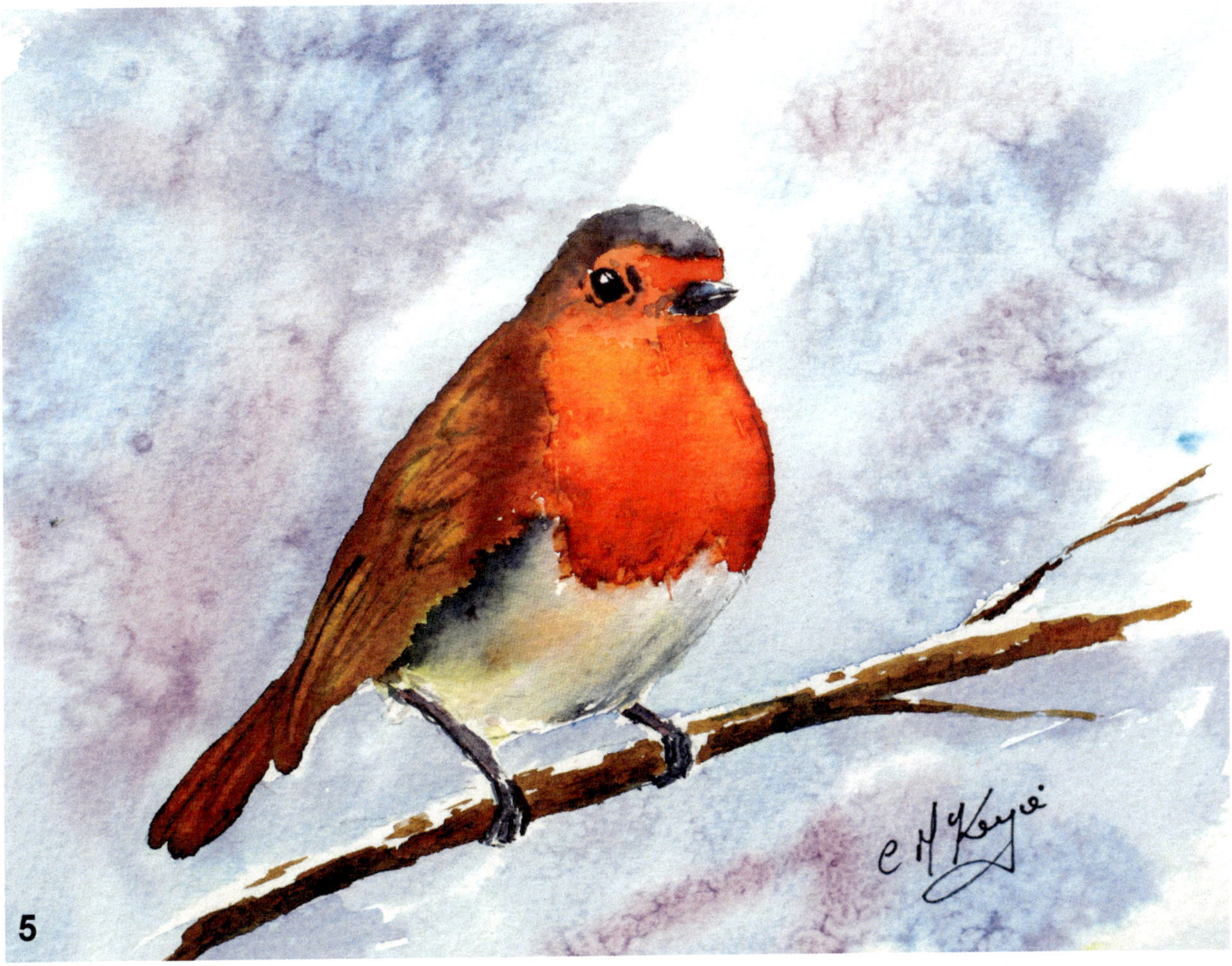

Demonstration
TREE STUMP

MATERIALS
Yellow
Leaf Green
Dark Brown
Orange
Ultramarine

Masking fluid
Salt

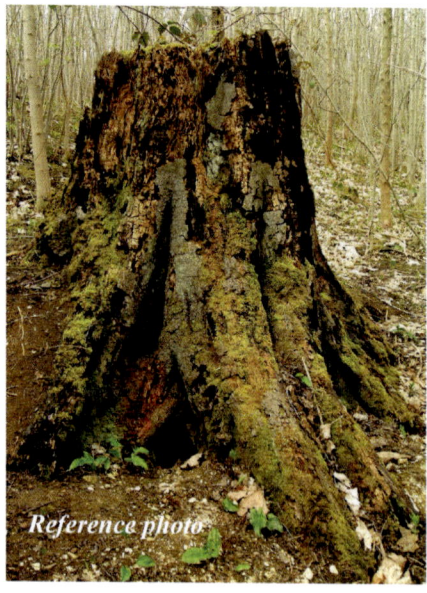

Reference photo

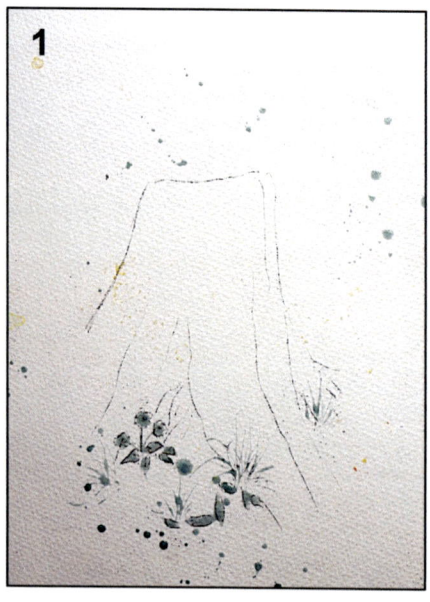

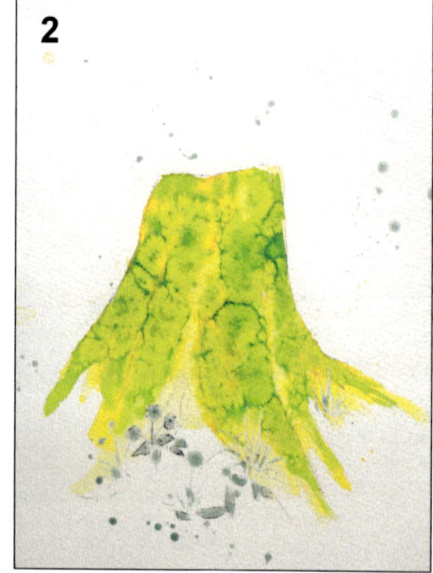

1 This project will combine the techniques of masking fluid and salt. Draw the tree stump and small leaves from the reference photo, but allow more space at the top. I've used a little artistic licence and added a few grasses and small flowers. Apply masking fluid to the leaves, grasses and flower heads. Then, with a small brush, old toothbrush or palette knife, splatter a few random spots of masking fluid on the foreground. Leave to dry.

2 Mix some Leaf Green and Yellow separately in your palette. Paint the trunk with Yellow. While this is still wet drop in some Leaf Green on top, allowing some patches of the Yellow to show through. Before the paint dries, sprinkle some salt into the yellowy-green wash to create lichen and moss texture.
   Leave to dry. Then, brush off any salt residue to reveal the patterns left in the wash.

3 Because both Brusho and salt are so unpredictable it is doubtful that you will be able to stick rigidly to the photograph. From this point, you need to follow the salt patterns that have emerged in your own painting.
   Mix some Orange in your palette. Look carefully at the textures and patterns that have formed in your painting and use these to guide your next steps.
   Paint Orange onto areas of the tree stump around the lichen patterns where you can see the bark. Soften the Orange here and there into the green lichen shapes, and at the end of the roots. Leave to dry.

44

4 Mix some Dark Brown in your palette and paint the dark areas of wood and the dark scratchy lines of the bark. Blend a few lines with a damp brush, but leave some hard edges as well.

5 Sprinkle some Orange, Yellow and small amounts of Dark Brown and Leaf Green sparingly on the foreground area, and just behind the tree stump at each side. Spritz lightly – don't over-do it, you want this foreground area to retain lots of texture. Leave to dry. Use a clean finger or putty rubber to remove the masking fluid from the foreground.

Paint the white leaf shapes and grasses with Yellow and Leaf Green. Put a Yellow dot in the centre of each white flower head. Leave to dry.

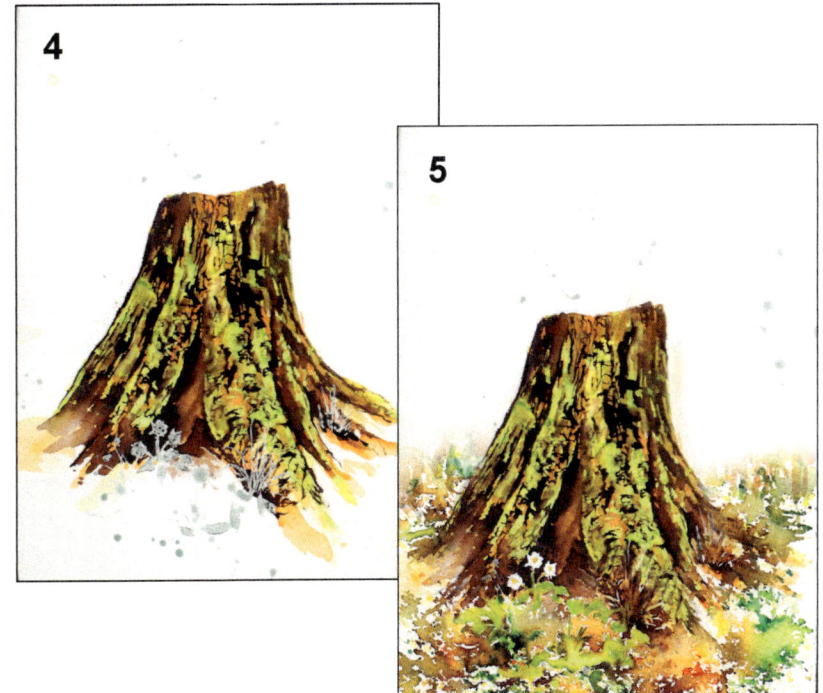

6 Turn the painting upside down. Wet the area above the foreground and around the tree stump (don't wet the tree stump itself or the foreground).

While the paper is still wet, use the tip of your brush to drizzle in some Yellow, Orange, a little Leaf Green and a little Dark Brown - use vertical strokes as if these are distant trees.

Whilst everything is still wet, lift the paper up from the bottom, and then holding it vertically, spray the colours down the paper.

Wiggle your paper and use gentle brush strokes to encourage the colours to blend a little and look like distant woodland.

If you lose too much colour through spraying, drop in some more and spray again. Work quickly so it doesn't go patchy or muddy.

When you are happy with the result, lay the paper flat again and leave to dry.

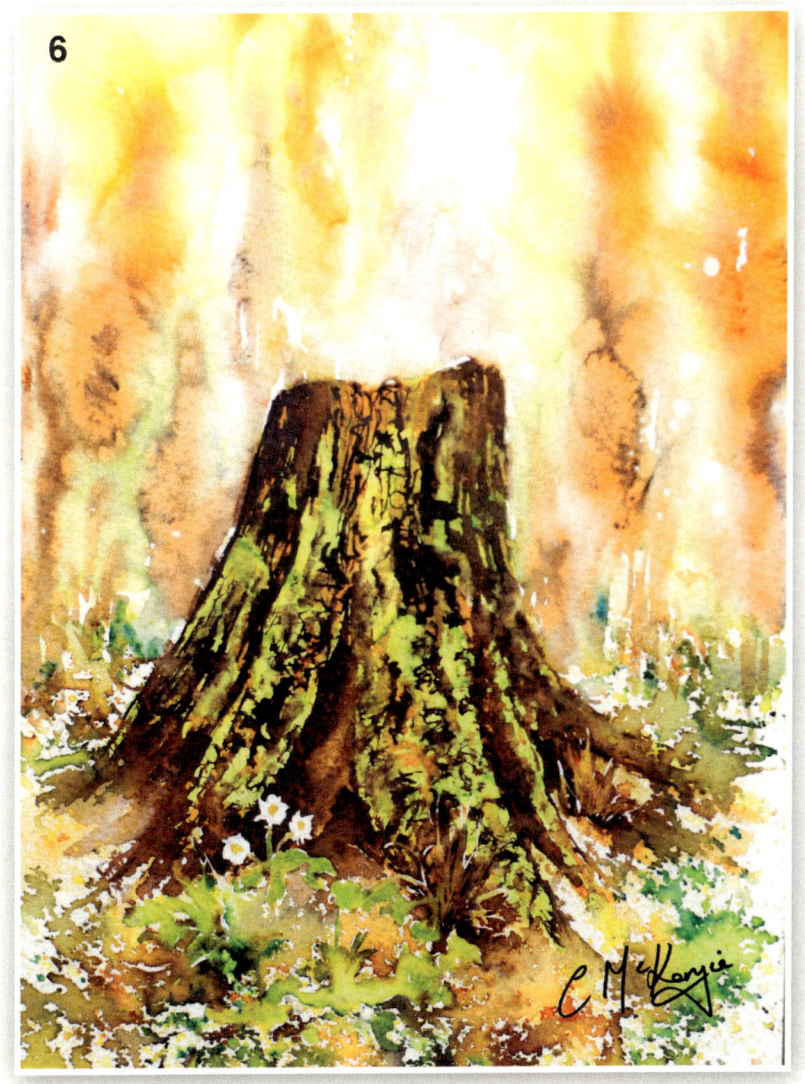

Demonstration
DRAGONFLIES ON THE WING

MATERIALS
Lemon
Leaf Green
Emerald
Purple
Black

Masking fluid
Salt

We will now incorporate some of the techniques you've learned so far to paint lovely dragonflies dancing round hogweed and other wild flowers. Dragonflies have beautiful almost transparent wings, which will contrast nicely with the textured foliage.

This painting is based on several reference photos of dragonflies and hogweed, along with my imagination, so there's no set reference photo. I think it's important not to rely on photos to create your art, and allow your own creativity and ideas to surface. You can use my drawing and the finished painting as a guide but feel free to develop your own interpretation. This is intended to be a loose, impressionistic painting so don't worry about trying to complete a botanical study.

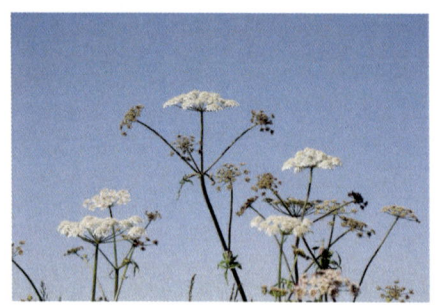 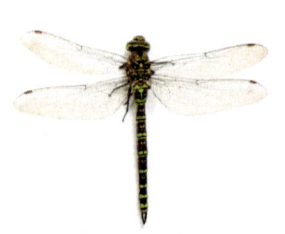 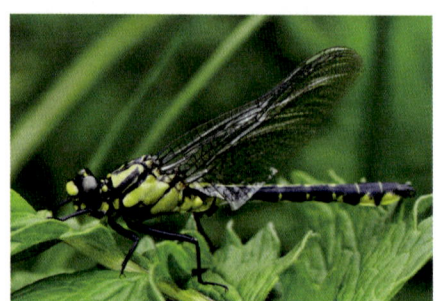

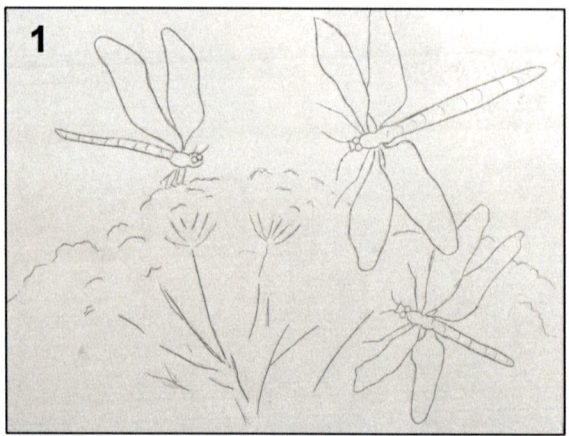

1 Copy the outline of the drawing on a large sheet of paper at least quarter imperial size - it's much easier to work loose with Brusho on larger pieces of paper

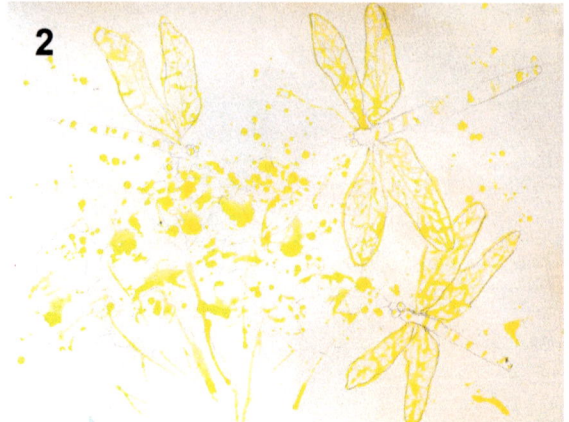

2 Use a ruling pen or other pointed tool to apply a fine line of masking fluid around each dragonfly wing and the network of lines inside their wings. Add a small dot of masking fluid in the centre of each eye. Make small linear marks with masking fluid to retain white paper at intervals along each dragonfly body.

Then using an old brush, apply masking fluid in a fairly random way to the foliage areas that you want to keep white or light – this will particularly apply to the hogweed heads. Mask a few stems and leaf shapes where they catch the light. Finally, dip your brush into the masking fluid and spatter a few small drops randomly just above the foliage/hogweed head.

Let this dry completely.

3 Mix some Ultramarine and Turquoise in separate palette wells – don't make either of these too strong, you are aiming for a soft pale-blue summer sky.

Wet the sky area of the paper with a large brush, and also wet the two dragonflies at the top of the paper. Working quickly, drop some Ultramarine and a little Turquoise onto the wetted paper and spray horizontally to keep the colour at the top of the paper.

Pick your paper up and tilt it horizontally left and right to allow the colours to blend. The colour should flow into the parts of the dragonflies that are not masked so that the background sky colour shows through their transparent wings. If it doesn't, pick up some colour on your brush and use the brush tip to gently stroke it into the wings.

If you get any runs of colour into the foliage area, just blot with some paper towel. Remember not to spend too long fiddling with the sky or it will look overworked and lose its freshness – set a time limit of 10 minutes max!

As soon as you are happy with the look of it, lay it flat and leave it to dry.

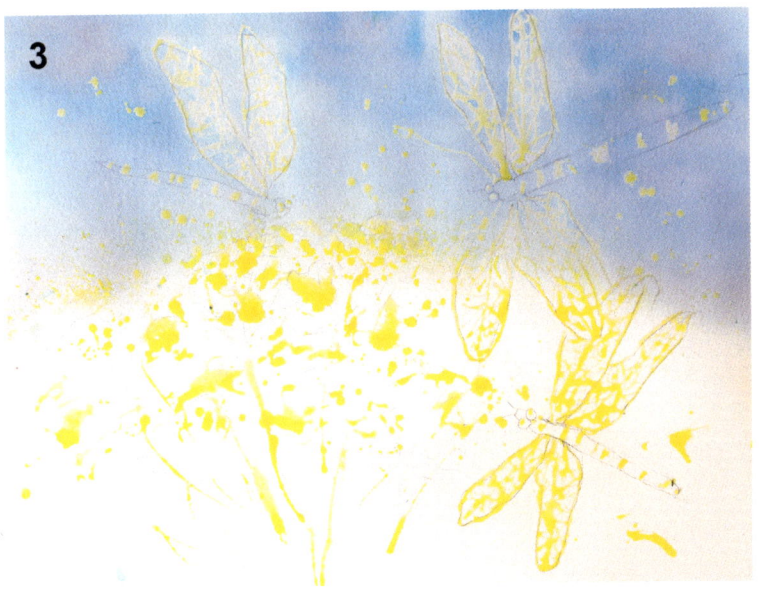

4 Protect the dry sky area with some paper towel to avoid contamination from this next step. Keeping the top of the foliage area where the flowers are catching the light mostly Lemon, sprinkle some Lemon, Leaf Green and little touches of Emerald around the foliage section of the paper, and including the third dragonfly.

Spritz just enough to obtain a nice foliage texture. Scatter in a few household salt crystals here and there to add more texture. Leave to dry.

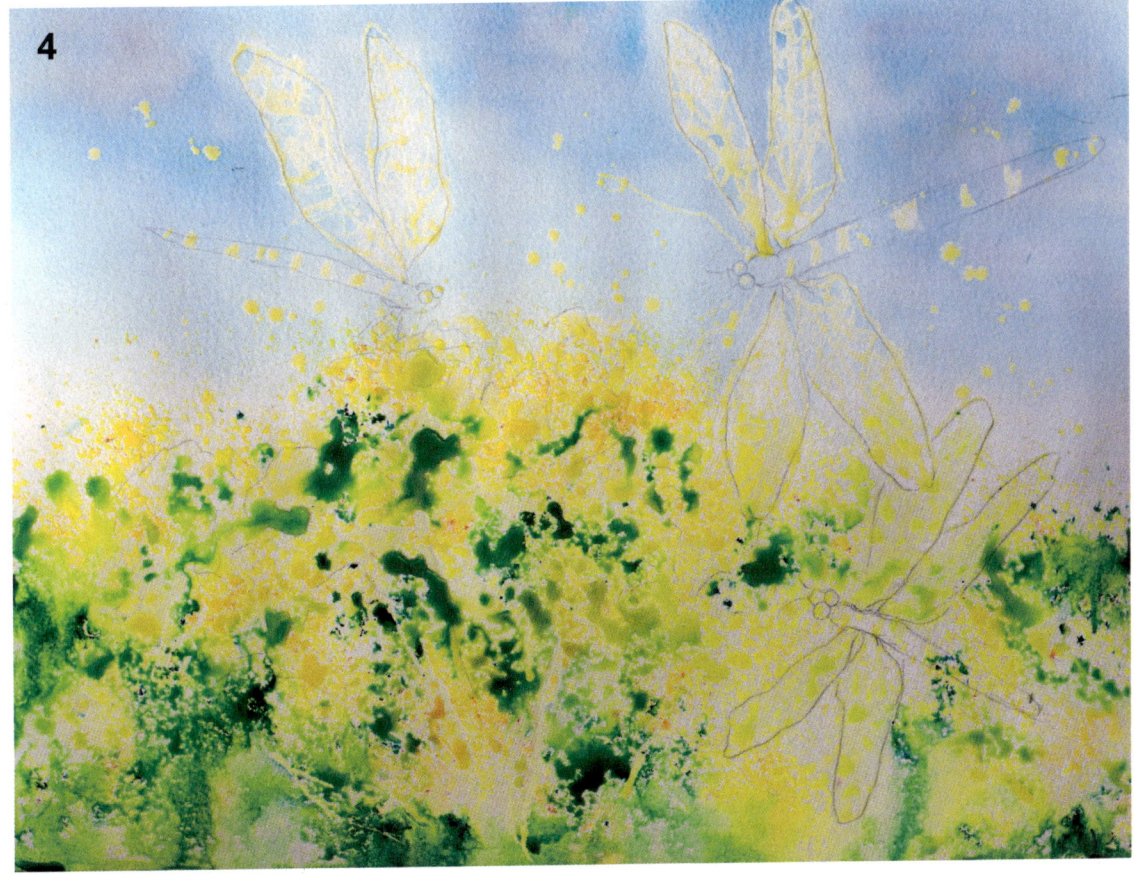

5 Remove the masking fluid with a clean finger or putty rubber. Soften any hard lines on the dragonfly wings left by the masking fluid by rubbing them with a clean damp brush If there is too much white showing, paint over it.

Paint the bodies of the top two dragonflies with Ultramarine and Black stripes, retaining the little stripes of white paper in between (preserved by the masking fluid). Repeat using Emerald and Black for the lower dragonfly. Paint the legs, antenna and eyes of all the dragonflies with Black, leaving a small dot of white paper for the catch lights in the eyes.

To 'knock back' the white stems of the foliage, paint them with Lemon and Leaf Green, but leave little touches of white highlights here and there. Emphasise some of the stems by painting them darker at one side with a mix of Leaf Green and Ultramarine.

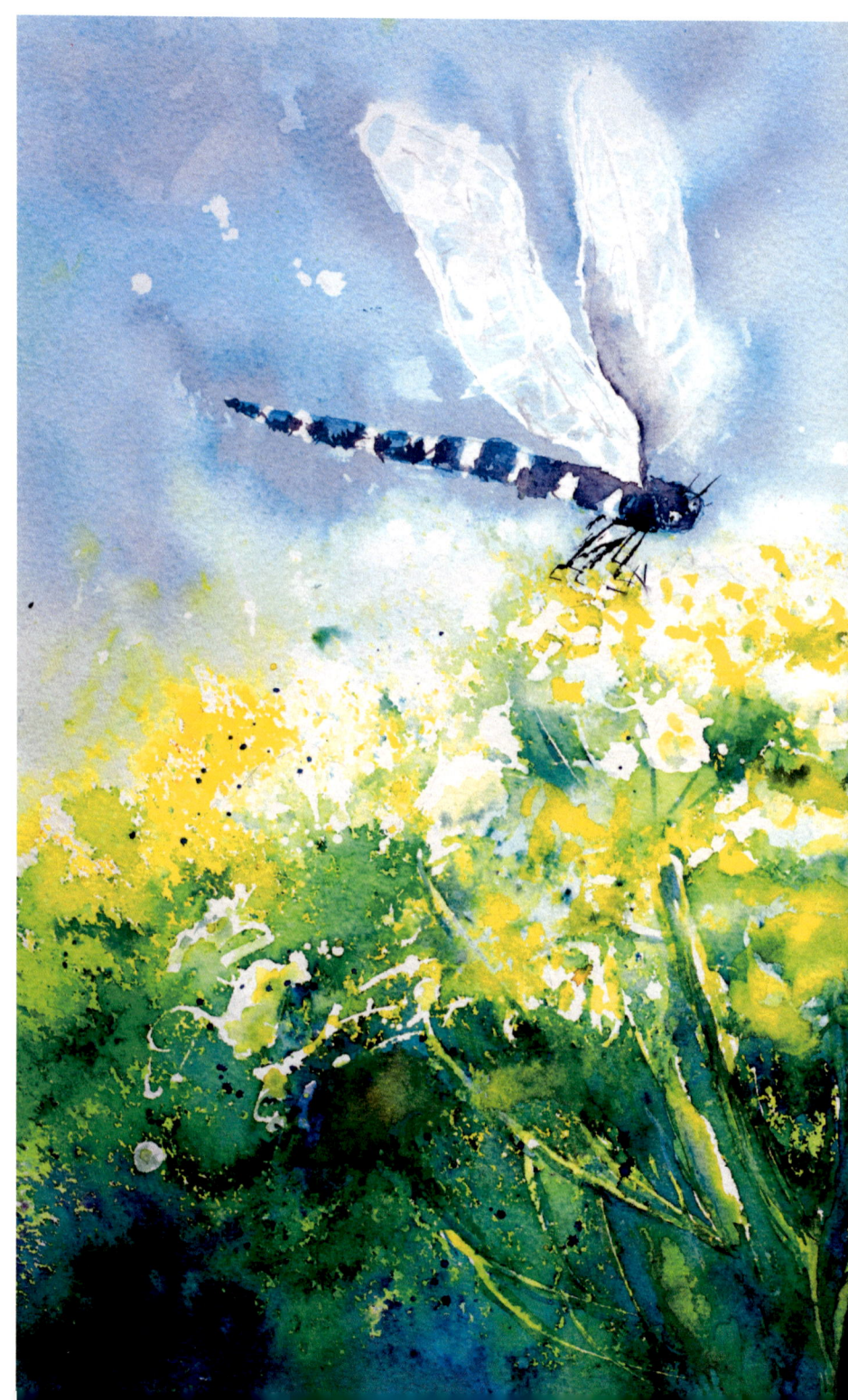

Mix a little Ultramarine with Emerald in your palette and drop this into a couple of places at the bottom of the page to 'anchor' the painting - use the blending technique to soften them in.

Leave to dry. Define the dragonfly wings by painting a slightly darker background colour the outer edges of the wings using the same colours you applied to the background area (ie, either the sky or the foliage colours). Blend and soften the paint to avoid a hard edge in the sky. Don't be tempted to paint around a whole wing or it will look unnatural.

I hope you enjoyed this chapter and are beginning to feel more confident using Brusho. There are some more exciting techniques to try out in the following pages. Beautiful Brilliant Brusho

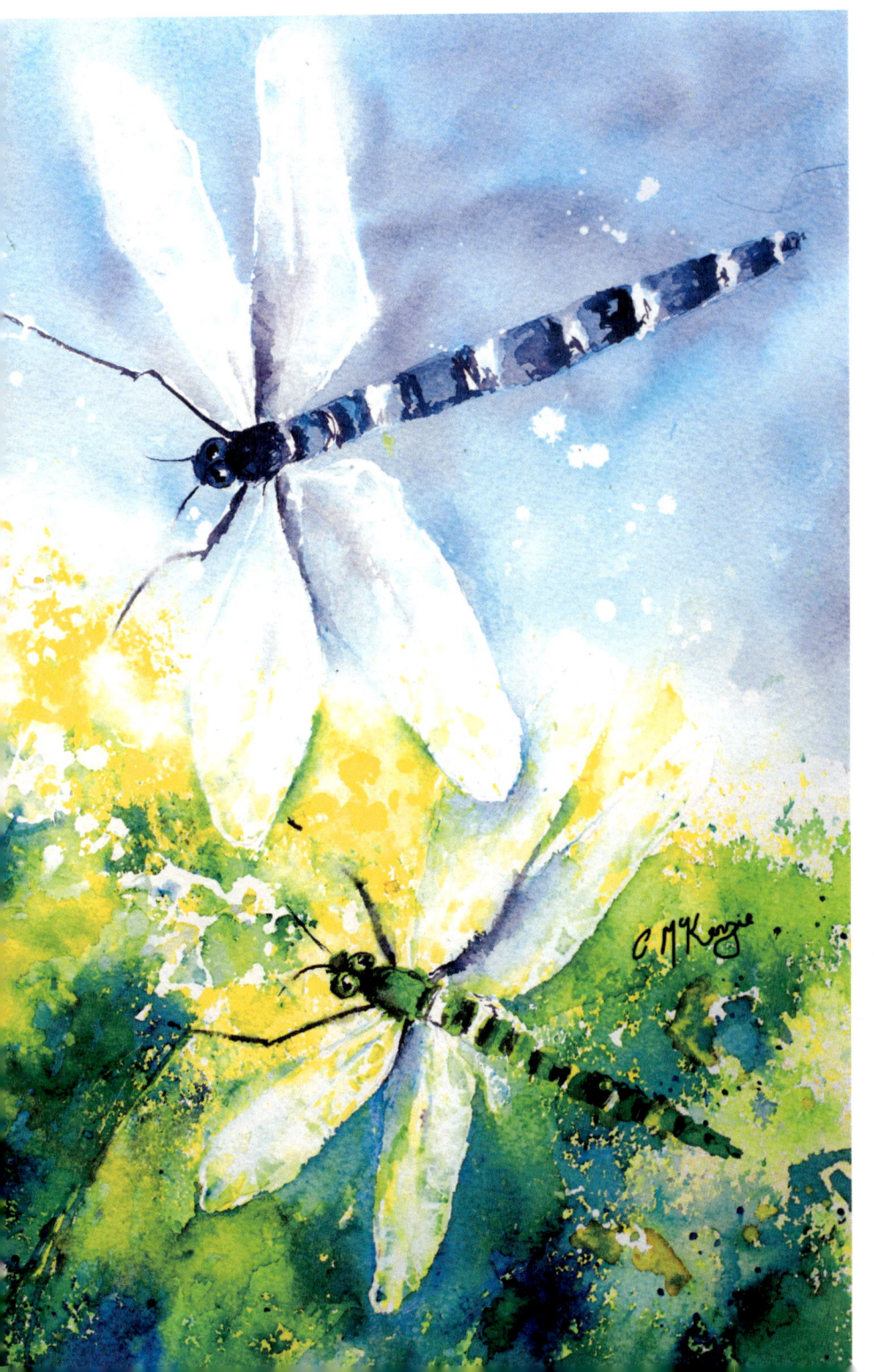

GALLERY

STEPPING OUT

In this painting, I preserved the white paper with wax to define the feather shapes and to break up the foreground. The swirls of wax in the tail feathers help to indicate movement

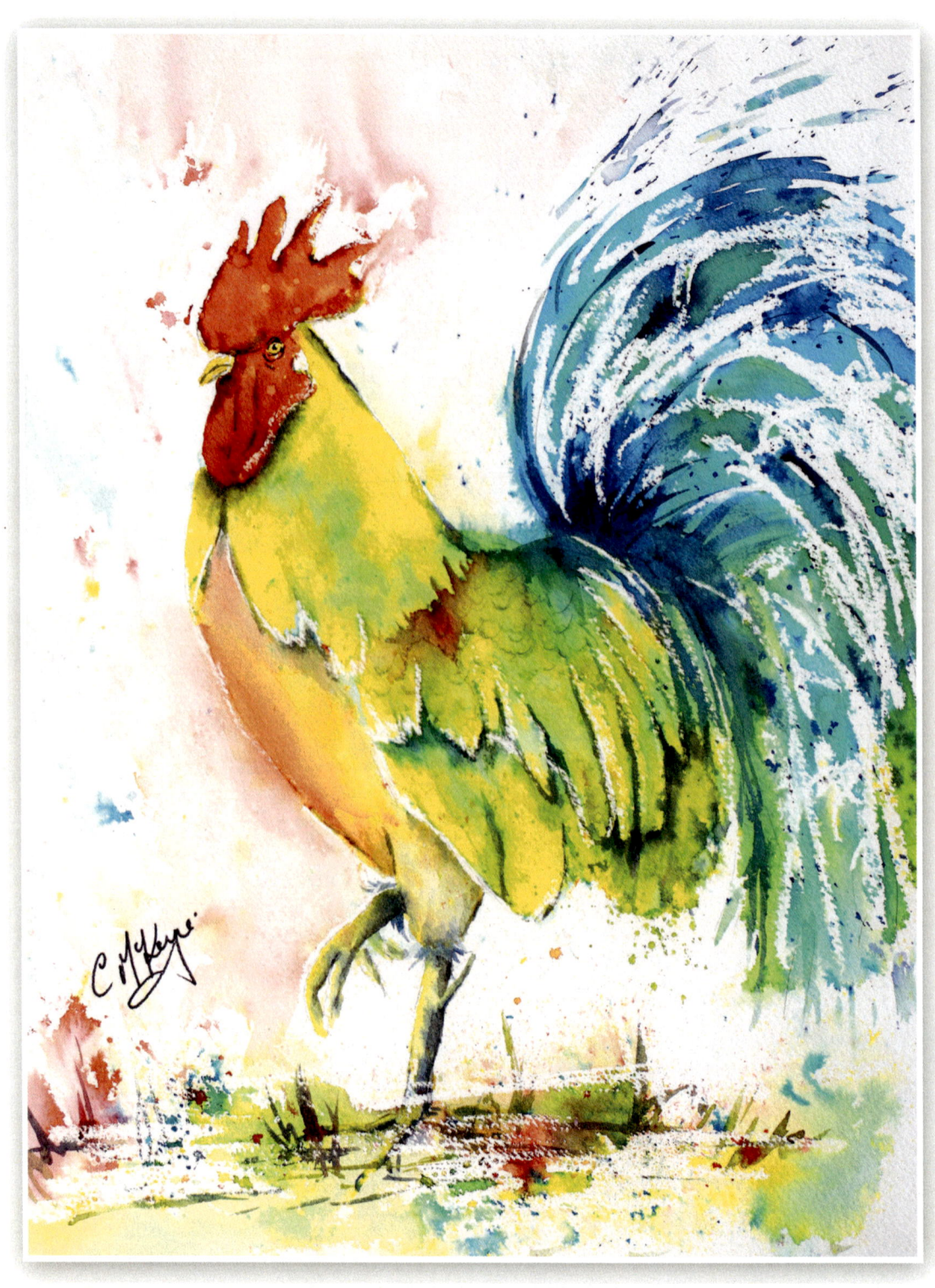

POPPIES ON FIRE

I preserved some of the white highlights in the centres of the poppies with wax. I preserved other highlights on the petals with masking fluid

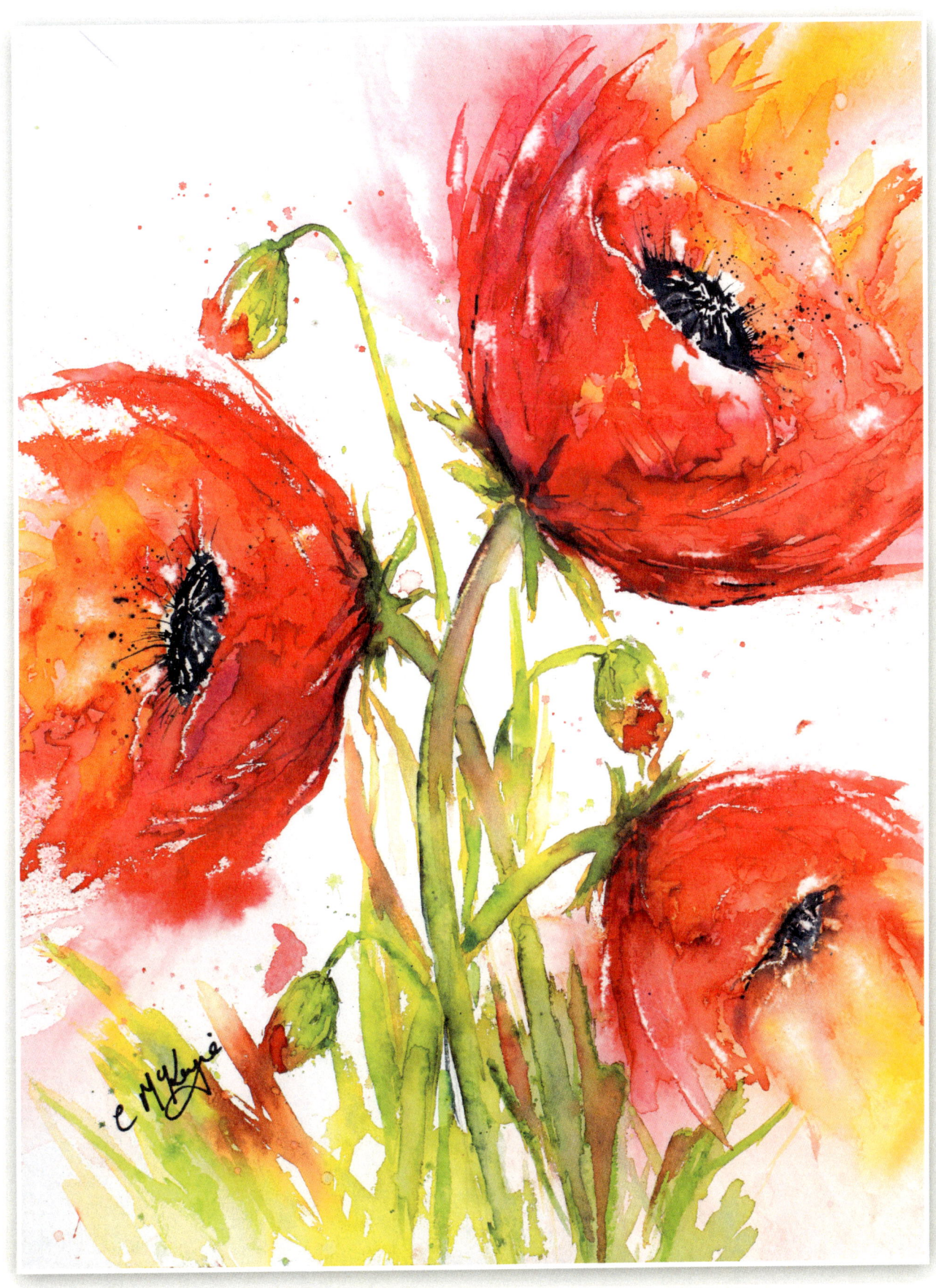

A WALK IN THE RAIN

I used masking fluid and clear wax to preserve white paper on the umbrella, its handle and highlights on the man's clothes, some falling raindrops, and parts of the little dog. I sprinkled a little salt into the background wash for interest.

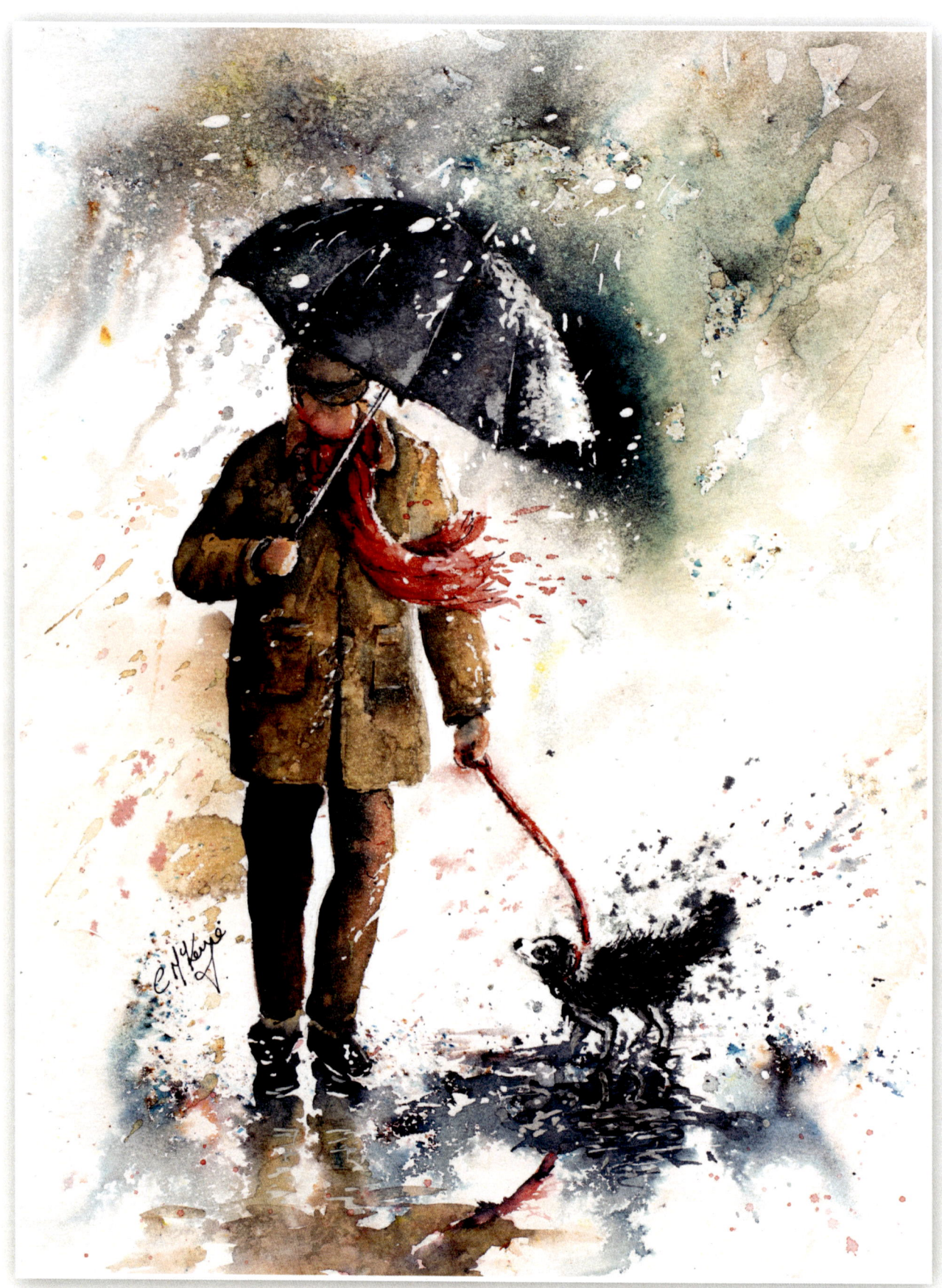

OFF TO THE SHOPS

In this painting, I used wax and masking fluid to preserve the white paper on the umbrella and the girls clothing. I used wax and salt to break up the background wash.

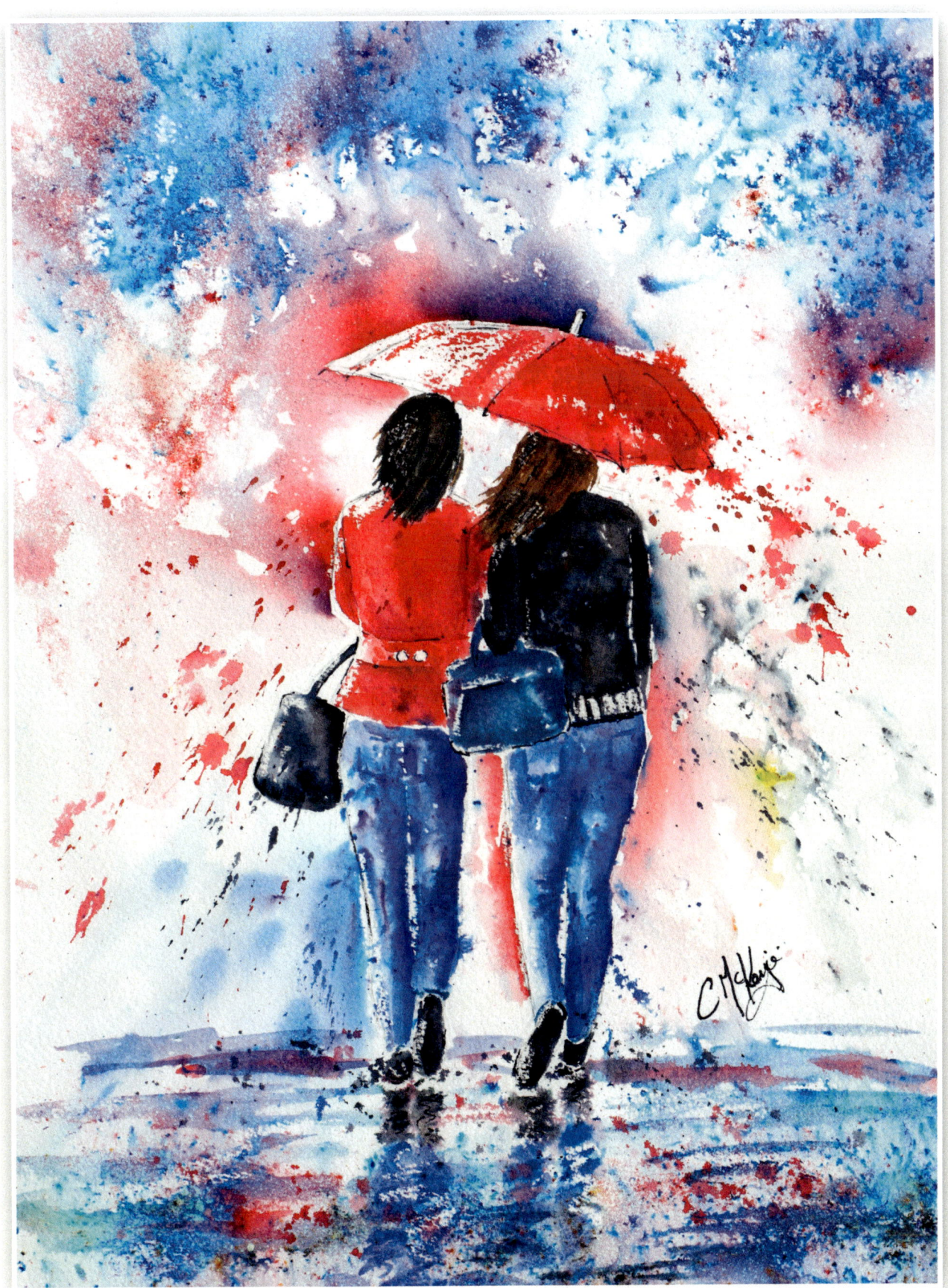

4 : INKS & GRANULATION

Line and wash is an expressive and exciting technique. It combines precisely drawn pen lines that give structure and lively emphasis to the drawing, with the fluidity and transparency of paint that suggests form, movement and light.

The loose, impressionistic effects of Brusho make it an ideal medium to use for a pen and wash painting.

The essence of a good line and wash painting is simplicity. It should have a sketchy, unfinished quality — remember the saying "less is more".

There is no hard rule about whether to use the ink or the paint first. However, if you use water-soluble ink first, beware that it will run and bleed into the paint when you put a wash over the top. So if you want the pen marks to be permanent it makes sense to use waterproof inks.

Because it is permanent, however, it can't be removed so you need to spend a little more time thinking before inking!

You can use steel-nibbed dip pens, quill pens or reed pens, with a pot of ink, all of which make lovely spontaneous lines. It can be frustrating to keep re-loading the pen as they don't hold a lot of ink, but you do get lovely, expressive lines that give a lot of visual interest.

You can use fountain pens that have an ink reservoir. Or you can simply use a ready-made waterproof pen, which come in different point sizes. I have even dipped the ends of broken twigs into a pot of ink, which give some lovely energetic lines that are perfect for drawing tree branches!

You can use any colour of ink, but the most usual one is waterproof black indian ink. For the purpose of this book, I have suggested using a black 0.5 ready-made waterproof ink pen, but feel free to experiment with other tools if you wish. Try these different pen and ink shading methods on a piece of cartridge or watercolour paper.

Technique 12 – Pen and ink

➢ LINEAR HATCHING – the lines mostly go in the same direction, usually parallel to each other. The closer together the lines are, the darker the value.

➢ CROSS HATCHING – the same as hatching but the lines cross over each other.

➢ CROSS CONTOUR – the lines follow the outline of the object and fill its shape, making your drawing look more 3-D.

➢ RANDOM or SCUMBLING – the lines go in various 'crazy' directions, allowing you to create a variety of textures.

➢ STIPPLING – use countless dots to create the value, although a little tedious this provides more control and gives a very neat effect.

➢ INK WASH – you apply the ink with a brush, and just like watercolour the amount of water that you dilute it with determines the tonal value

➢ SPATTER – gently tap a brush or pen that's been dipped in ink and let the drops fly onto the paper - great fun but it can be a little messy and unpredictable

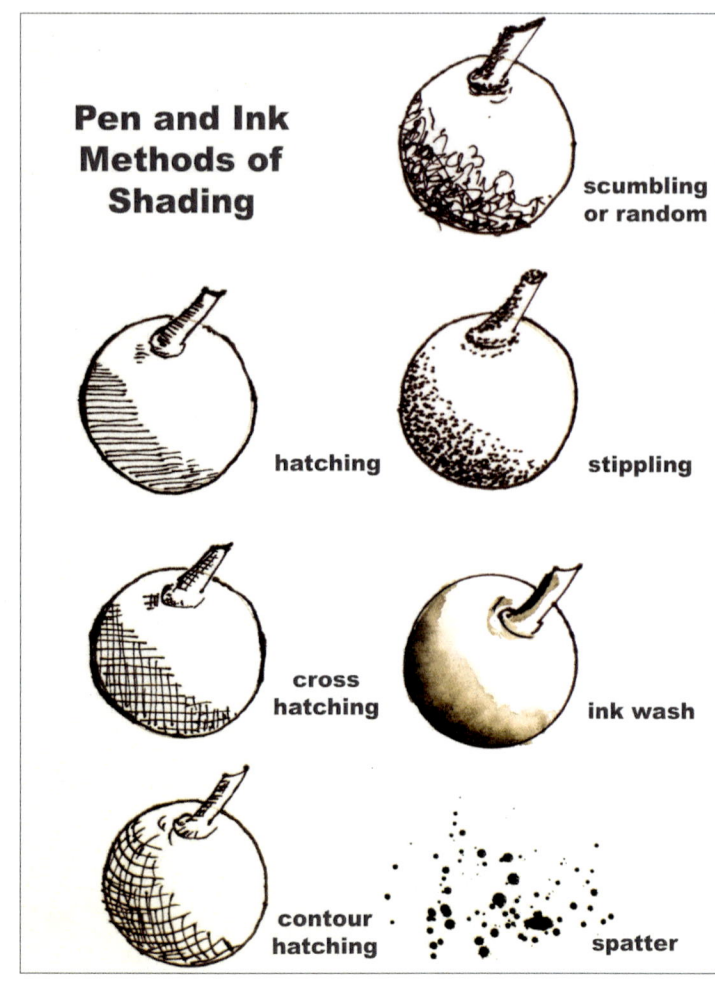

Pen and Ink Methods of Shading

scumbling or random

hatching

stippling

cross hatching

ink wash

contour hatching

spatter

Demonstration

PEN & WASH COUNTRY SCENE

MATERIALS
*Lemon
Leaf Green
Brilliant Red
Purple
Ultramarine*

*Waterproof black
pen 0.5*

1 Use a black waterproof ink pen (or pen and waterproof ink) for this simple sketch of the countryside.

If you are not confident in drawing straight onto paper with a pen, first use a pencil to sketch the outline. Then go over your drawing with a waterproof pen, or pen and waterproof ink.

Avoid too much neatness, keep it loose.

2 Paint the sky with a very watery Ultramarine, following the cloud shapes and leaving plenty of white paper.

Paint the hills mostly with Lemon and a little Leaf Green – make the hill furthest away lighter in tone to convey a sense of distance.

Use Leaf Green with a touch of Ultramarine for the trees and bushes.

Sprinkle some Lemon, Leaf Green and a touch of Brilliant Red across the foreground and spritz lightly to retain texture.

Above all, keep it simple, light and spontaneous throughout. When the painting is dry, you can always go over any black lines that you think need strengthening.

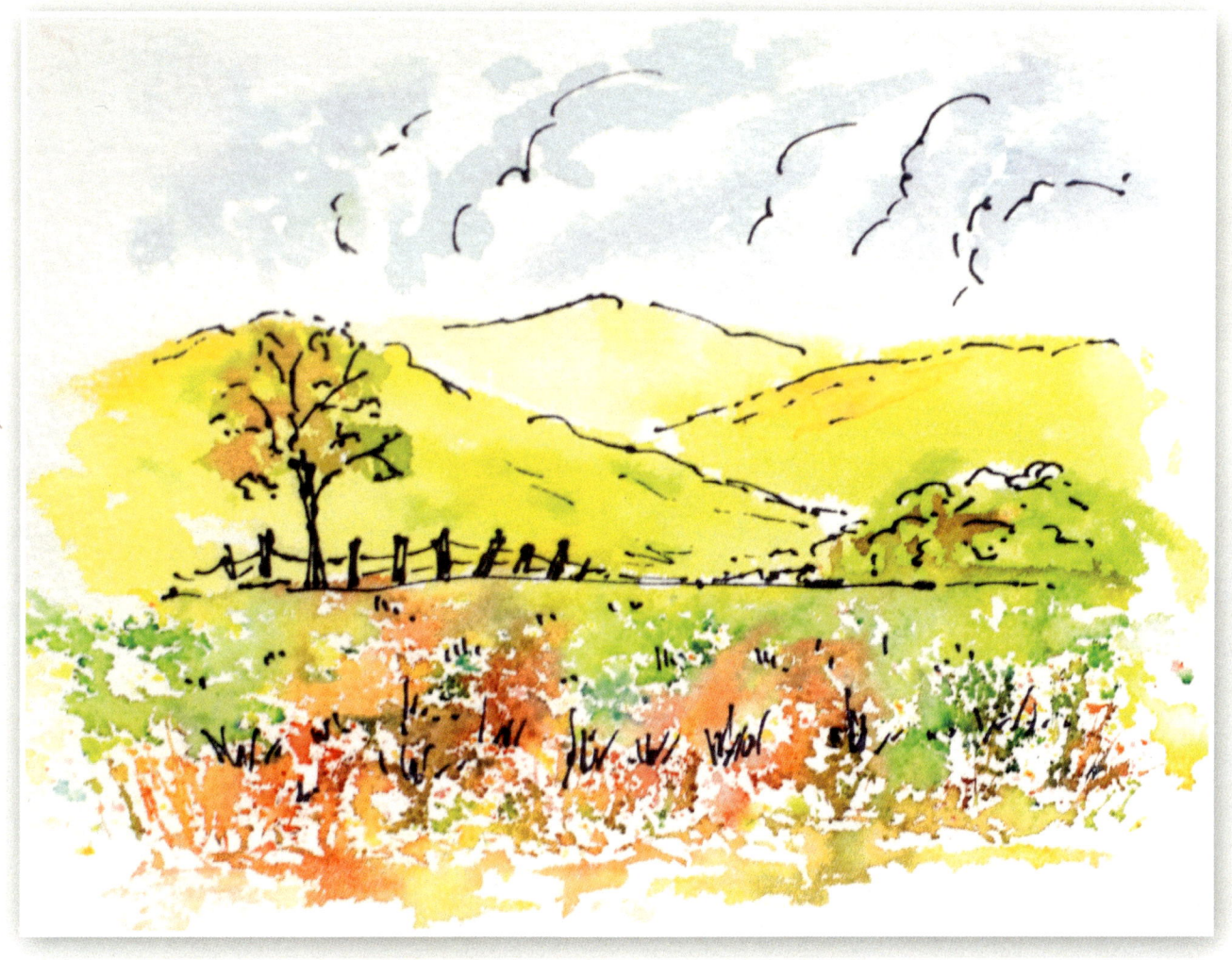

Demonstration
RAINBOW COTTAGES

MATERIALS
Lemon
Brilliant Red
Ultramarine
Purple

Waterproof black pen 0.5

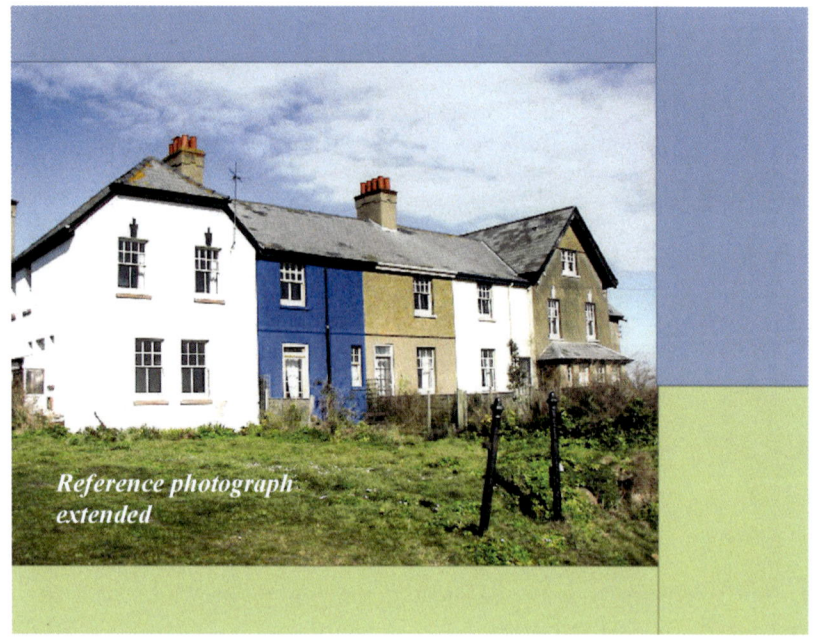

Reference photograph extended

Sometimes you need to alter a reference photo to improve the composition. In this example, I've extended the sky and foreground areas as shown by the blue and green L-shapes.

We are going to replace the complex fencing with a simple line of bushes running in front of the houses.

We will completely ignore the posts dominating the foreground

1 Simplifying the detail, draw the outlines of the houses, bushes and foreground in waterproof pen.

Add a couple of trees at the far right of the painting, and a few grasses and stones in the foreground.

Use the cross-hatching technique for the shading under the eaves of the houses, in the windowpanes and at the bottom of the bushes.

Use the scumbling technique for the bushes (replacing the fencing). Keep it simple, loose and sketchy.

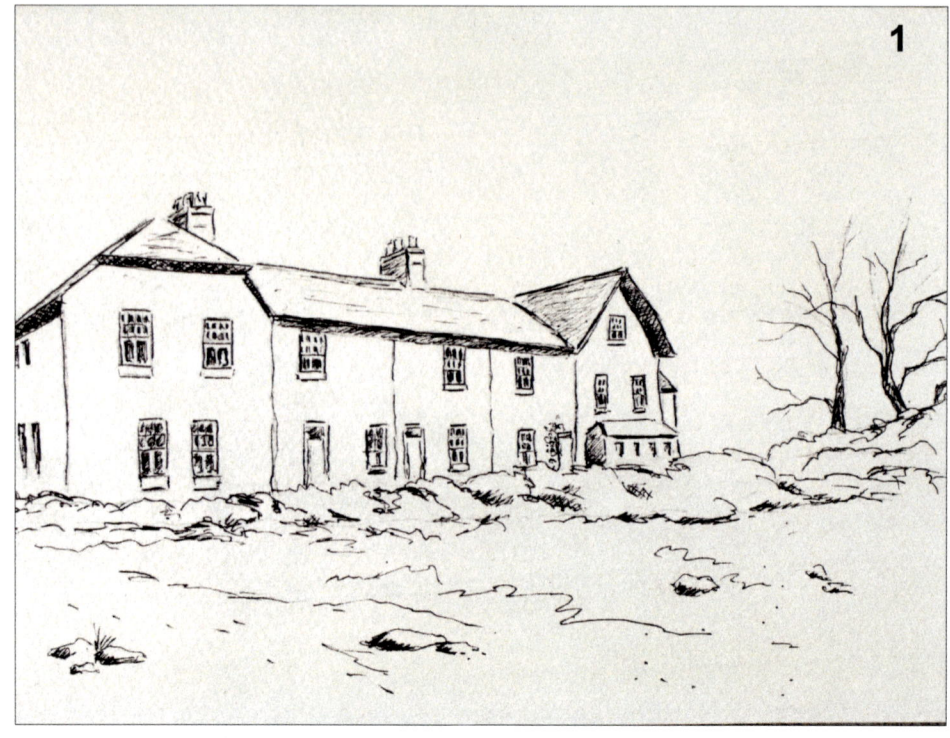

2 Mix some Ultramarine, Purple, Lemon and Brilliant Red in separate palette wells. Wet the paper thoroughly from the top sky area to the bottom of the bushes. Drop the colours you mixed onto the top of the paper. Then, lifting the paper up at the top left hand corner, spray downwards and diagonally to blend and soften the colours to the bottom of the bushes. Wiggle the paper around to encourage the paint to spread.

Use a piece of kitchen towel to dab out a few white areas on the roofs and house fronts. Drop a little extra colour onto the bushes to bring them forward. Don't worry if you get a few dribbles running into the foreground, just blot with a paper towel and leave. Lay the paper down horizontally and leave everything to dry.

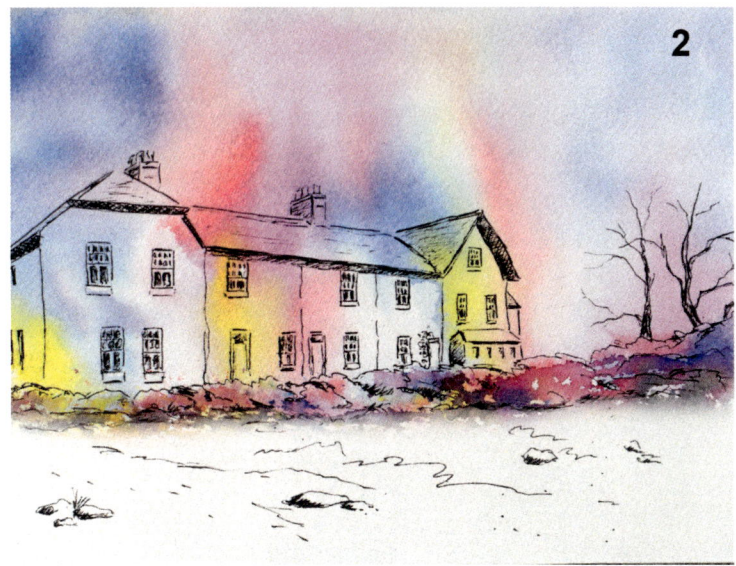

3 Mask the houses and sky areas with some paper towels. Sprinkle the same colours that you used in the previous step across the foreground, Spritz lightly to obtain a grassy foliage texture. Use the point of a rigger brush to 'join up' some of the speckles to give the foreground a more solid look but don't lose all of your texture.

While the paint is still wet, use the point of a brush to drop in touches of Ultramarine and Purple here and there amongst the foliage in the foreground to add depth, allowing them to mingle. Remove the paper mask. Add the same watery colours for the leaf area around the trees. With a mix of Ultramarine and Purple, add a little shading to the left sides of the chimney pots, the far side of the house at the far left, and some of the roof areas.

Leave to dry. Use your waterproof pen again to emphasise any pen lines that have got lost in the paint, or to add any final details. You can also use it to add your signature to your painting!

RAINBOW COTTAGES

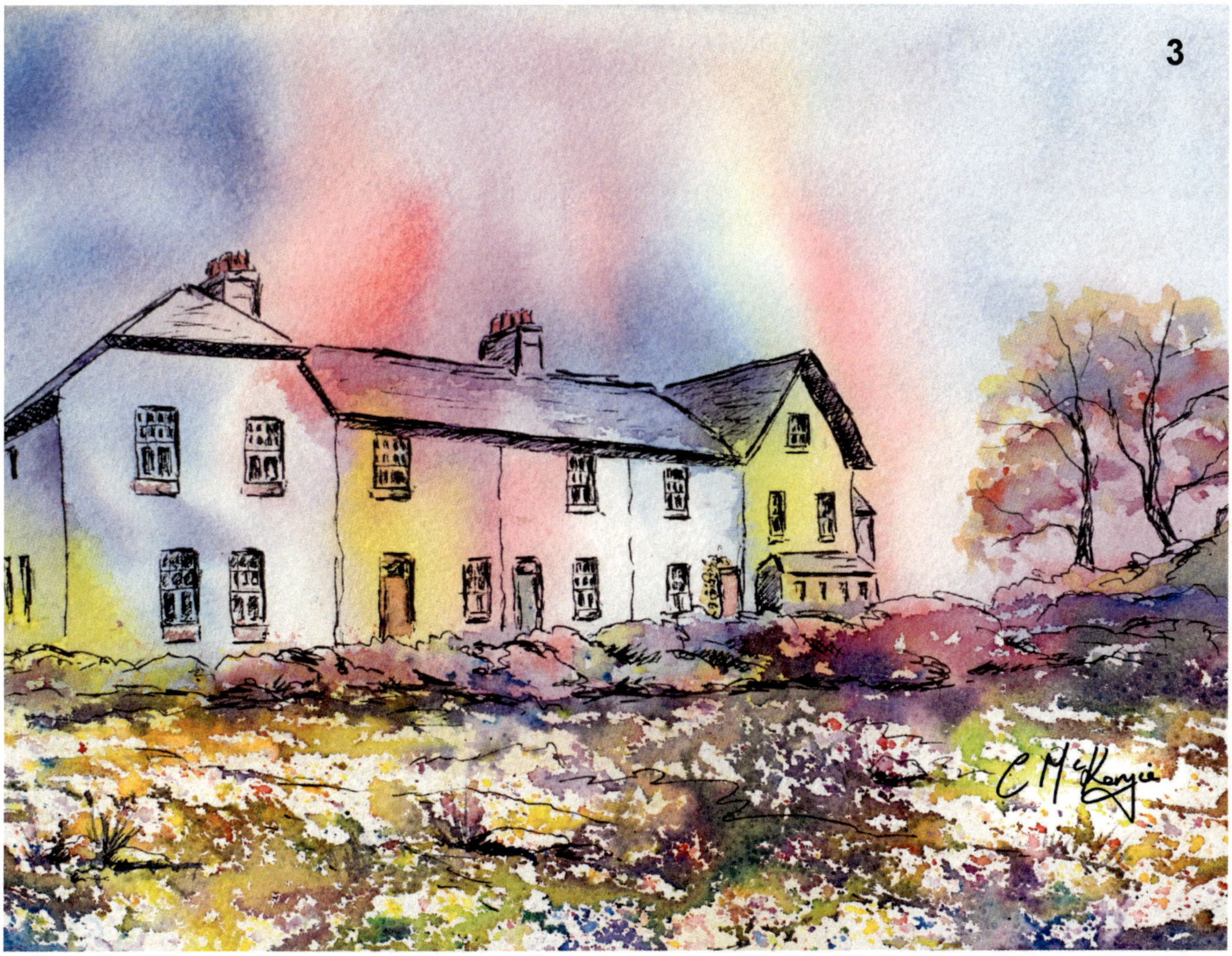

Demonstration
COCK-A-DOODLE

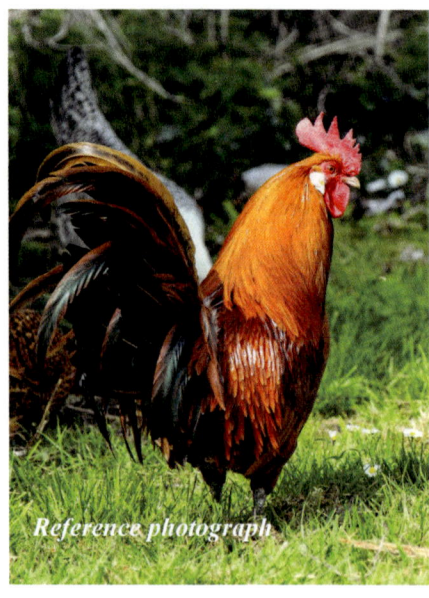

Reference photograph

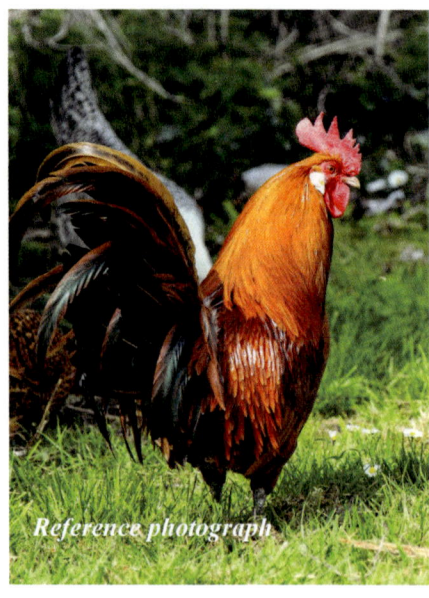

1

MATERIALS
Lemon
Brilliant Red
Ultramarine
Purple
Orange
Turquoise

Waterproof black pen 0.5

1 Draw the cockerel in pencil first if you wish, then go over it in black waterproof pen. Note how loose and scratchy the lines are – this is to try and create a sense of movement, particularly in the feathers. Add a little shading underneath the tips of some feathers and in between the tail feathers.

Apply some clear wax around some of the feather shapes and the gaps in between them, and also to catch the highlights on the right side of each leg. Apply masking fluid to the beak, eye and giblet. Spatter some masking fluid on the foreground area to retain some white paper to represent stones on the ground.

2 Mix some Lemon, Orange and Brilliant Red in separate palette wells. Paint everything except the tail feathers with Lemon - vary the strength of colour in places to add tonal value to the painting. Keep the colour on the legs very pale.

Whilst the paint is still wet, drop Orange on top, but leave some areas of Lemon showing through. Add a touch of Brilliant Red in a couple of places, letting this mingle with the Orange and Lemon.

Leave to dry.

3 Paint the chicken head with a strong mix of Brilliant Red, but keep it weaker and paler round the eye area. Paint the legs with a pale watery Brilliant Red. Leave to dry.

Use paper towel to protect all the painting except the tail feathers.

Sprinkle mostly Turquoise and a little Ultramarine and Purple onto the tail feathers then spray in the direction of the feathers.

Mix some Turquoise, Ultramarine and Purple in your palette. Remove the paper towel and use the point of your brush, loaded with Purple, to emphasise the curves of the feathers with a few flamboyant curved lines.

Spatter a little of the Turquoise colour outside the pen lines to convey movement. Leave to dry.

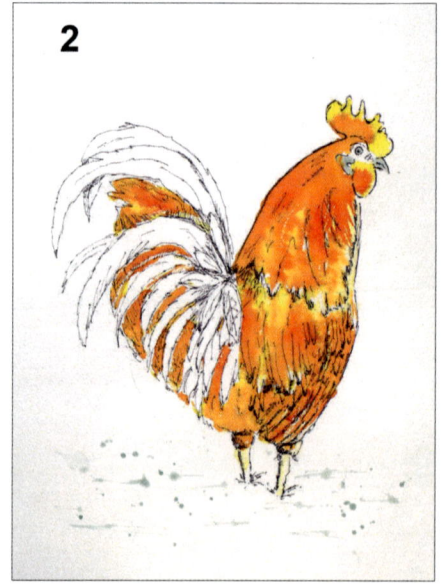

2

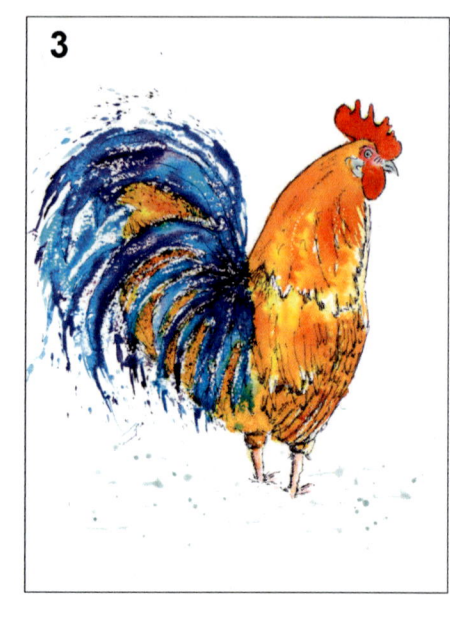

3

4 Use a clean finger or a putty rubber to rub away the masking fluid from the eye, beak and giblet. Paint the iris of the eye with a mix of Lemon and Orange. Paint the Beak with Lemon. Leave the giblet white, but soften the edge where it meets the head with a damp brush. Sprinkle all the colours across the foreground and spritz lightly to create grassy texture. Use the tip of a rigger brush to join up some of the speckles with linear marks and also flick upwards to represent grasses.

Apply a little Purple with the tip of your brush to create some depth in the foreground. Leave to dry.

With your waterproof pen, draw the black pupil in the eye; try to leave a small white dot of white paper as a catch light. Sprinkle just a few grains of Lemon, Brilliant Red and Orange in the white background space around the cockerel, spritz lightly then blot with a paper towel to keep the colour lighter than the rest of the painting.

Finally, when the painting is completely dry, use your waterproof pen to re-draw any lines that have become lost in the painting or where you want to add extra emphasis or shading.

COCK- A-DOODLE

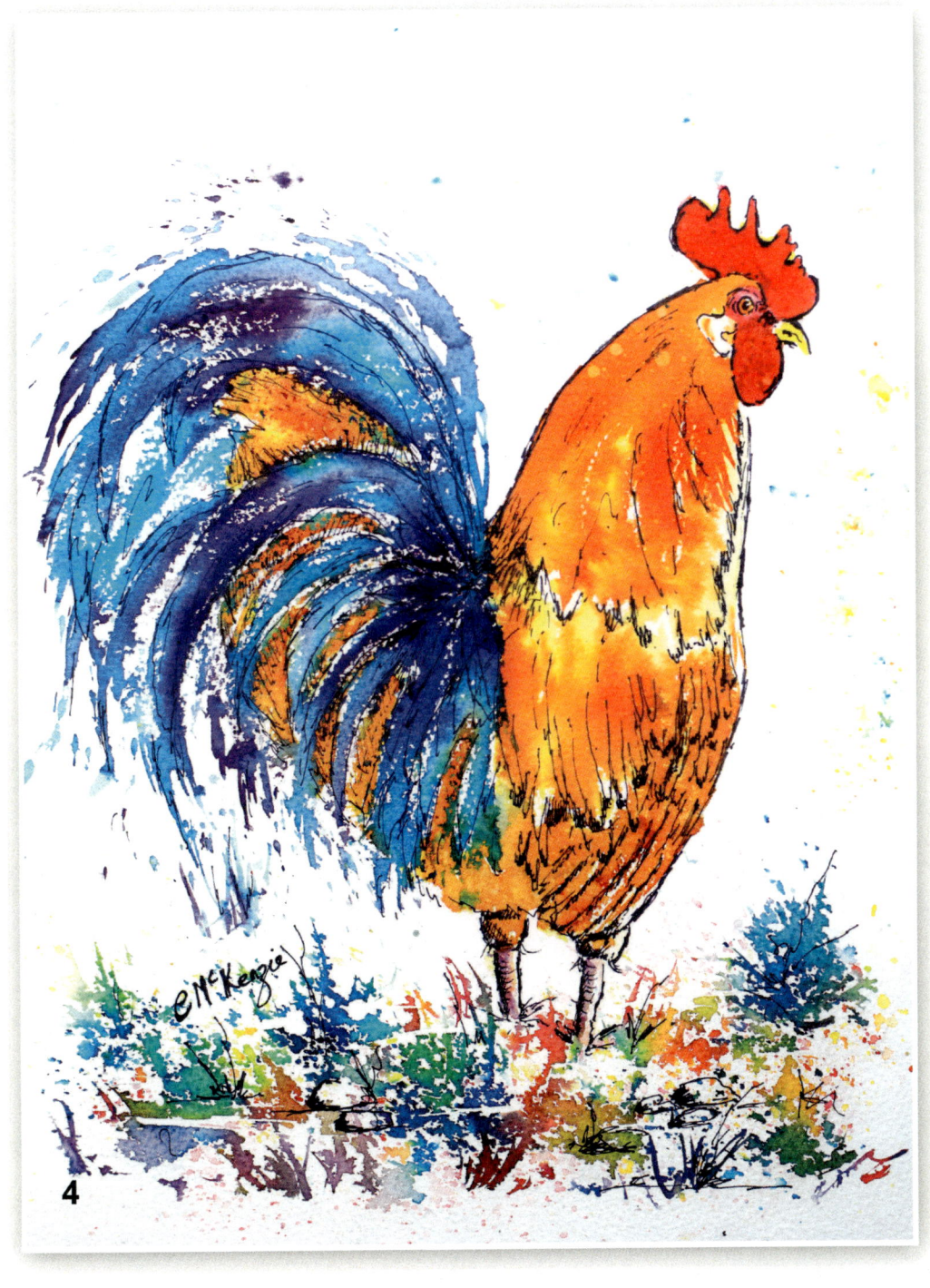

Technique 13 – Acrylic inks and granulation medium

Acrylic inks

Acrylic inks are great in mixed media pieces and are an ideal companion for Brusho. Vibrant and bright in colour, they do not fade when dry. They usually come in little bottles with their own eyedroppers. You can use them neat out of the bottle, or dilute them with water. Inks work best when you let them flow and find their own edges. Unlike Brusho, once the ink dries it is completely insoluble.

I tend to use earth coloured inks for most of my Brusho work – raw sienna, sepia, antelope brown – these add interest and depth to landscapes, flower centres and backgrounds. White acrylic ink is useful for adding white highlights especially those that have become lost in the painting. I also use black India ink as it reacts beautifully with wet washes, giving feathery or mossy effects that imitate lots of organic effects in nature.

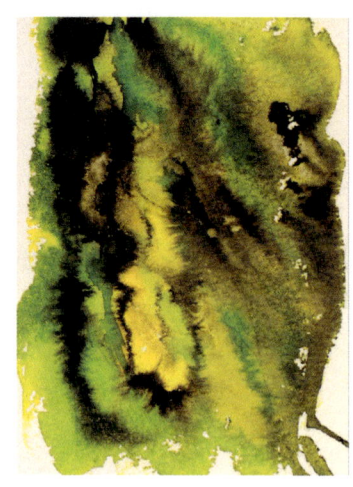

Black India ink and Granulation Medium trickled onto Yellow, Leaf Green and Ultramarine Brusho

Granulation medium

The addition of granulation medium gives a mottled or granular appearance, which adds interest or dimension to otherwise flat areas. It is especially useful for landscapes and seascapes. You can either mix it with paint in the palette, or brush granulation medium onto the paper and drop paint into it whilst it is still wet - or vice versa drop it into wet paint that is already on the paper.

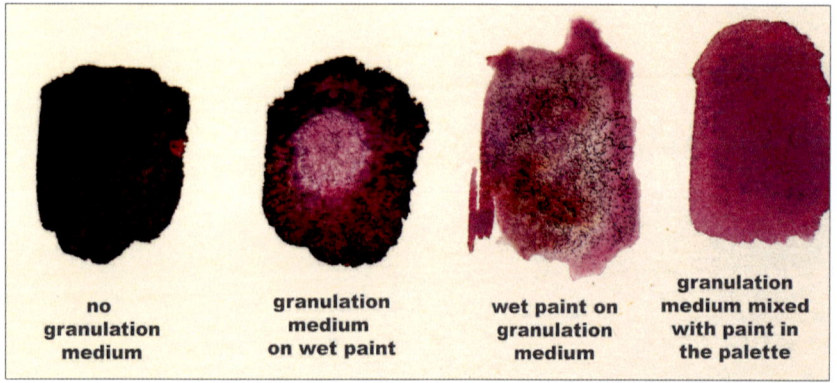

no granulation medium   granulation medium on wet paint   wet paint on granulation medium   granulation medium mixed with paint in the palette

Antelope Brown acrylic ink and granulation medium trickled on Yellow and Brilliant Red Brusho

Raw Sienna acrylic ink and granulation medium trickled on Turquoise and Yellow Brusho.

Sepia acrylic ink and granulation medium trickled on Yellow and Leaf Green Brusho.

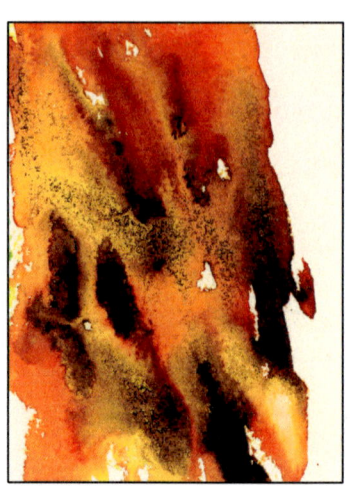
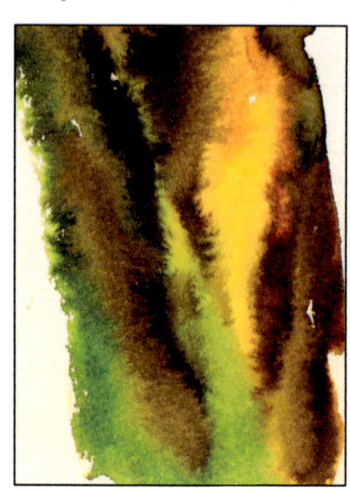
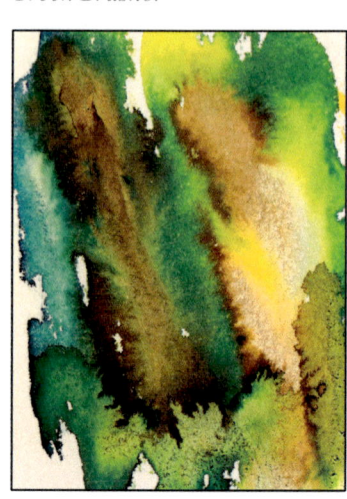

Ink and granulation on a coloured wash
Hillside 1

➤ Draw a simple hillside that takes up approximately two-thirds of the paper. Wet the top third sky area. Paint a watery Ultramarine sky in the top third of your paper, leaving a few cloud shapes. Leave to dry.

➤ Mix some Leaf Green, Yellow, Emerald and Dark Brown in your palette wells. Using these colours quite randomly, paint the hillside on the bottom two-thirds of the paper using downward and diagonal strokes for the hill contours. It doesn't matter if the colour looks patchy at this stage; the next step will take care of it.

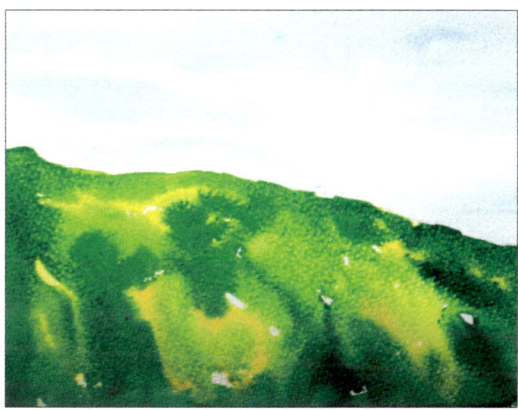

➤ While the paint is still wet, drop in some sepia acrylic ink – you can use the eyedropper that comes with the bottle to draw linear contour lines curving down the hillside. Drip granulation medium on top of the ink while it is still wet. Tilt your paper up vertically and let the ink and granulation medium trickle down the paper – let it find its own way; use the tip of your brush to encourage it if you need to. You can keep adding ink and granulation until you are happy with the result. (Put a towel underneath to catch the runs.) Lay the paper flat and leave to dry

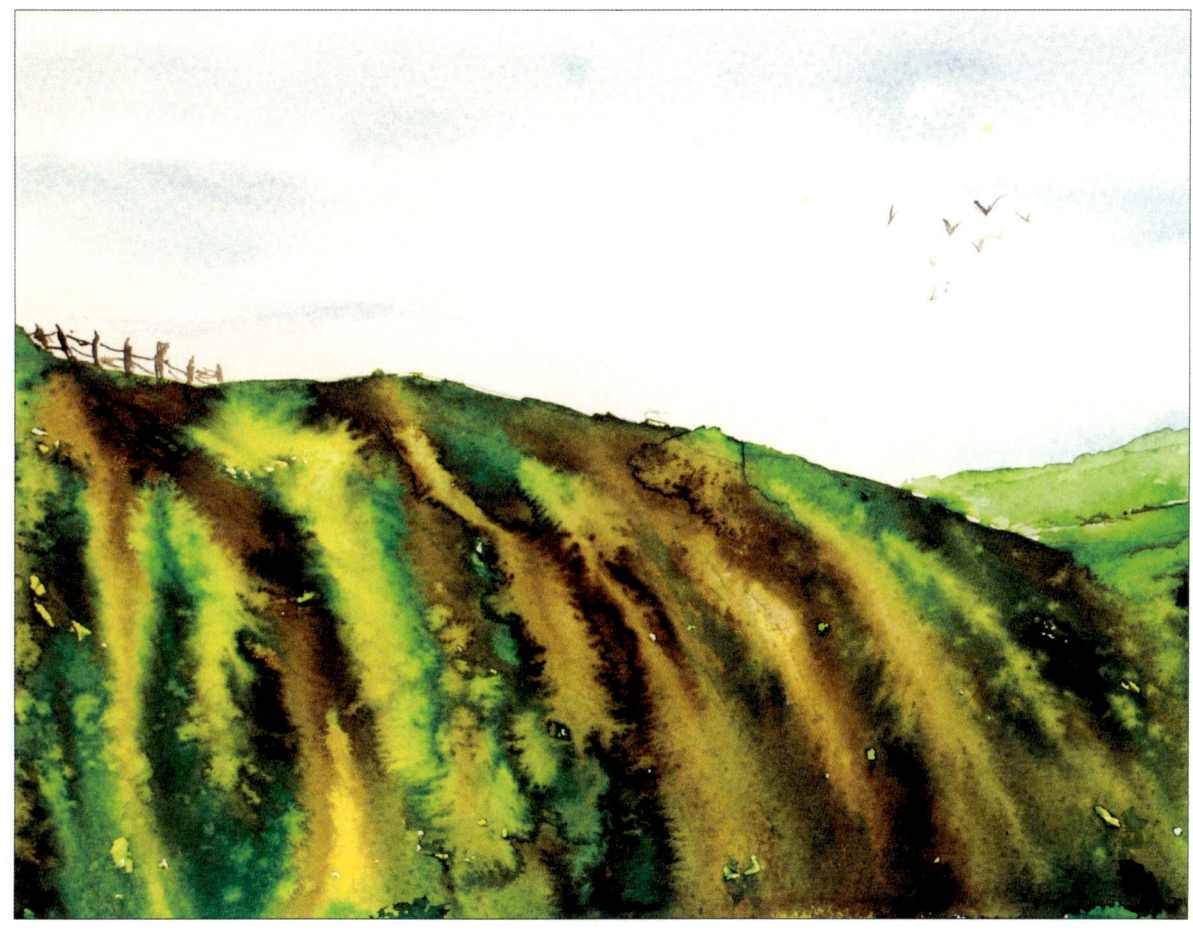

Ink and granulation on spritzed Brusho
Hillside 2

➢ Make a similar drawing as the previous exercise and paint a watery Ultramarine sky in the top third of your paper as you did previously. Leave to dry. Protect the sky area with paper towel. For the hillside, sprinkle the Leaf Green, Yellow, Emerald and Dark Brown directly on your paper. Spray lightly to blend some of the colour whilst also retaining some texture.

➢ While the paint is still wet, drop in the ink and granulation medium as you did before, letting them trickle their way through the wet brusho–

use the tip of a brush to encourage the flow. Add more ink and granulation if you need to. Lay the paper flat and leave to dry.

➢ Compare the slightly different result of this exercise with the previous one. Notice the difference in texture that results from spritzing or spraying the sprinkled Brusho before adding the ink and granulation medium. Neither method is right or wrong – it all depends on the look that you want to achieve - as you are beginning to find out the possibilities are endless!

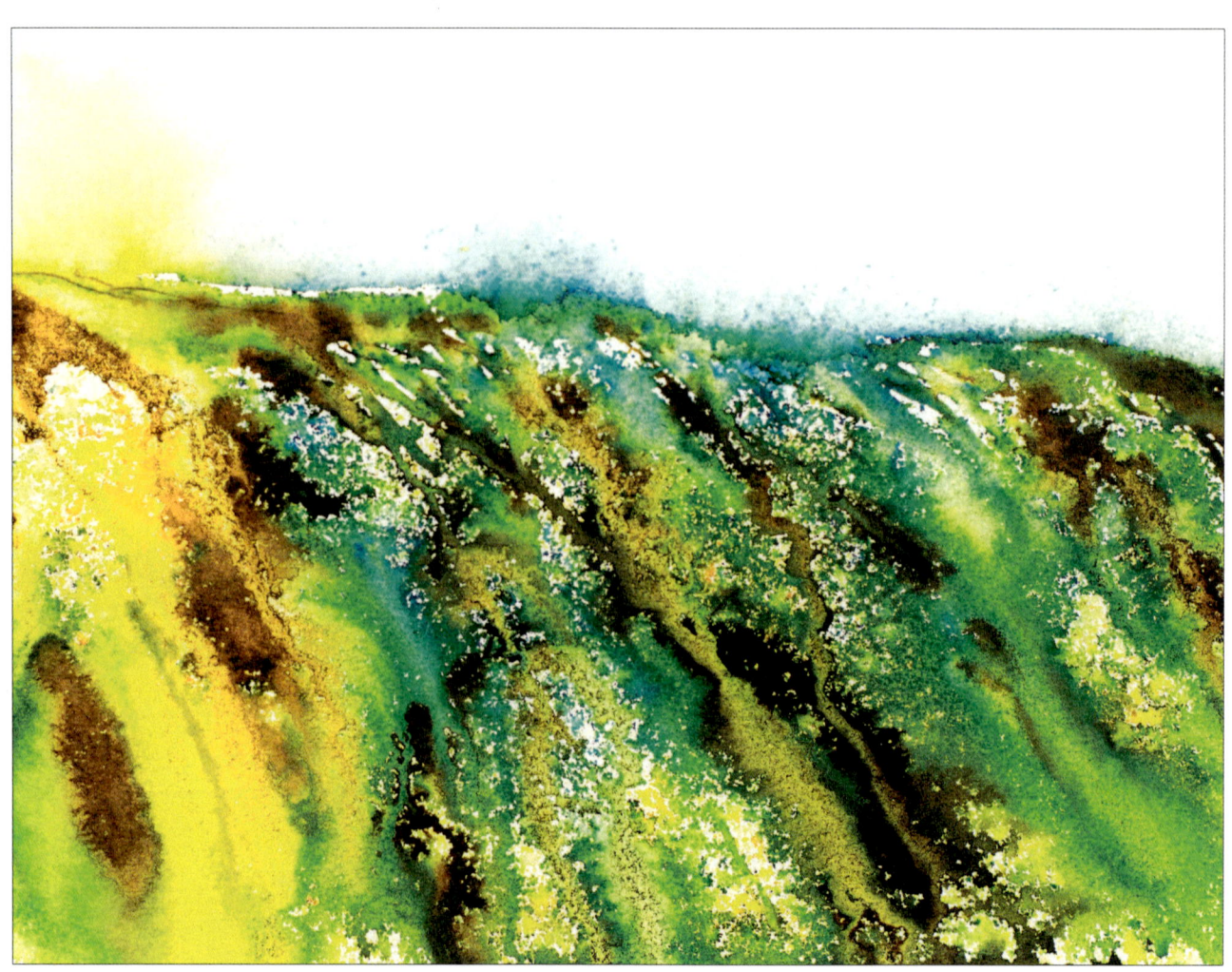

STUDIO TIP

Because of their permanency it is very difficult to clean acrylic inks from your palette, so I usually keep a stash of old bottle and jar lids for mixing inks in – I can then just throw them away after use.

Demonstration
MOORLAND AND HEATHER

MATERIALS
Lemon
Purple
Leaf Green
Ultramarine

Sepia acrylic ink
Granulation
medium

1 Copy my simple moorland and heather line drawing – I've over-emphasised the lines so you can see it more clearly than in my actual painting where I've kept the lines quite light. Mix a watery Lemon, and a watery mix of Ultramarine with a touch of Dark Brown, in separate palette wells. (Ultramarine on its own is a bit too blue for a natural sky, a touch of Dark Brown will just 'knock it back' a little.)

2 Wet the sky area with a clean brush and some clean water. With the paper still wet, work quickly and paint a few streaks of Lemon across the sky, then paint in some streaks of Ultramarine mixed with a touch of Dark Brown. Tilt the paper from side to side to encourage the paint to mingle on the paper, leaving some areas of white cloud – don't be tempted to fiddle, remember the 5-10 minute time limit for skies! As soon as you like the result, lay your paper down flat and leave to dry.

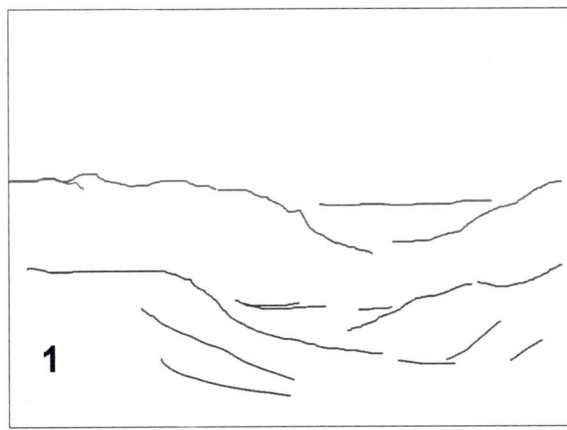

2

1

3 Paint the land in the far distance with a watery blue-green mix, leaving the central area very pale where the light is shining down on it. Paint the middle hills with a watery wash of Lemon, again leaving a pale area in between the left and right hills for the light. Drop in some streaks of Leaf Green while the wash is still wet and allow it to mingle. Leave a minute or so until the wash is semi-dry, then add in some streaks of Purple softening these in at the base. Add a little granulation medium in one or two places at the top of the hills. Lift the paper up from the top, hold it diagonally, and let the granulation medium trickle down the hill in rivulets. Add a couple more streaks of paint in Purple if you need to define the contours of the hill. Leave to dry.

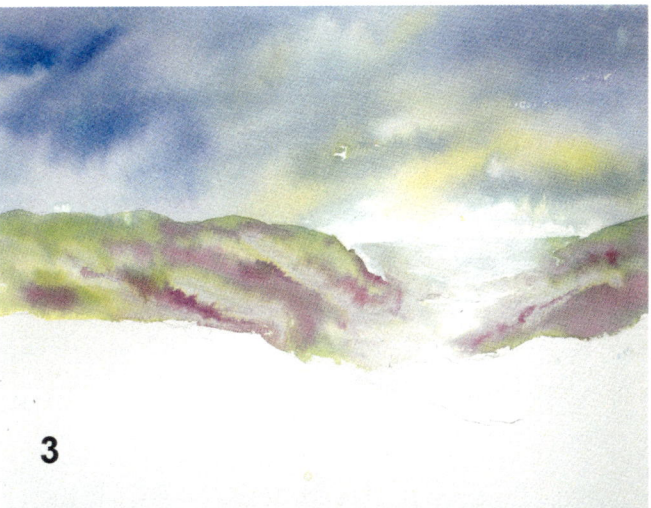

3

4 Protect the sky and middle distance with some paper towel. As above, try to leave the area below the light area in the sky paler than elsewhere – blot with a paper towel if you need to remove some paint. Paint a Lemon wash across the foreground, and then add a few streaks of Leaf Green. While the wash is still wet, sprinkle in some Purple. Use the water sprayer to spritz the foreground so that you get a soft edged texture. Remove the paper towel so you can see the full painting. Load your brush with Purple and tidy up the top outline of the foreground hill.

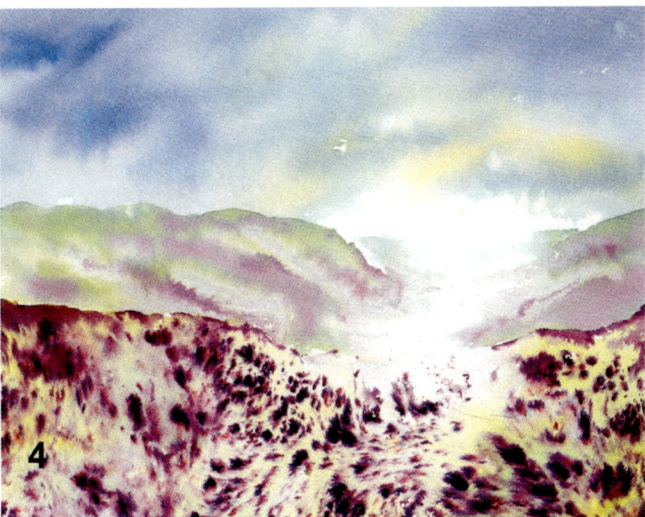

4

5 Using the Sepia Acrylic Ink eyedropper, draw some lines going downward and diagonally across the foreground hill. Stop and start these in random places – you don't want them to appear uniform. If you wish, you can also add a few dashes and lines of Black Acrylic Ink, again using the eyedropper to place your marks, but be sparing with this colour. While the ink is still wet drip some granulation medium on top of it and tilt your paper diagonally.

Let the granulation medium mingle with the ink so they both run diagonally across the paper towards the bottom.

Use a rigger brush to encourage the ink to flow where you want it to go and to draw more lines. Soften some of the lines with your damp rigger and allow the diluted brown ink to spread a little. Use your rigger brush to flick some of the paint and ink at the top of the foreground to represent some grasses. Leave to dry. Your painting may now look completely finished. If not, add a few more contour lines in Dark Brown and Purple, blending and softening these in places with a damp brush so they become part of the background.

You can also paint over any areas that have been left too white with a damp/wet brush – remember Brusho can be reactivated – your brush will pick up any paint crystals lying on the paper and spread the colour. You can even add more paint, ink or granulation medium. Because this technique is so experimental, it really is a matter of trial and error so don't be disheartened if it doesn't work out well the first time. The thrill from experimenting comes when you produce a masterpiece almost accidentally!

MOORLAND AND HEATHER

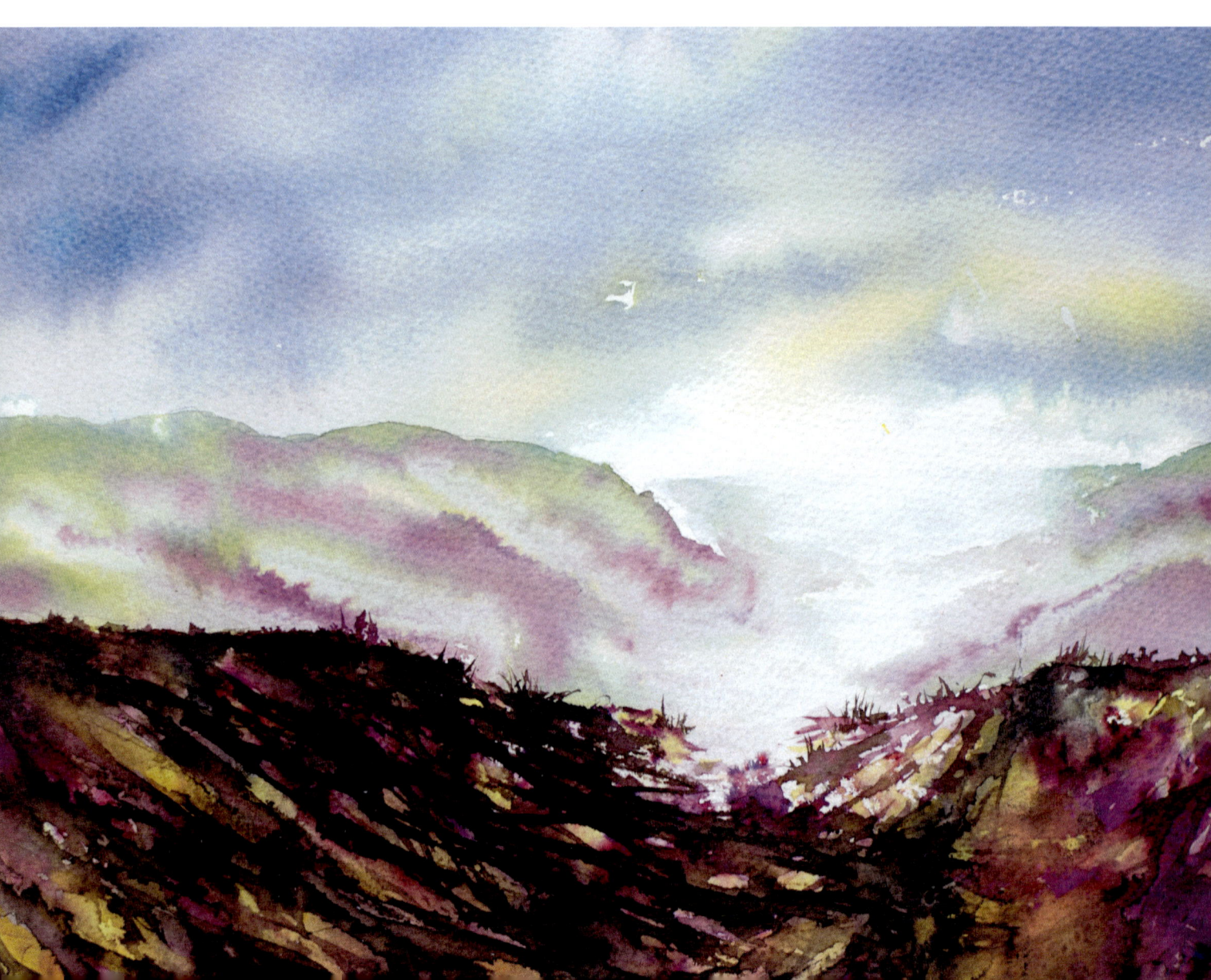

GALLERY

Halifax Town Hall was designed by Charles Barry, the same architect who designed the Houses of Parliament, hence the highly elaborate detail. In order for the painting not to look like a laboured technical drawing, I have deliberately left out areas of detail both in the pen work and in the coloured washes. I've also used a few additional Brusho colours: Gamboge, Sandstone, and Burnt Sienna.

HALIFAX TOWN HALL

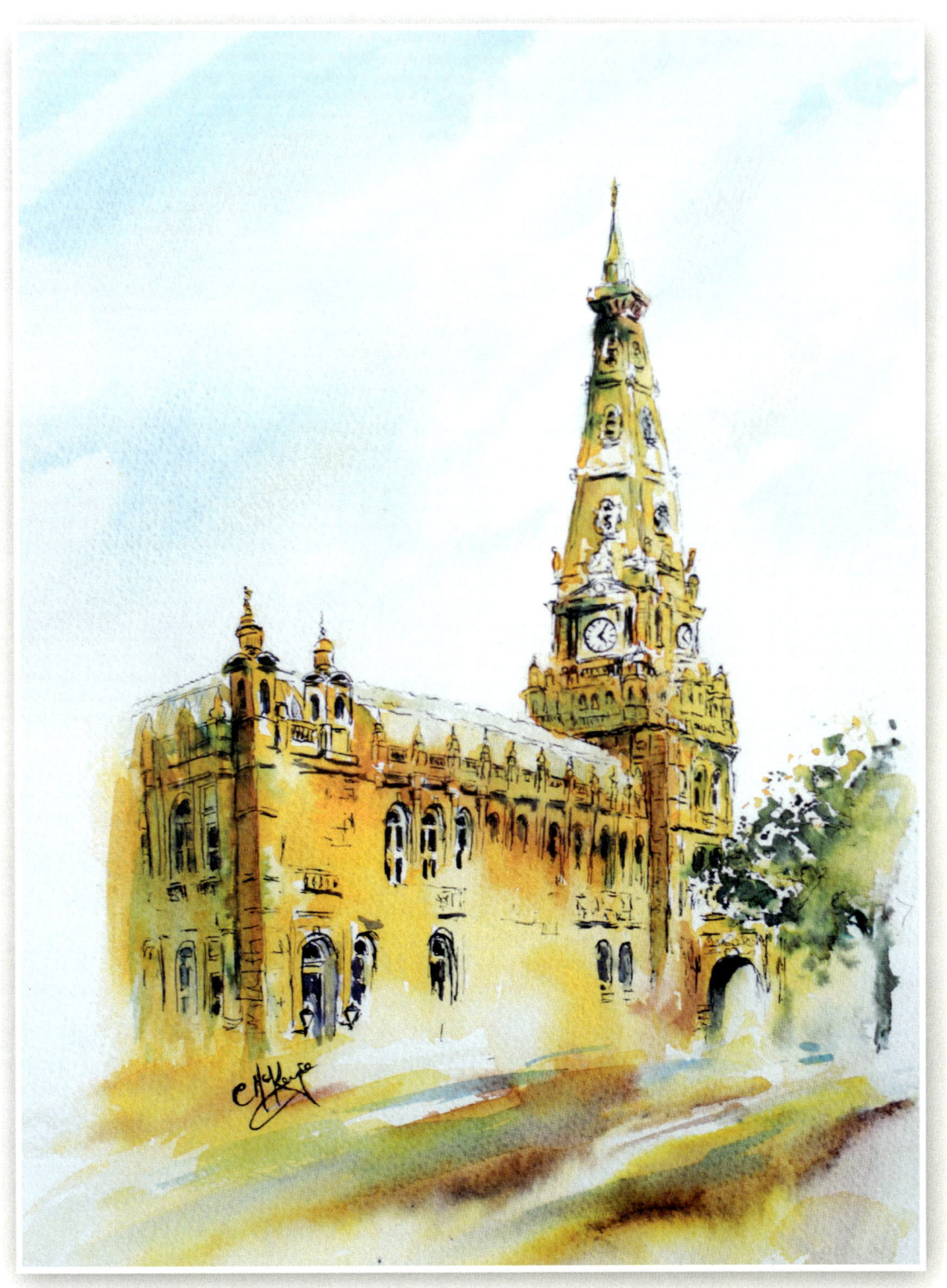

5 : NEGATIVE PAINTING

Negative painting is a technique that takes the approach of painting around an object to define it in a composition.

Instead of painting the main subjects of a painting, such as a flower, building or person, you paint the space around and in between the subjects.

The spaces around the main subjects are called "negative spaces".

The main subjects are the "positive shapes".

By painting the negative spaces, you reveal the positive shapes, without actually painting them. The crucial point is to see the negative spaces as shapes that add zest and depth, rather than unimportant, empty holes.

When commencing a drawing you need to be aware of the space and shapes between the main objects — ie the negative spaces. The interrelationship between the positive shapes and the negative spaces is key to good composition. It is important not to over-do the drawing, so that you can allow opportunities for more shapes to be discovered in the painting process.

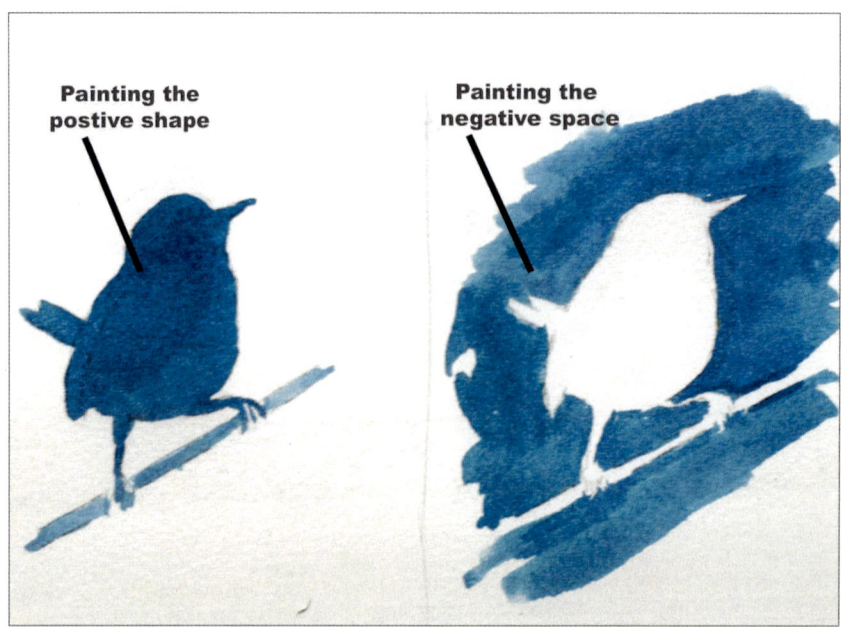

Painting the positive shape

Painting the negative space

Technique 14 –Negative painting on white paper: Snowdrop

Paint the negative space
➤ Draw this little snowdrop extracted from the reference photograph
(I've exaggerated the darkness of the lines so you can see it more clearly).
➤ Mix Ultramarine and Purple in separate palette wells.

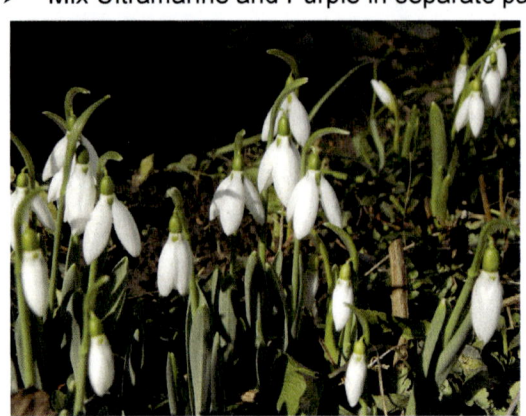

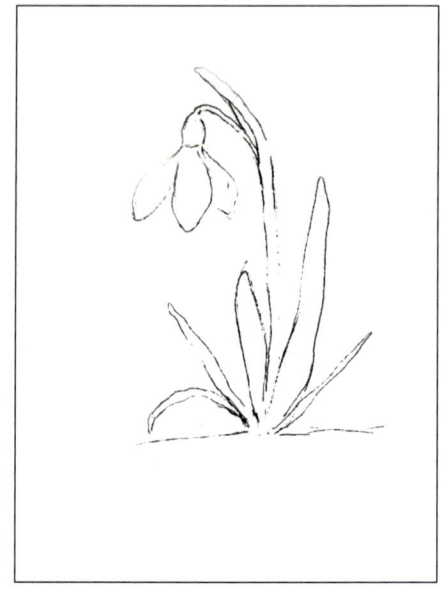

Wet the paper all around the snowdrop, but don't wet the snowdrop or its leaves. Brush Purple and Ultramarine into the wet paper right up to the outer edges of the snowdrop shape. Vary the colour in places for interest. Keep it darker at the bottom. Let the paint blend and mingle into the wet paper – wiggle the paper about if you need to get the paint moving. Blend with clear water to the top and sides of the paper.

Sprinkle a few salt crystals on the wet paint before it dries, and add a little paint spatter, to add interest to the background. Leave to dry. Can you see how you have brought out the shape of the snowdrop without actually painting it?

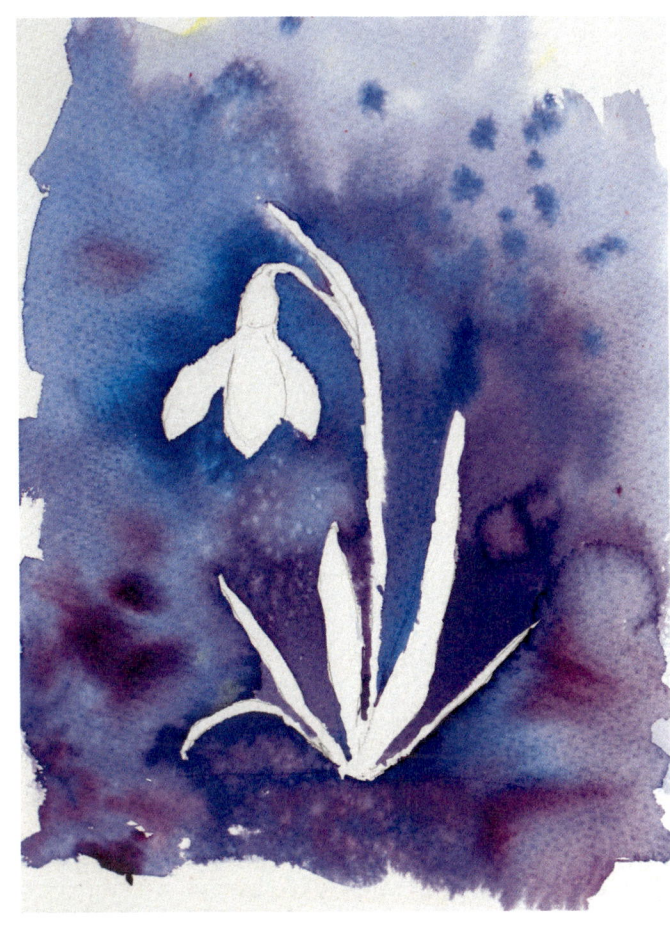

Paint the positive shape

Before painting the positive shape of the snowdrop, brush off any salt residue.

Paint the stem and leaves with a mix of Yellow, Leaf Green and a few strokes of Ultramarine in the shadow areas.

Add a little shadow between the petals with a very watery mix of Ultramarine.

Add a few linear marks in Purple and a little Leaf Green at the bottom of the flower to represent the soil.

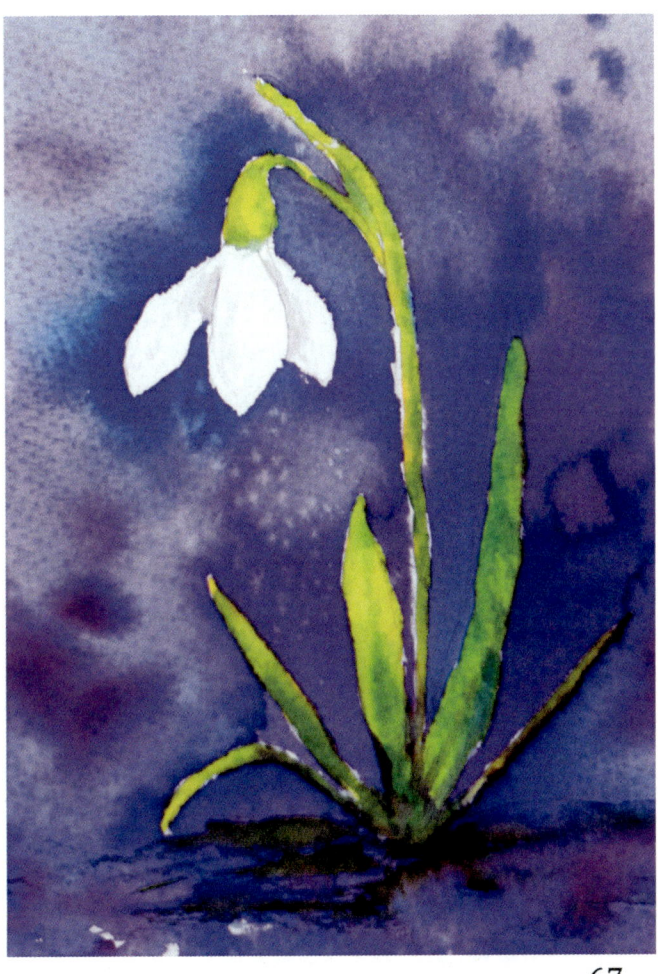

Technique 15 – Negative painting on a coloured background – Mushrooms

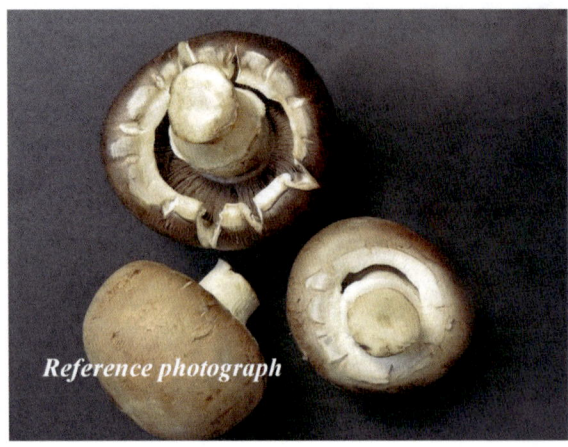

Reference photograph

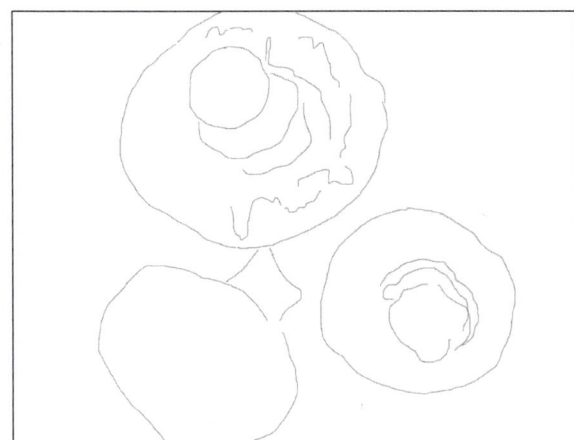

Paint the background

➤ In this exercise, we are going to use negative painting on a coloured background wash instead of white paper. Unlike the snowdrop exercise, with this method you hardly need to paint the positive shapes at all! First, draw the 3 mushrooms shown in the reference photograph.

➤ Sprinkle Yellow and Scarlet over all the paper. Then spray lightly to get a loose blended wash with a little texture. Leave to dry.

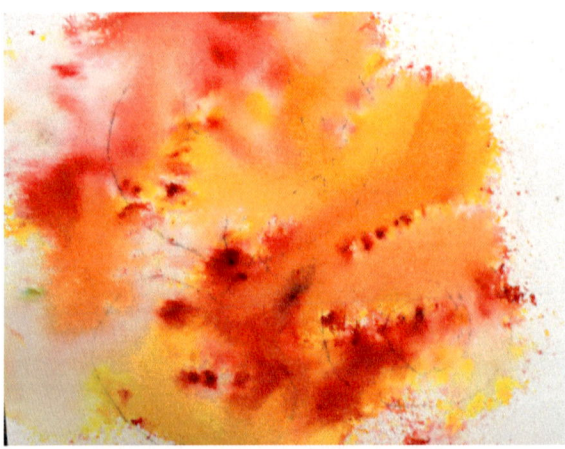

Paint the negative space

➤ Using Dark Brown in some places and Scarlet in others to add variety, paint the negative spaces around the outside, and in between, the mushrooms. Use the blending technique to soften and blend the paint and spread it to the edges of the paper, covering all the negative space.

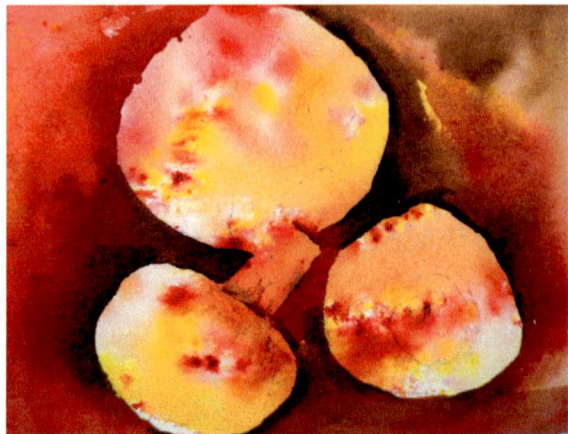

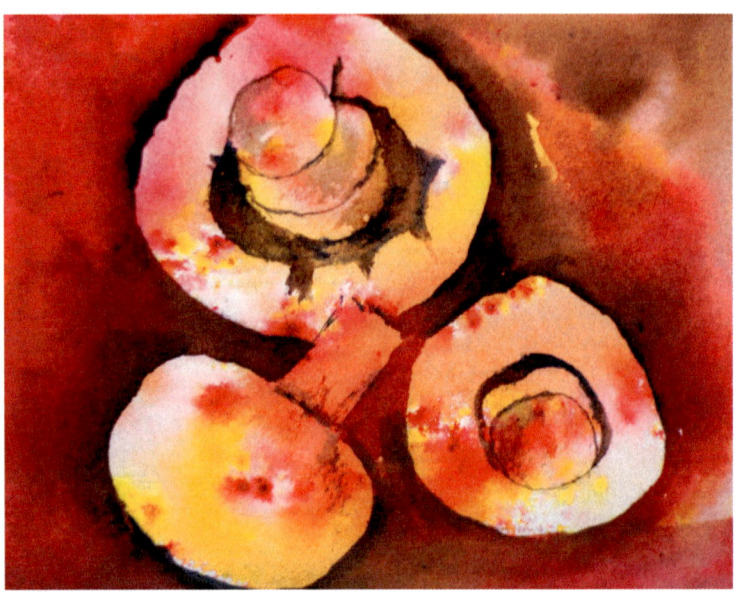

Paint the positive shapes

➤ Note how painting the negative space has brought the mushrooms out of the background wash without you actually painting them.

➤ Because the background wash has already given the mushrooms some colour, all you need to do now is to add a few dark accents and contour lines to the mushroom shapes with Dark Brown.

Demonstration

A NEW DAY DAWNS

MATERIALS
Lemon
Dark Brown
Purple
Scarlet
Ultramarine

Waterproof black
ink pen

1 We are going to combine pen and wash with negative painting. Make a simple line drawing using a black waterproof pen. Keep the drawing 'scratchy' and vary the strength of the line in places. Ignore the bikini in the reference photo.

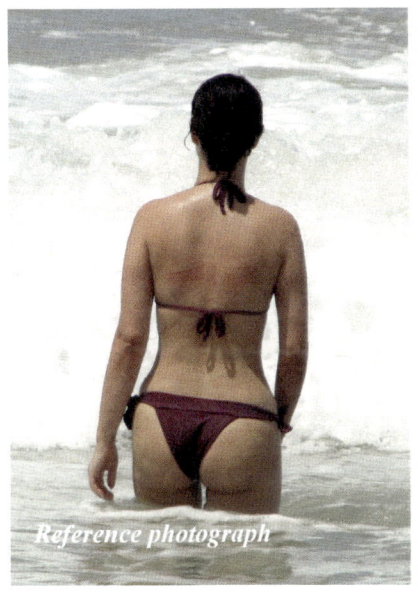

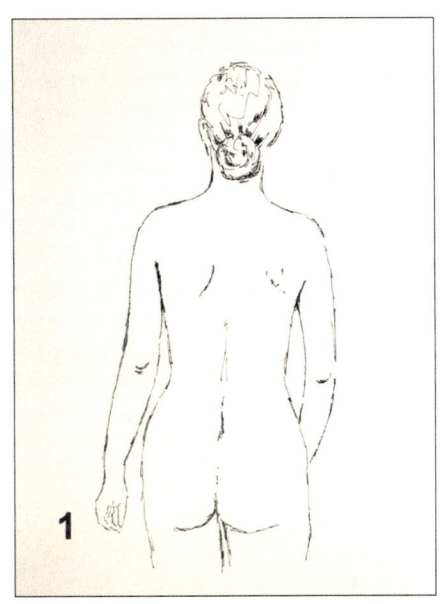

Reference photograph

2 Sprinkle the paper with Lemon, Scarlet and Turquoise, reserving the Turquoise for the bottom two-thirds of the paper.

Spray lightly to get a soft blend with a little texture. Don't worry if your background looks different to mine – that's the nature of Brusho – it's impossible to replicate so just go with what you've got. Leave to dry.

3 In the mushroom exercise, you applied negative painting to all the outer edges of the positive shapes. However, it is not always necessary or attractive to paint around every single edge, especially when you have used pen and ink which has already defined most of the edges. Negative painting can be applied to just a few select places to bring out the shape. This 'hit and miss' approach tends to give a softer appearance that is more unified with the background.

Bring out the shape of the woman by applying negative painting to some, but not all, of the outline. To keep in harmony with the background, use the same mix of colours - Lemon, Scarlet, Turquoise - plus Dark Brown. Look at my example to see where I have omitted negative painting, mainly in the head and right shoulder areas.

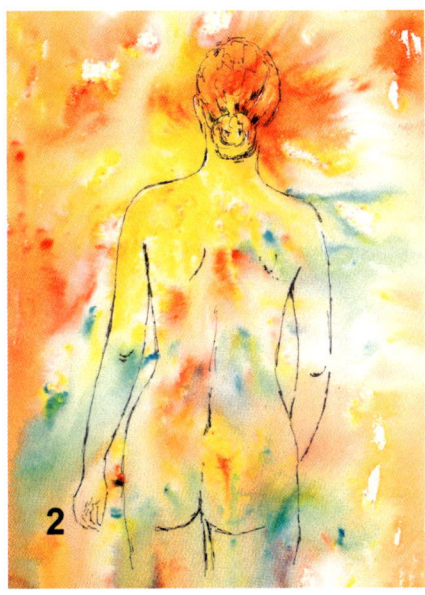

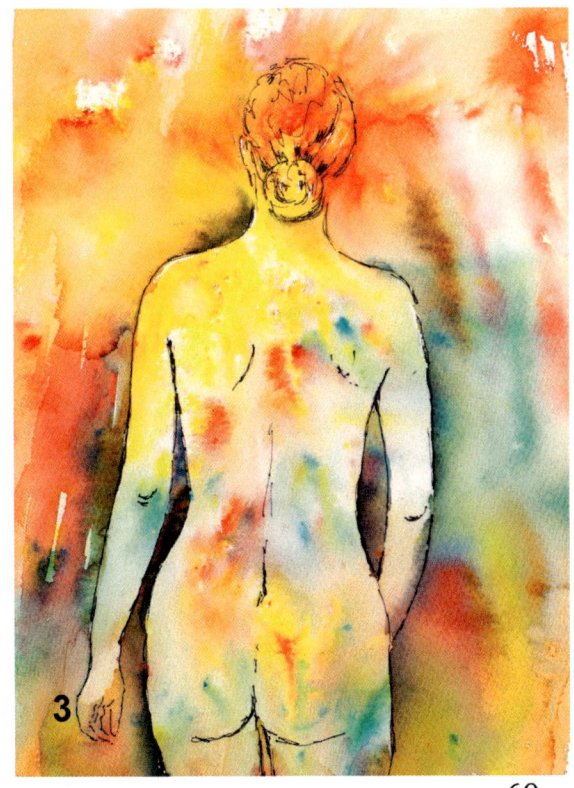

69

4 Paint the hair loosely with Dark Brown, allowing some of the underlying colour to show through. Add a little shadow to the left side of the neck below the hairline.

It's up to you how much painting you want to apply to your positive shape – but don't overdo it, remember, less is more!

A NEW DAY DAWNS

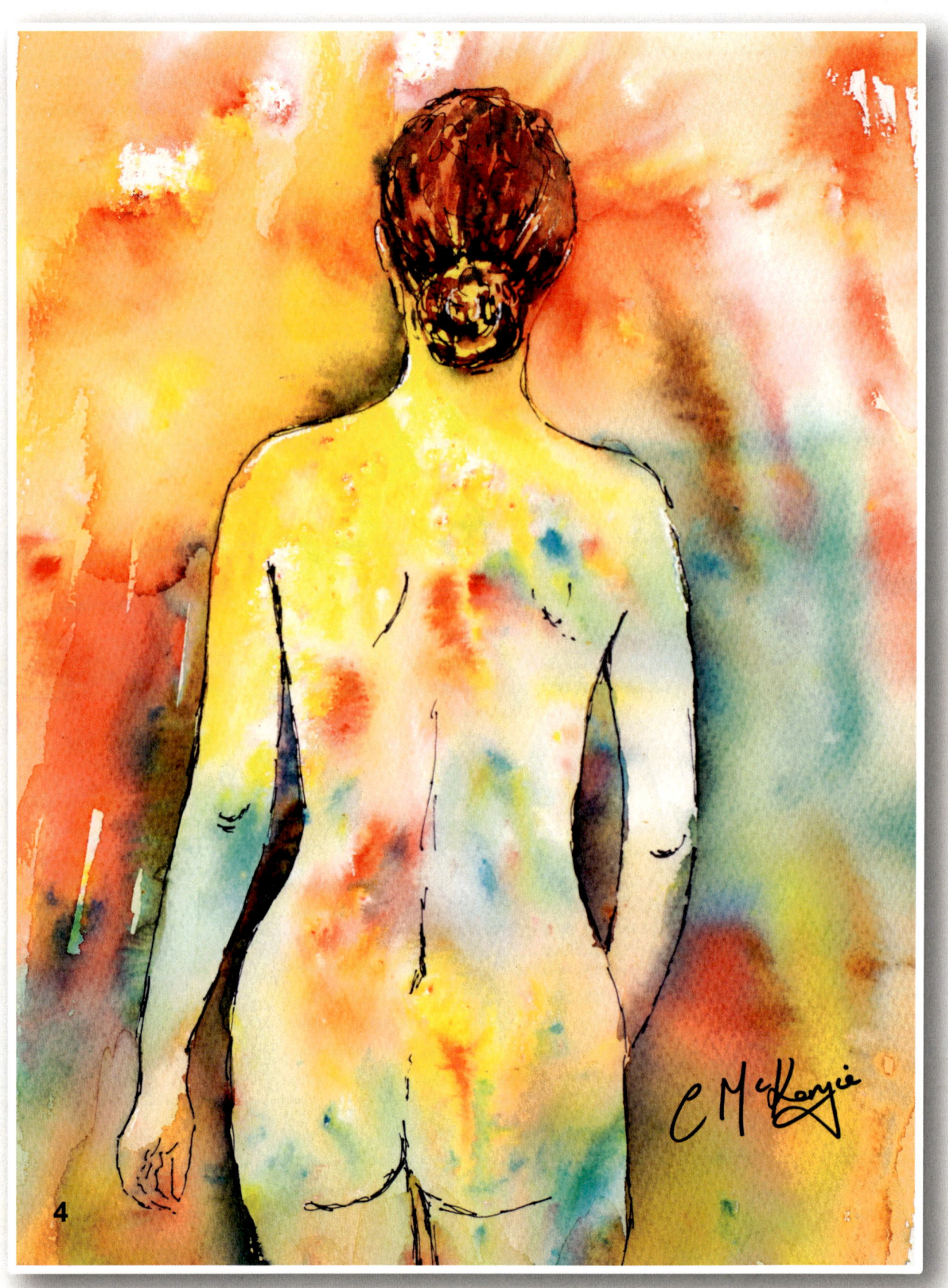

4

Demonstration

A MOMENT WITH MUM

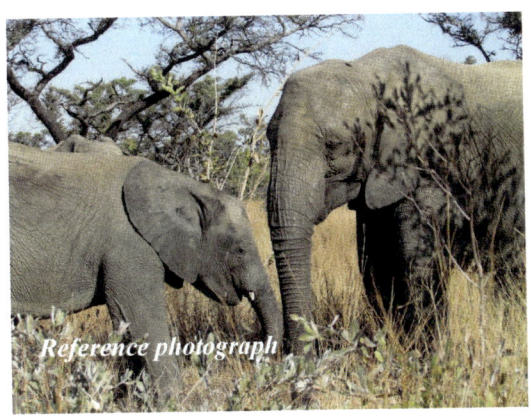

Reference photograph

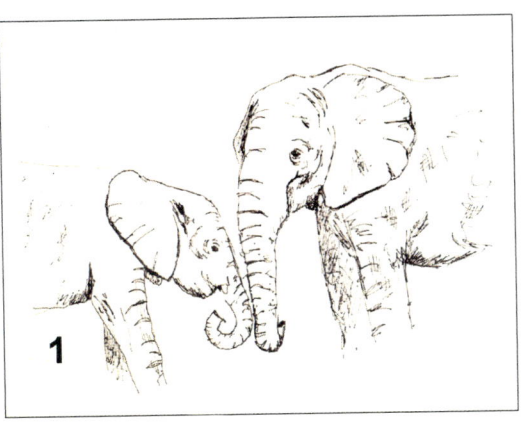

1

MATERIALS
Lemon
Dark Brown
Purple
Brilliant Red
Ultramarine
Turquoise

Clear wax
Waterproof black
ink pen

1 In this project we are going to combine negative painting with pen and wash and clear wax. Make a simple line drawing using a black waterproof pen. Keep the drawing 'scratchy' and vary the strength of the line in places.

Use the pen to add a little shading to the elephant's legs that are furthest away and to indicate the rough markings on their skin, particularly on the trunks.

To preserve a few white areas, apply some clear wax to the young elephant's tusk.

Apply a few more touches of clear wax to catch some highlights on both of their trunks, and anywhere else that the light is catching their bodies – but don't overdo the wax – just a few small touches will suffice.

2 Sprinkle Lemon, Brilliant Red, and Turquoise over the entire paper, keeping the central area around the trunks and heads mainly Lemon.

Spray lightly to get a soft blend with a little texture. Use a damp brush to move the paint around if you need to, and wiggle the paper to spread the paint to the far edges.

As before, don't worry if your background wash looks different from mine – it's inevitable that it wilℕote how the waxed areas repel the paint, giving you some nice white highlights. Leave to dry

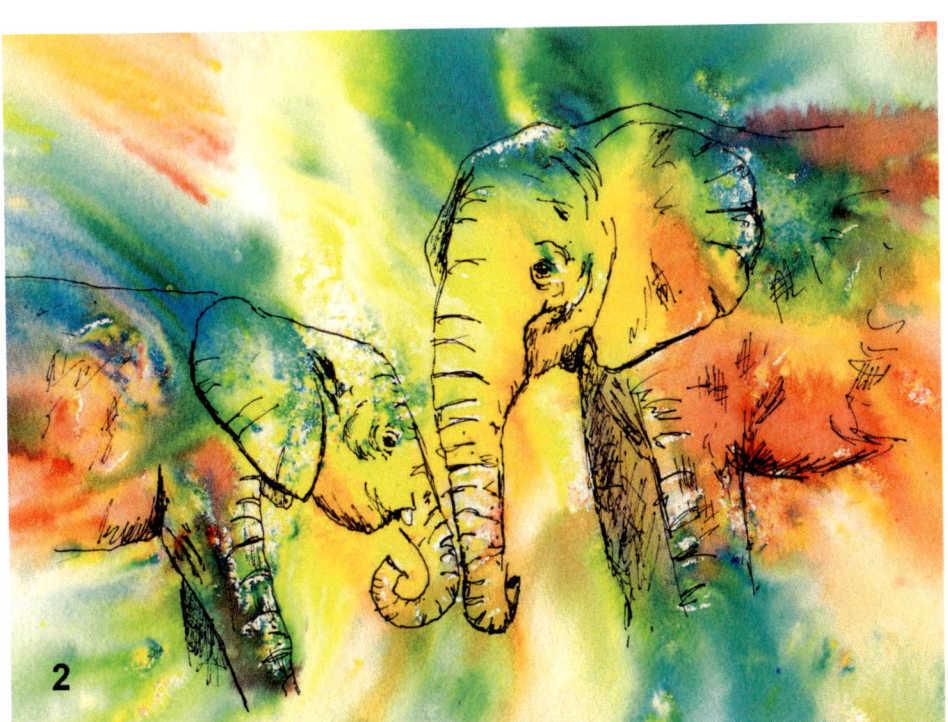

2

3 You are going to use the negative painting technique to bring out the shapes of the elephants.

For more control, ***turn the paper upside down*** and gently wet the area outside the elephants' backs and heads. Using the same colours that you used for the background wash plus a mix of Ultramarine and Purple, apply paint to the outer edges of the elephants' backs and heads, continuing down the outer edge of the trunks.

Lift the paper up so that the paint flows downwards.

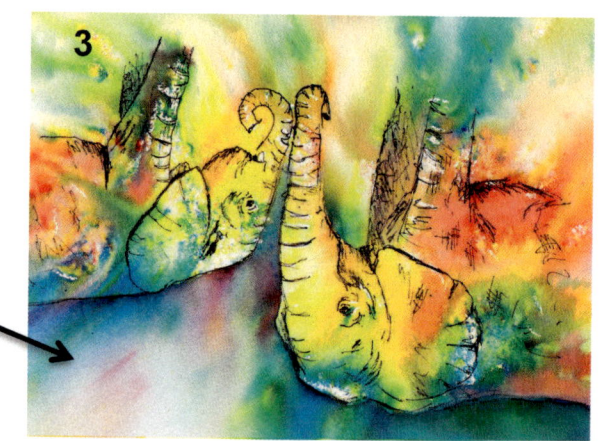

4 Turn the paper back round and repeat for the bottom half of the painting.

While the paper is still damp, sprinkle a little Dark Brown across the foreground. Spray the foreground lightly if you need to blend the brown speckles more, and then use a rigger to flick the Dark Brown paint upwards to represent grasses.

Because we used pen and ink to add shading to the elephant positive shapes, and clear wax to add white highlights, I feel this painting doesn't really need any more doing to it. But it's now your painting, so it's your decision on just how much you want to add to complete.

A MOMENT WITH MUM

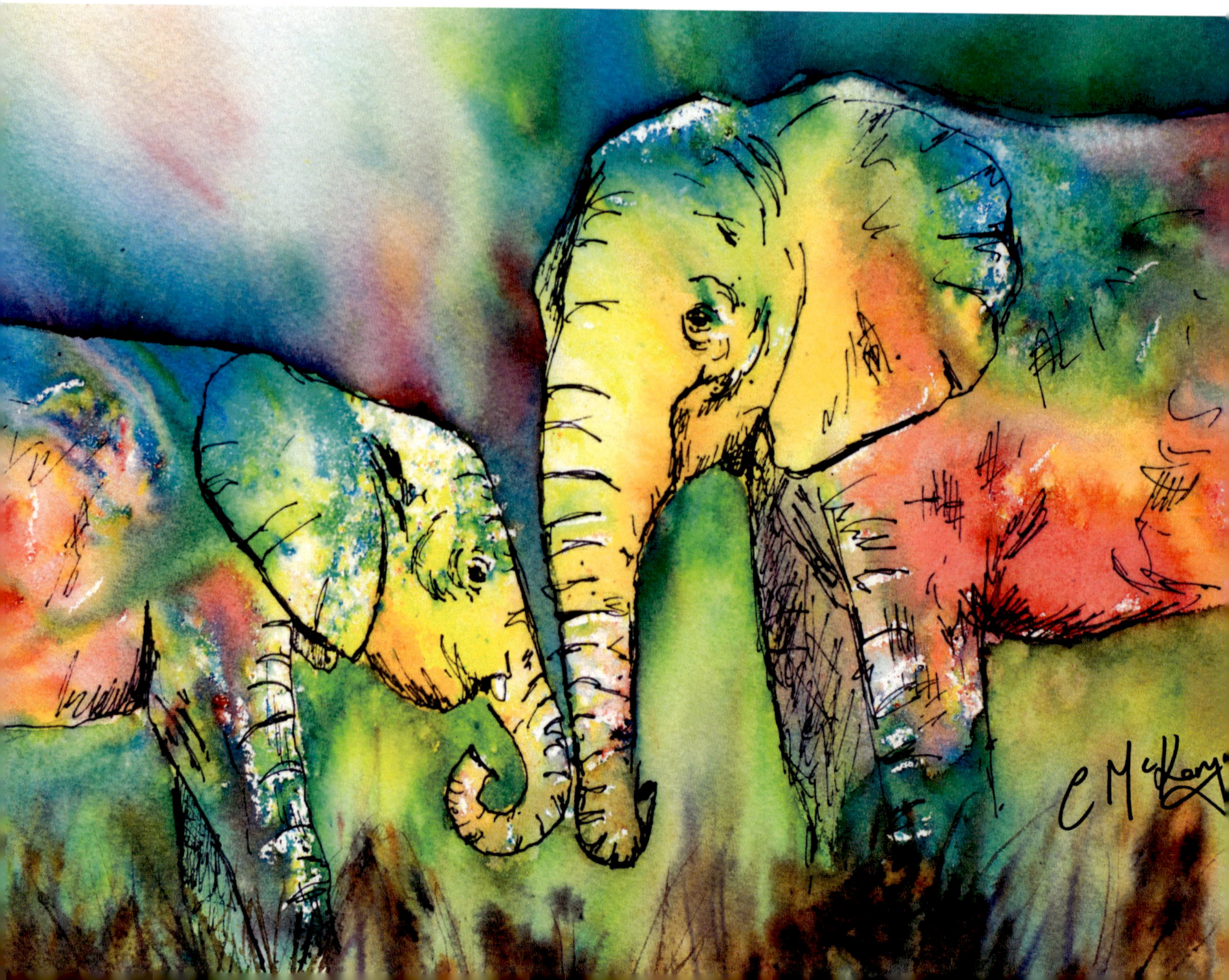

GALLERY

WAITING FOR A KISS

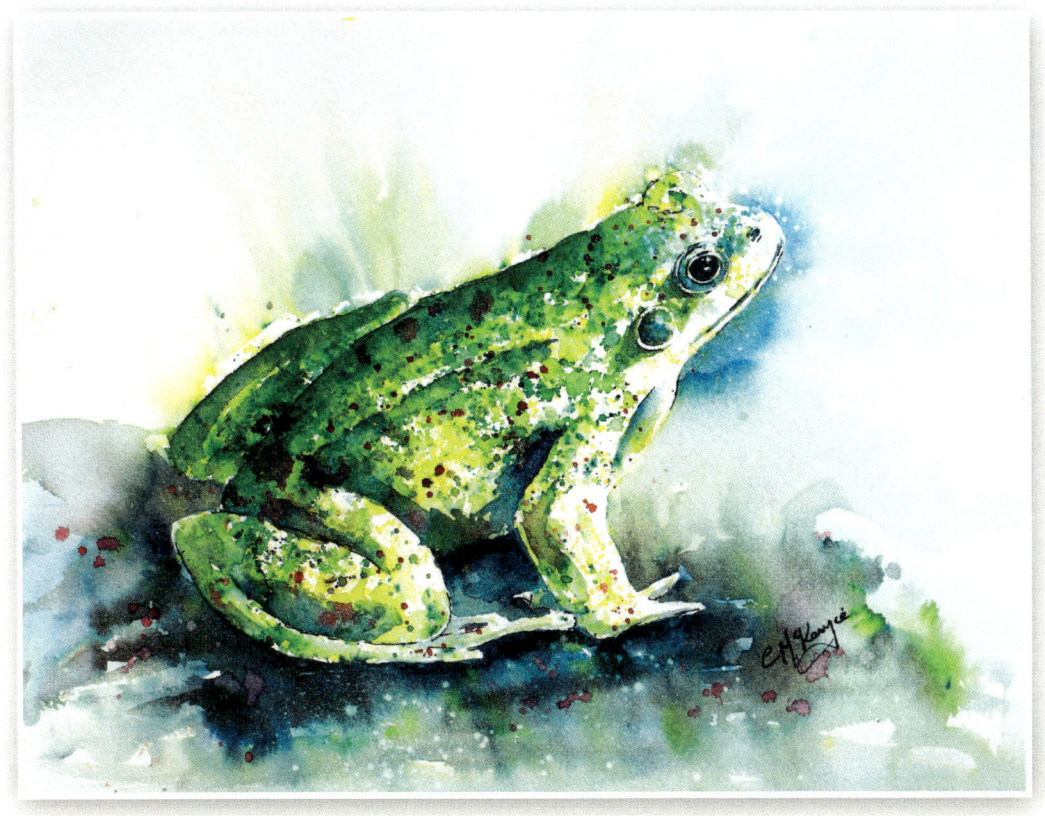

I used negative painting around the right side of the frog's head to emphasise it as the focal point. I've also painted dark pigment in the negative shadow spaces beneath the frog. In this painting the negative space has been painted in analogous colours, to produce a harmonious overall colour scheme.

FREDDIE

In "Freddie" complementary colours have been used for some of the negative space painting to produce more contrast in the overall colour scheme. Neither is right or wrong – it's all down to artistic choice

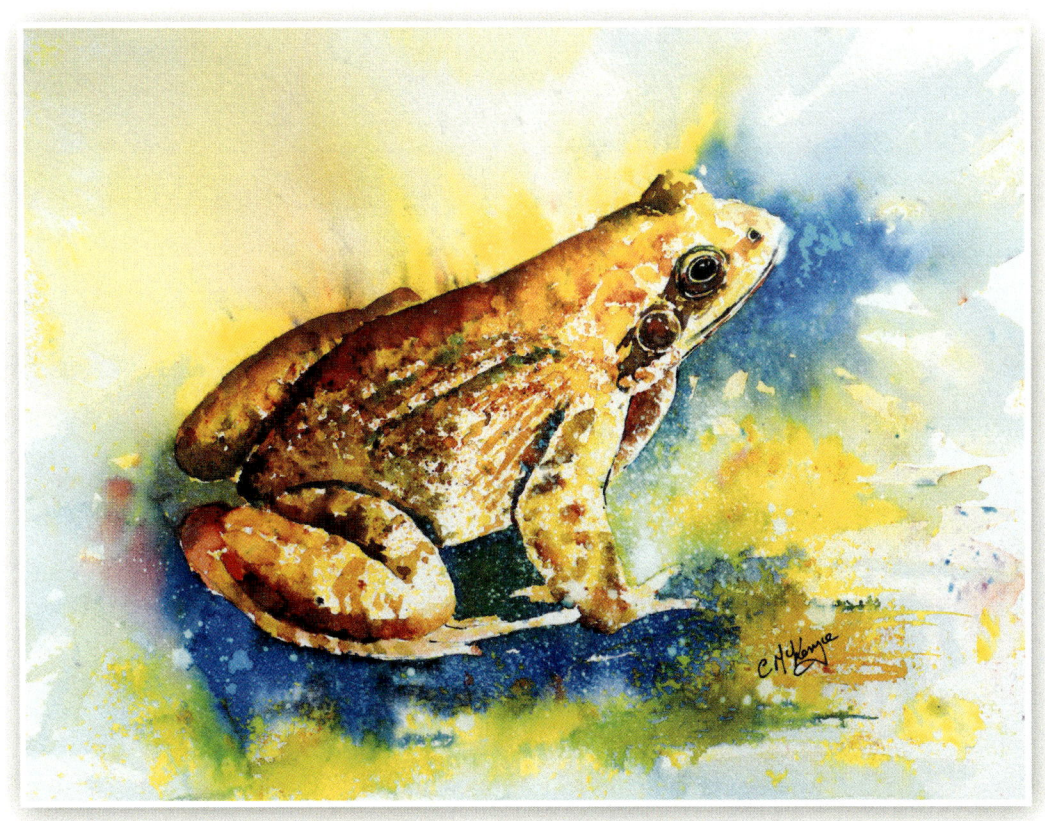

AMARYLLIS

I sprayed Brilliant Red, Orange and Yellow across the entire page, leaving pale areas for the highlights on the petals.

When this was dry, I used negative painting to add more colours around the flower head, varying the tonal value in places to avoid too much intense heavy colour in the background.

When the background was dry, I added more colour to define the shapes and shadows of the petals and stamen, making this quite dark towards the centre.

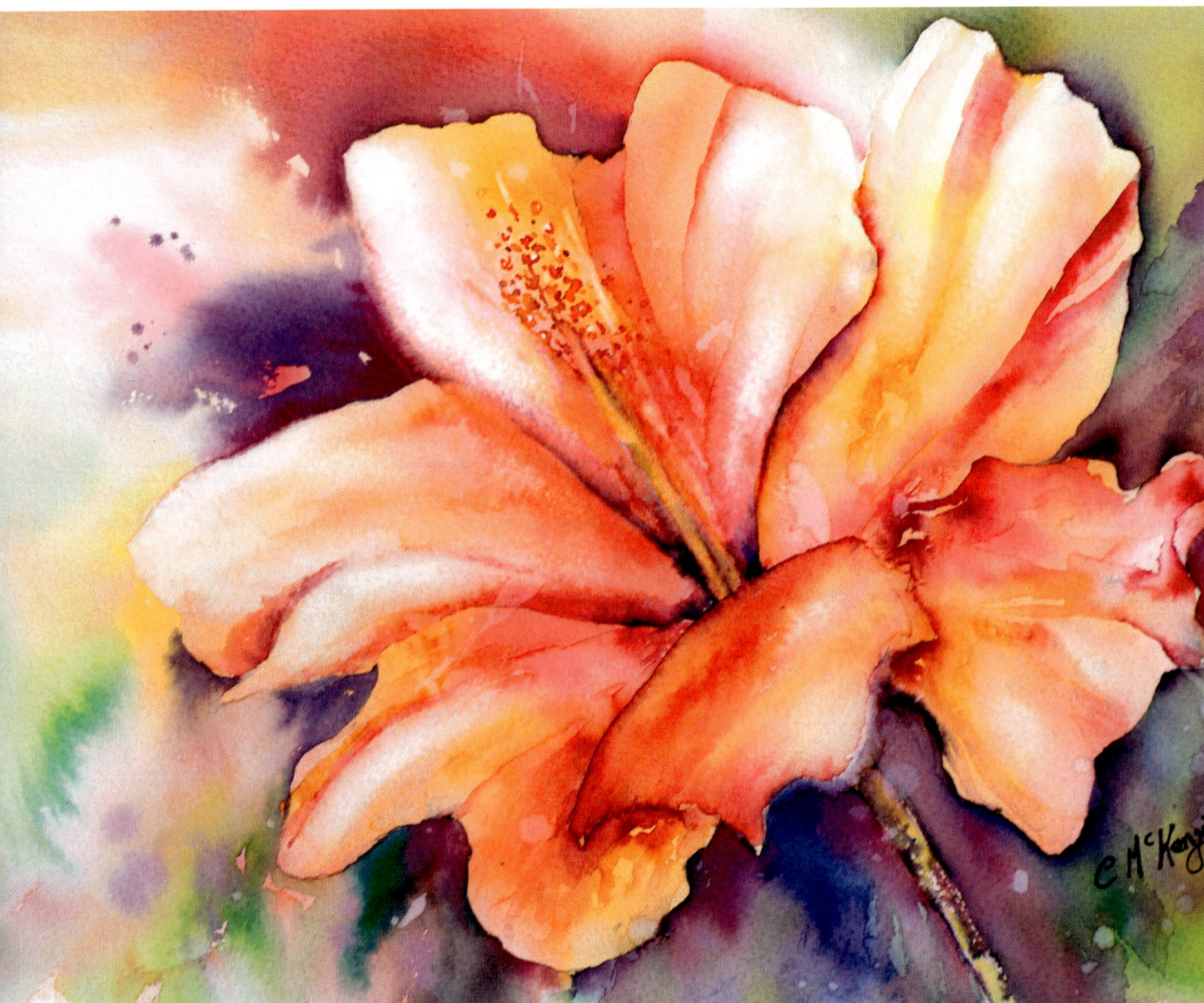

Beautiful Brilliant Brusho!

For these two paintings I used negative painting to complete the dark background first in order to bring out the white flower shapes. I then painted the positive shapes – the flowers - using watery mixes of Cobalt Blue, Violet, Brilliant Red and Yellow to add shadow and shape to the petals.

GENTLE
WHITE

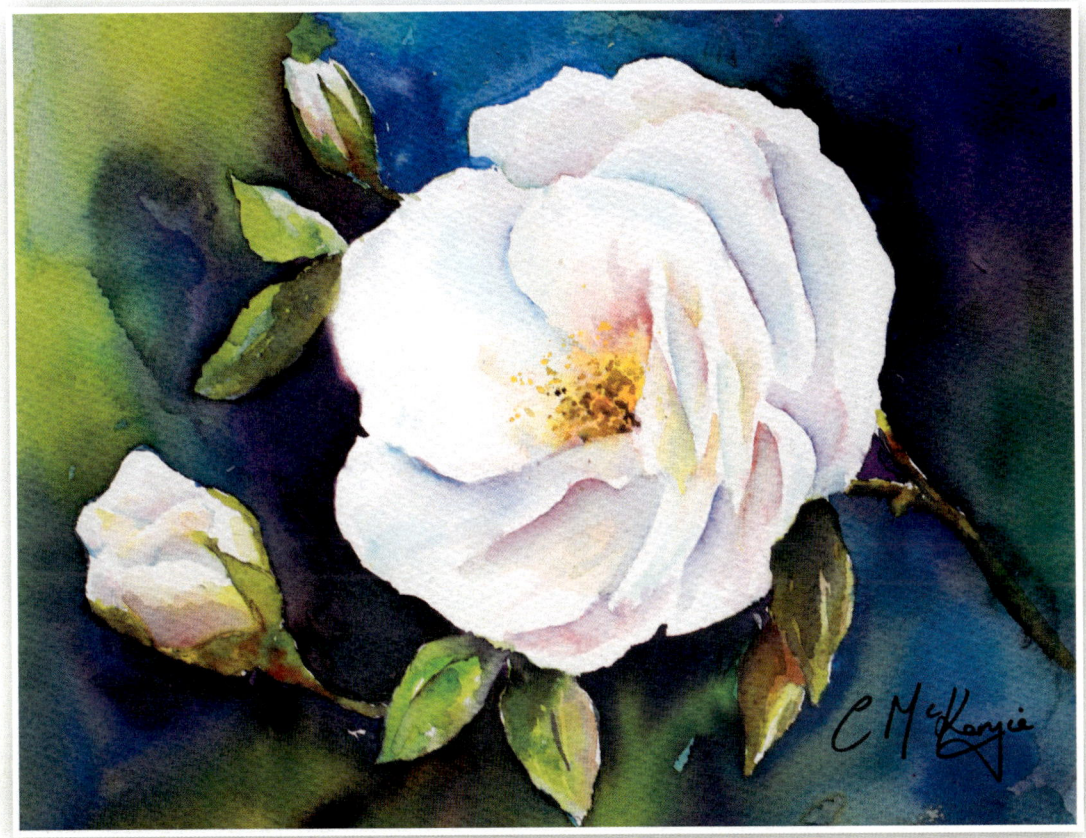

PRICKLE
POPPY

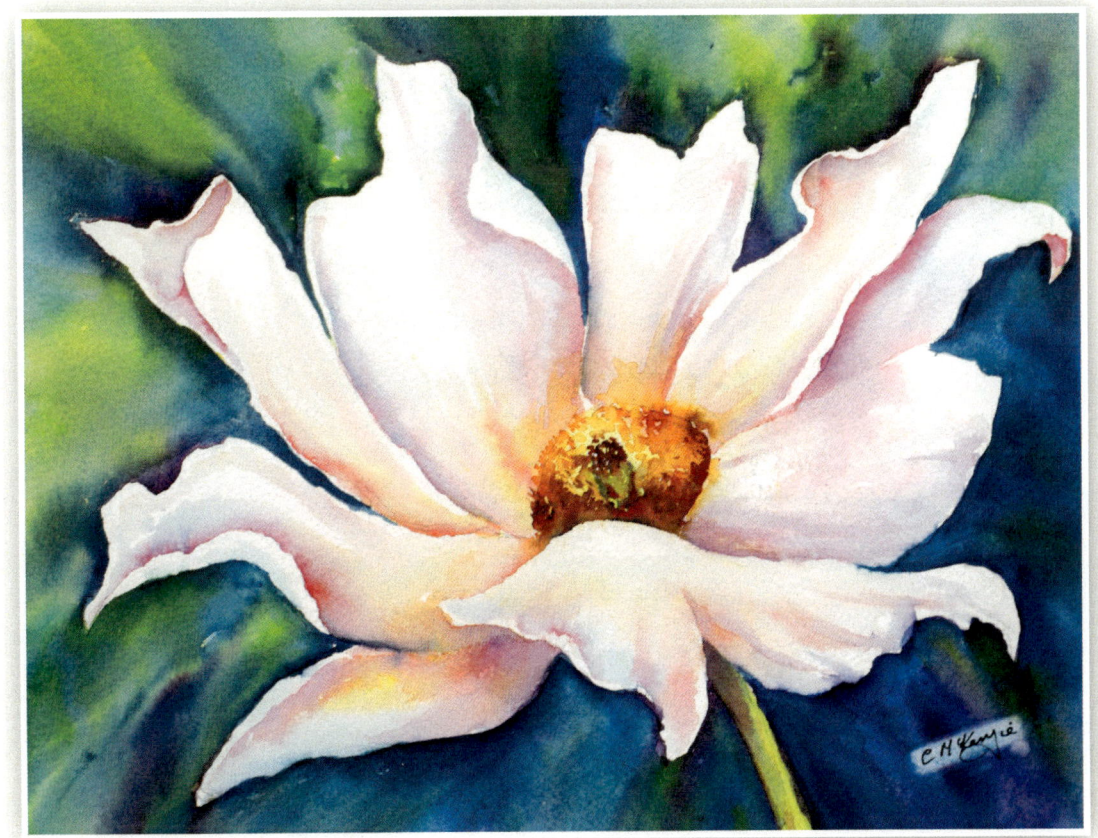

75

6 : BRUSHO & BLEACH

USING BLEACH

In addition to some ordinary household bleach, you need a spray bottle that can be clearly labelled and used solely for bleach so that you don't accidentally spoil any other artwork. If you prefer, you can substitute Milton for bleach.

Don't use your good brushes — the bleach will ruin the fibres, so either use your old ones or buy some very cheap synthetic ones. For finer detail, you could use a mapping pen, cocktail sticks, or even twigs.

Bleach is far more effective on Brusho paint than it is on watercolour paint. Some fantastic effects can be achieved, from subtle highlights to intense bright stars:

- Used on wet paint, the bleach can strip the colour right back to white paper.
- Used on dry paint, the bleach will strip some colours back to a pale yellow-brown colour, others to a pale aqua.
- You can spritz or spray it from a spray bottle to obtain a speckled effect — different dilutions can be put into the spray bottle for a variety of effects and tones.
- The colour and density of the paint that was applied, the type of paper you are using, can all affect the end result so you need to experiment a little and test them out. When used in different dilutions, the bleach will strip the colour back to a range of different tones, depending on how much water is added.
- You have to be patient when using bleach. The final result can take quite some time to appear as the wet bleach continues to work and strip the colour until the paper is completely dry. Because you can't tell straight away, there is a temptation to keep on applying more bleach than you need to. To judge the full effect, it's advisable to leave it for at least a few hours, or even overnight, check the result first and apply more if necessary.

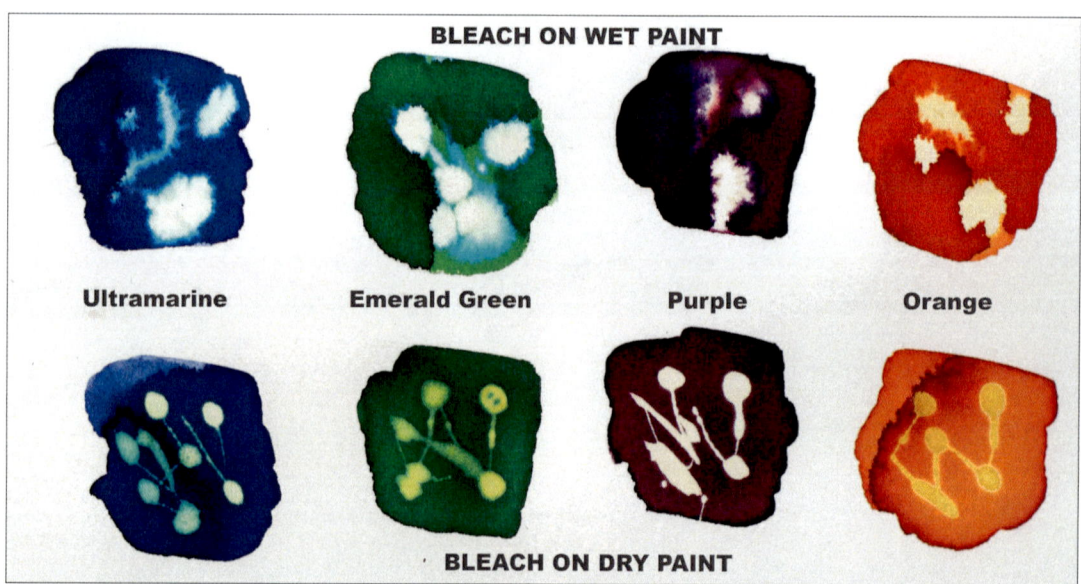

BLEACH ON WET PAINT

Ultramarine   Emerald Green   Purple   Orange

BLEACH ON DRY PAINT

STUDIO TIPS

To avoid spoiling your good brushes, buy cheap packs of children's painting brushes from local discount stores to use with bleach.

Save old jars with screw lids to mix different solutions of bleach in. Label these clearly with a waterproof pen and store upright in a safe place.

You may also choose to protect your mouth and nose with a mask.

Technique 16 – Apply bleach to Brusho

Apply neat (undiluted) bleach to Brusho

➤ Paint a small flower using Purple and put it to one side to dry.
➤ Paint another purple flower and, while the paint is still wet, dip a cocktail stick, small brush, or other pointed tool, into some neat bleach and dot it around the centre of the flower.
➤ Do the same thing with the first purple flower you painted; compare the results.

Spray bleach using a water sprayer

➤ Fill a water sprayer with approximately 75% bleach and 25% water. Paint two patches of Ultramarine. Spritz one patch with bleach while the paint is still wet, spritz the other when the paint is dry; compare the results.

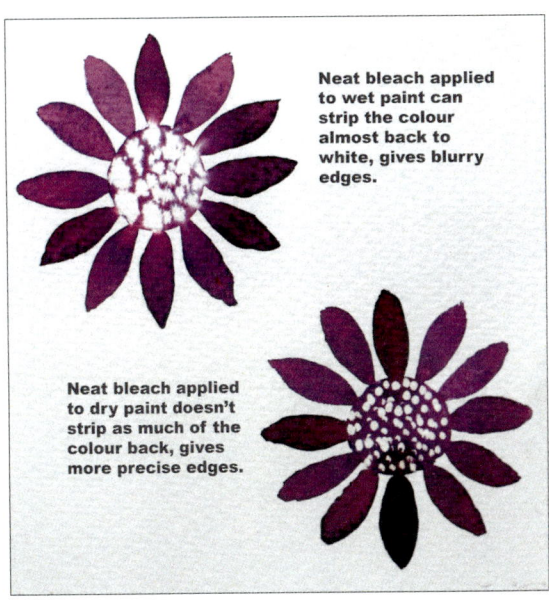

Neat bleach applied to wet paint can strip the colour almost back to white, gives blurry edges.

Neat bleach applied to dry paint doesn't strip as much of the colour back, gives more precise edges.

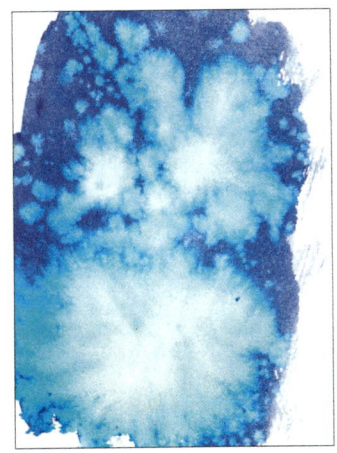

When sprayed on wet paint, the patterns left by the bleach are more fuzzy but whiter in colour.

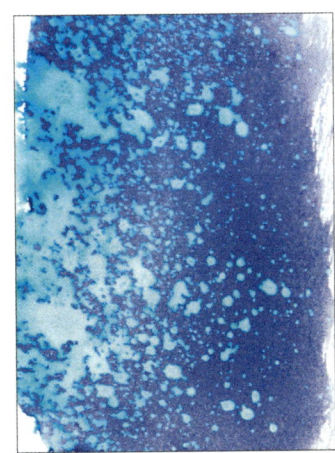

When sprayed on dry paint, the patterns left by the bleach are more defined but less white in colour.

Demonstration

BLEACHED TREE

1. Repeat the demonstration you did earlier for painting trees, but this time substitute Turquoise for Dark Brown and paint just a single tree. Use a mix of Leaf Green, Turquoise and Ultramarine for the trunks and branches. Use all the colours for the leaves and grasses. When the painting is finished leave it to dry.

Spray lightly with a mix of 25% bleach + 75% water - leave it for a few hours - if you spray too much bleach, you may bleach out your painting completely, You can always give it another spray of bleach solution if you need to. The results of using bleach are very unpredictable. Here's what my worked example turned out like.

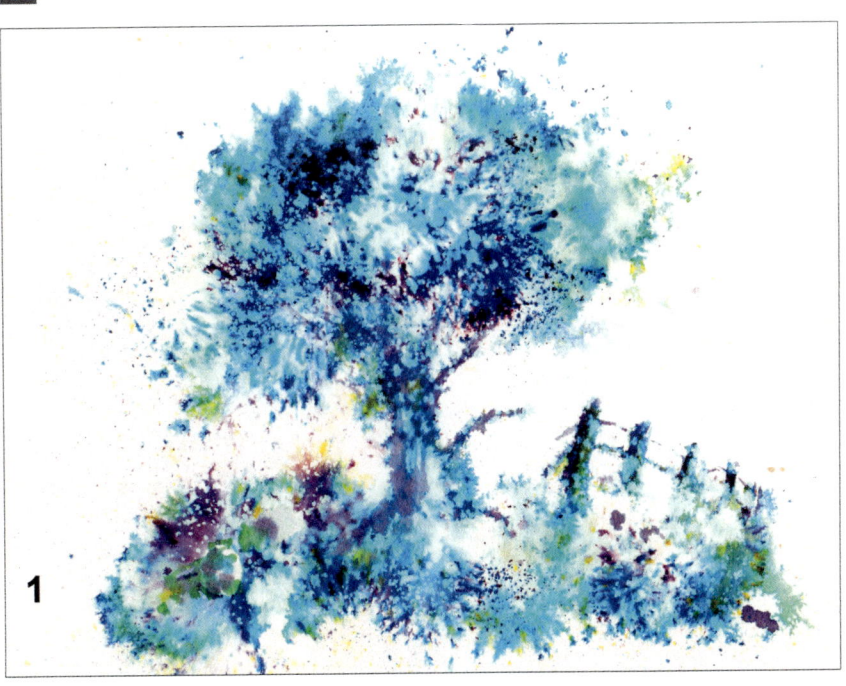

Demonstration
SILVER BIRCH TREE

MATERIALS
Yellow
Brilliant Red
Emerald Green
Ultramarine

Bleach

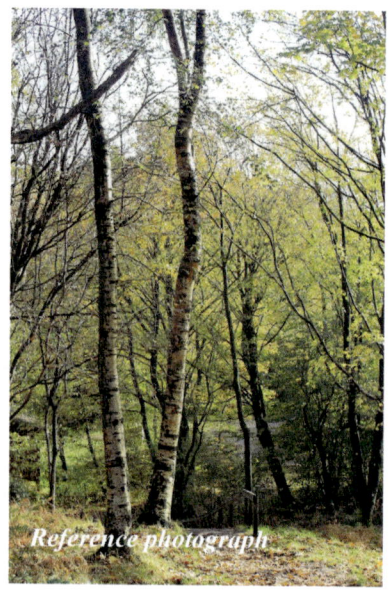

Reference photograph

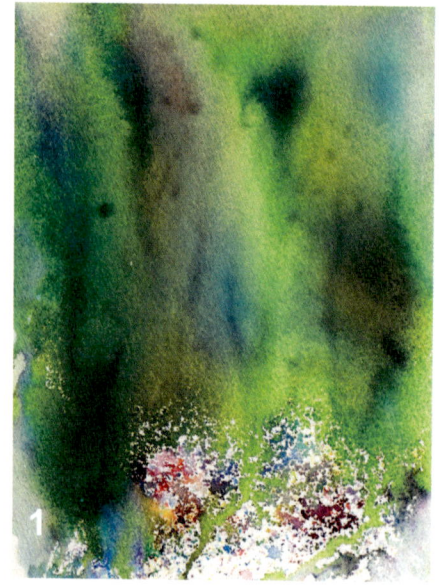

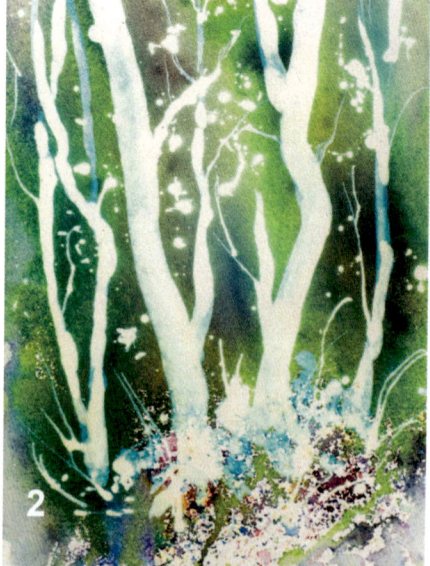

1 No drawing is needed for this project. The reference photograph will help you to define some of the tree shapes later on. First, create the background by sprinkling Emerald Green, Ultramarine, Yellow and a touch of Brilliant Red onto some dry paper.

Spritz lightly to get some texture. Then lift the paper up from the bottom and spray downwards towards the top, keeping some of the texture at the bottom to represent grasses. Leave to dry

2 Use some of the trees shapes in the photograph as a guide, but also use your imagination to move things around to make a good composition.

Paint some tree trunks and branches with an old brush dipped in neat bleach. Add a few dots, squiggles and curving grass shapes. Leave to dry.

3 Sprinkle a little more Emerald Green, Yellow and Ultramarine around the bottom of the trees and also in a few places higher up. Spritz lightly to preserve texture. While the paint is still wet, mix a dark colour with Ultramarine, Yellow and Brilliant Red and drop little touches in the foreground, allowing it to mingle with the other colours, to create some depth.

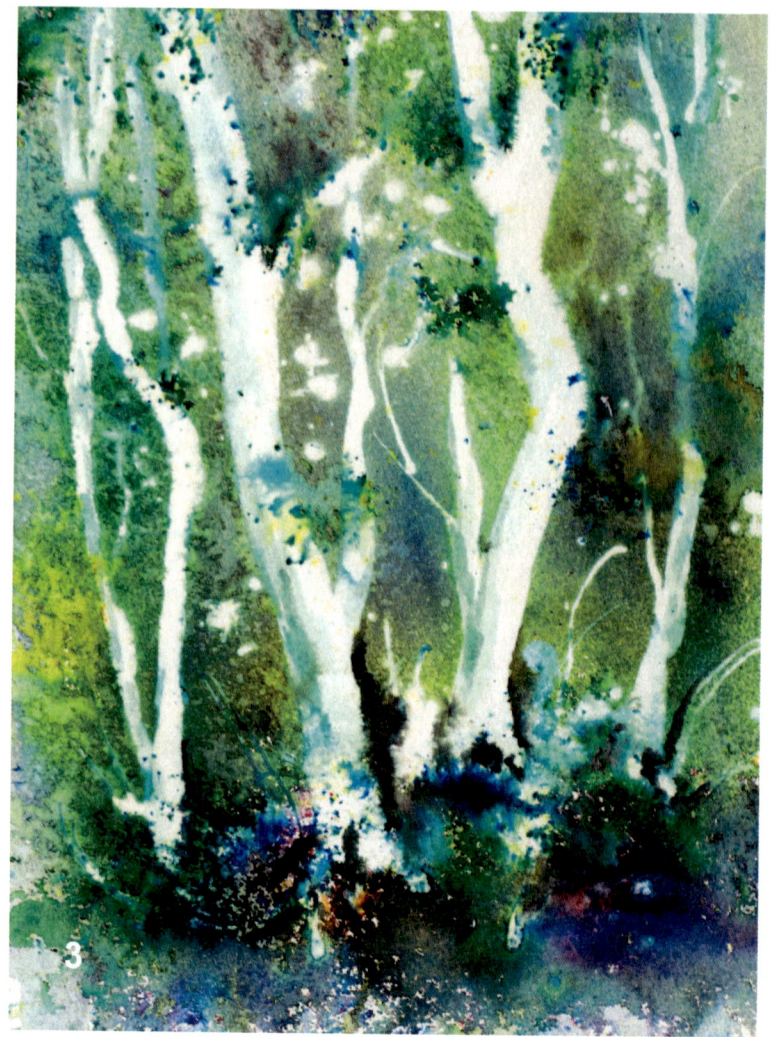

Demonstration
BRIGHT AWAKENING

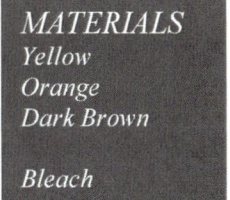

MATERIALS
Yellow
Orange
Dark Brown

Bleach

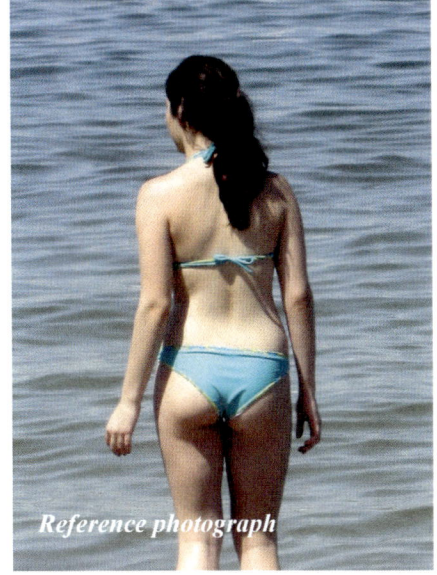

Reference photograph

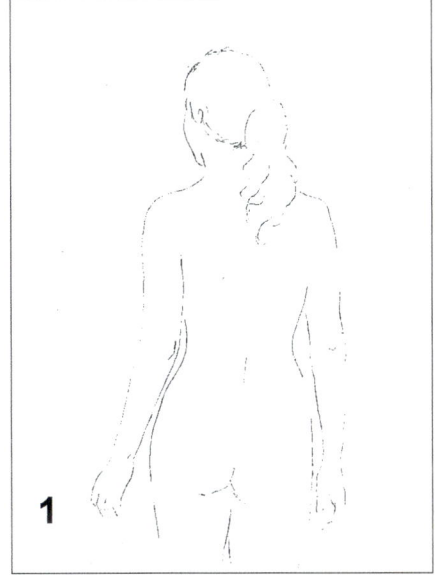

1 Draw the outline of the girl, ignoring the bikini.

2 Sprinkle Yellow, Orange and Dark Brown all over the paper. Spritz lightly to retain texture. Then, lift the paper up at the top and spray the paint downward in the centre section of the paper only. This will give you a nice, smooth blend across the body, which is more suitable for the skin areas, whilst leaving some texture in the surrounding areas.
   Leave to dry.

3 Mix 10% bleach with 90% water – you are aiming for a more soft, pale colour than a stark white. Working a section at a time wet an area of the skin that you want to lighten with a soft brush and clean water. Take the water a little past the area that you want to lighten so you can blend into it.
   Use an old paint brush to paint the bleach mix onto the skin area that you have just wet, blending it in to the wet paper to avoid hard edges. If the 10% bleach mix is not strong enough, add a little more bleach. If it is too strong, add some water. Continue working around the girl's body, applying the bleach to the parts that catch the light. Leave to dry.

4 In order to bring the girl's body out from the background and define it more, paint some of the negative space around the body with Dark Brown. Use the blending and softening technique to soften the darker paint into the existing background.
   Note that I haven't darkened the area around the hair. I will paint the hair darker in the next step so I want to keep the negative space around it light.

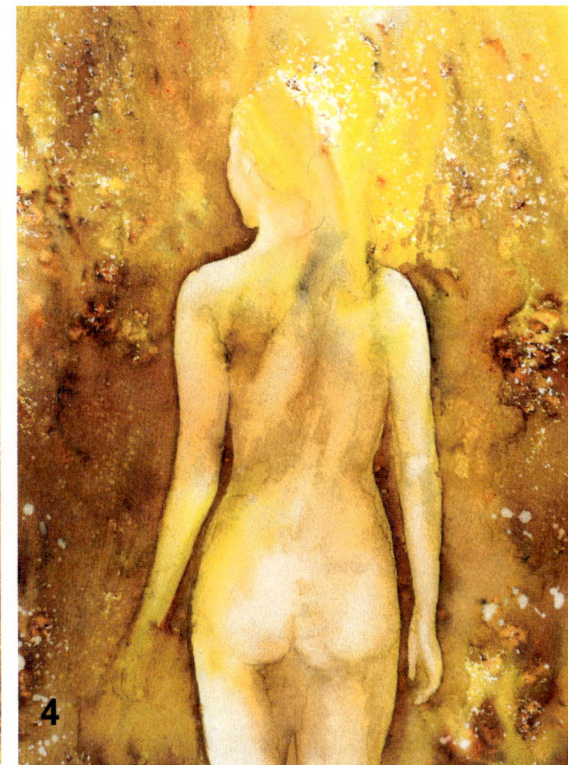

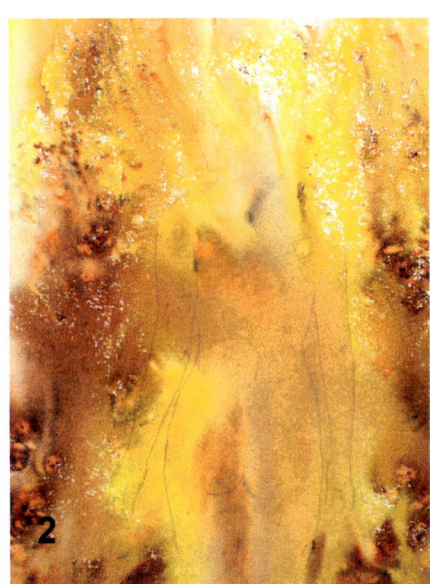

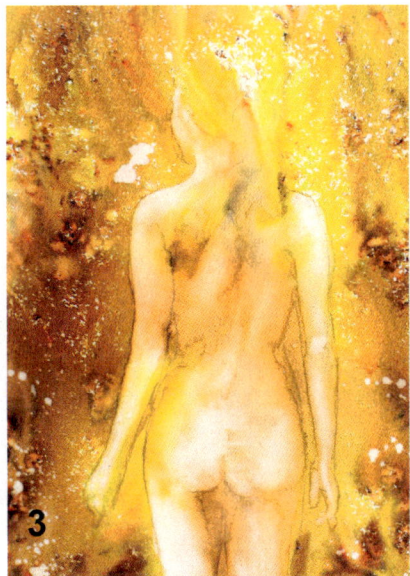

5 Add some darker paint to the shaded areas of the girl's body, blending and softening this away with a damp brush and clear water. Where the shadow is really dark, mix a little Ultramarine with the Dark Brown. Use the same colours to paint the girl's hair, allowing some of the underlying paler colour to show through.

STUDIO TIP

Converting an image to greyscale (black and white) helps to identify the highlight areas – this will help you to see more easily where to apply the bleach.

BRIGHT AWAKENING

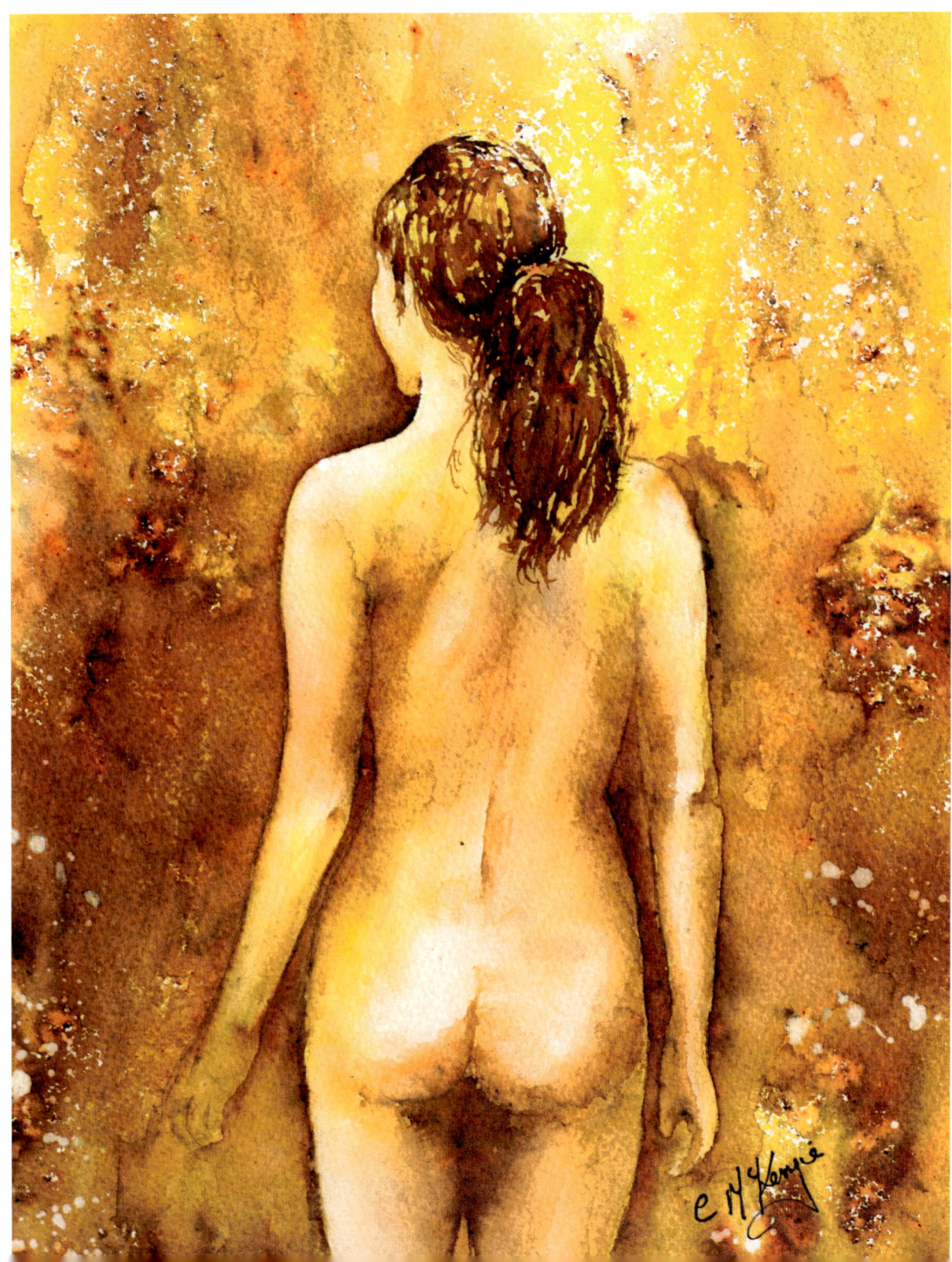

GALLERY

SWIMMING ALONG

Here, I wet the entire paper, and then dropped in some Turquoise, Ultramarine and Yellow letting these colours mingle randomly on the paper.

I sprinkled some coarse sea salt into the wet wash, which formed some of the bubble shapes.

I left it to dry, then sprinkled some Emerald, Turquoise, Ultramarine, Yellow and a little Brilliant Red along the bottom of the seabed and spritzed it lightly to retain texture. I painted the fish using the same colours.

When everything was dry, I spritzed the whole painting lightly with a mix of 75% bleach and 25% water, which gave the appearance of the fish swimming through lots of underwater bubble

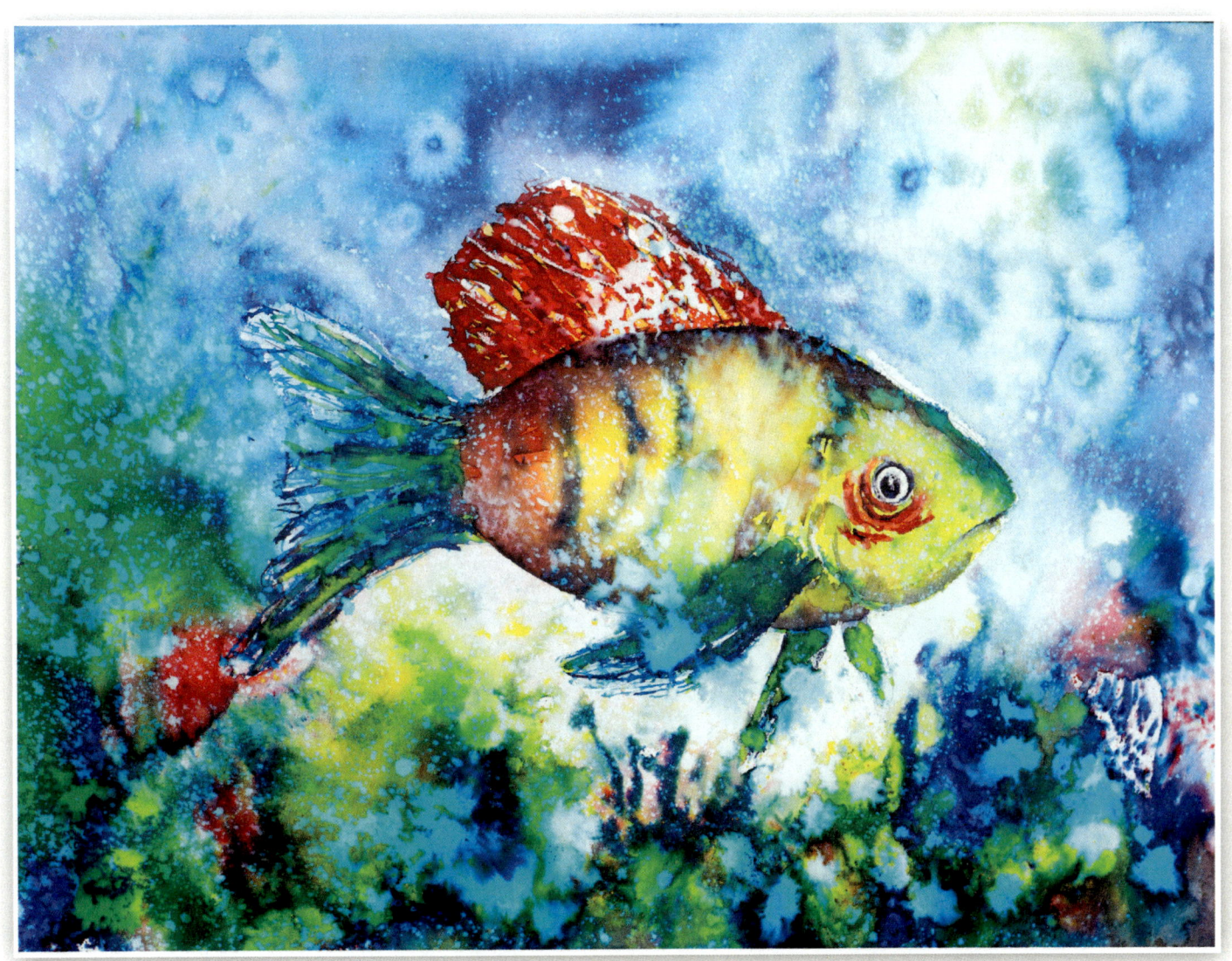

SOLITUDE

For this painting, I applied a few streaks of neat bleach with a cocktail stick to recover a few highlights on the water, and some diluted bleach to break up the dense background.

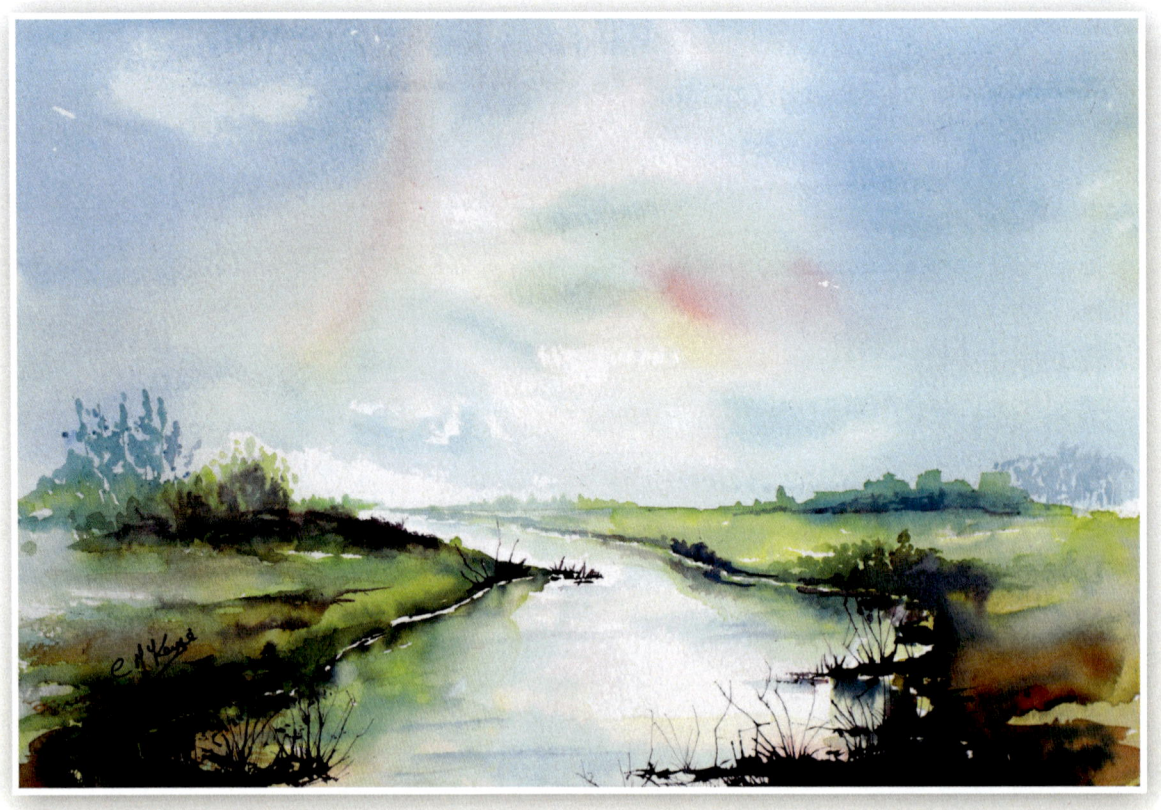

WHITE LADIES

When I finished this painting, I felt the background was a little uninteresting. To break it up a little, I masked the flower heads with some cellophane to protect them, then sprayed the background lightly with a mix of 50% bleach and 50% water.

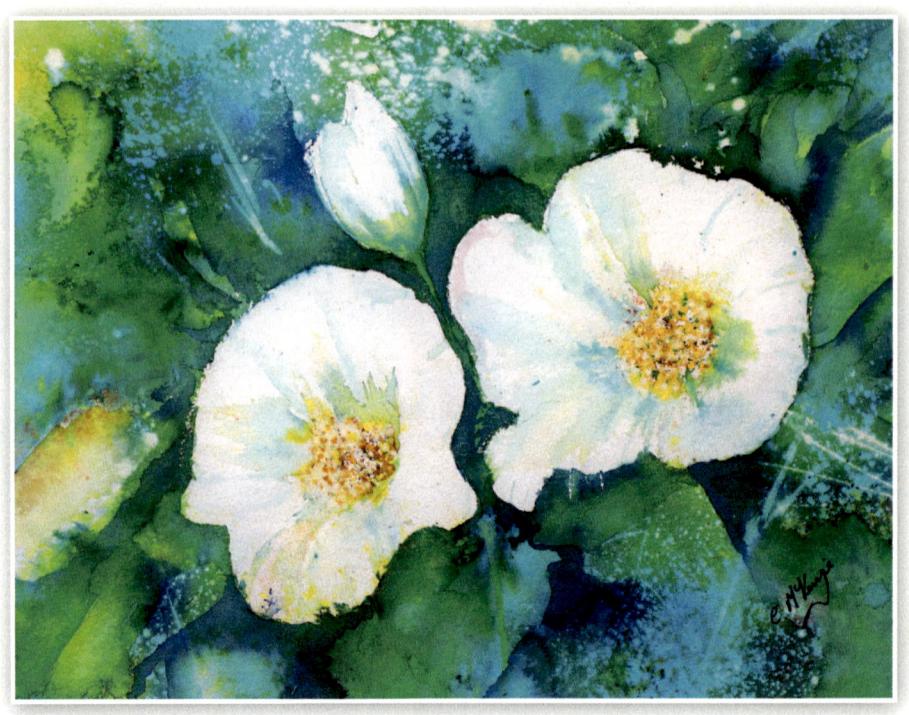

BLUESEY HYDRANGEAS

Unlike the previous flower painting, where I applied bleach to the background, for this painting, I applied it directly to the flower heads.

After painting the flower heads with Ultramarine and Turquoise, I dipped a small brush into the bleach (some neat and some diluted) and applied it using the brush bristles sideways on to make the little petal shapes, twisting and turning the brush to vary the shapes.

I used a cocktail stick dipped in neat bleach to paint a few small dots in the centres of some of the florets.

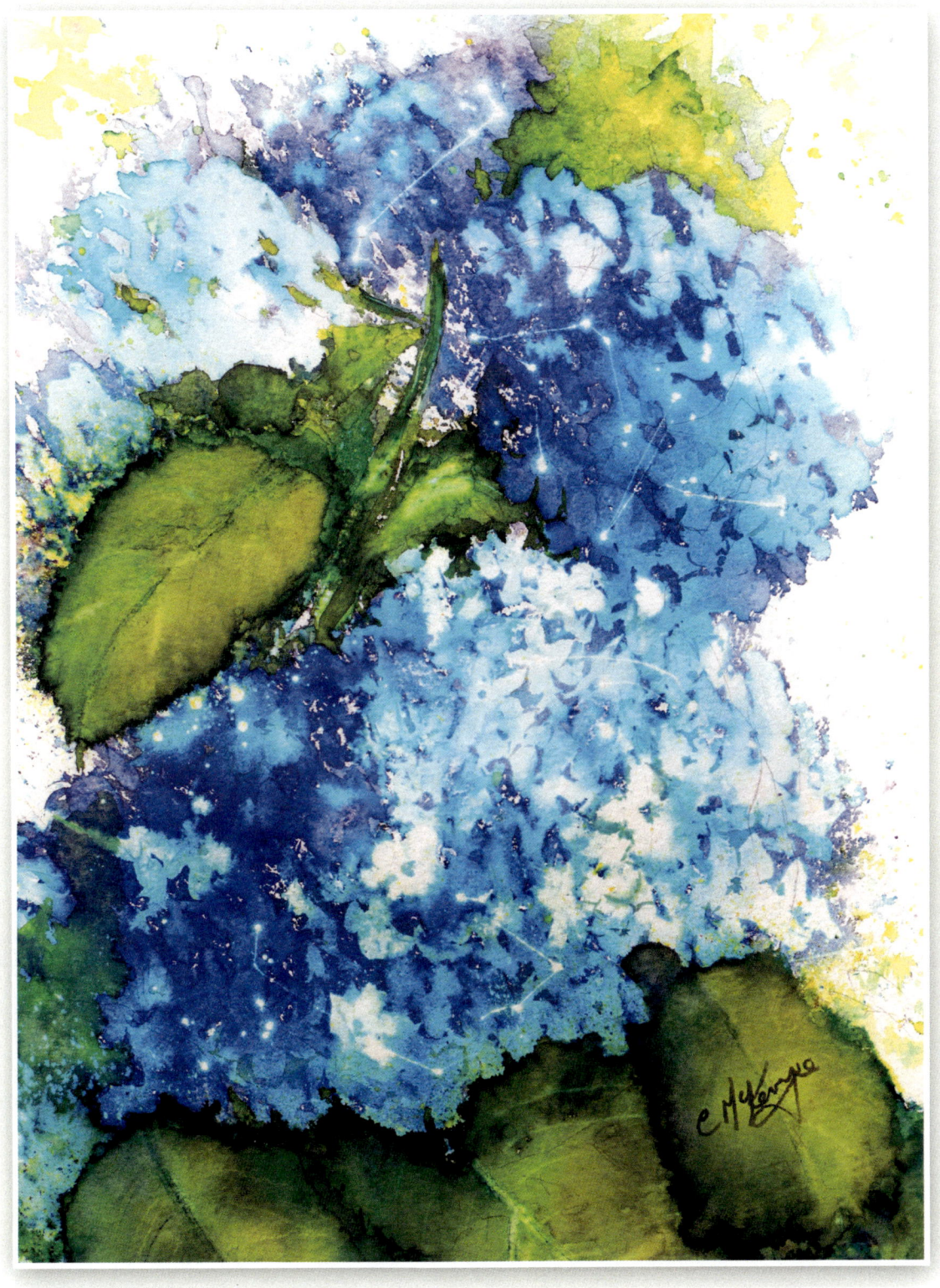

OFF TO THE PARK

These two paintings show how I've sprayed different dilutions of bleach to achieve a rainy effect in the background wash.

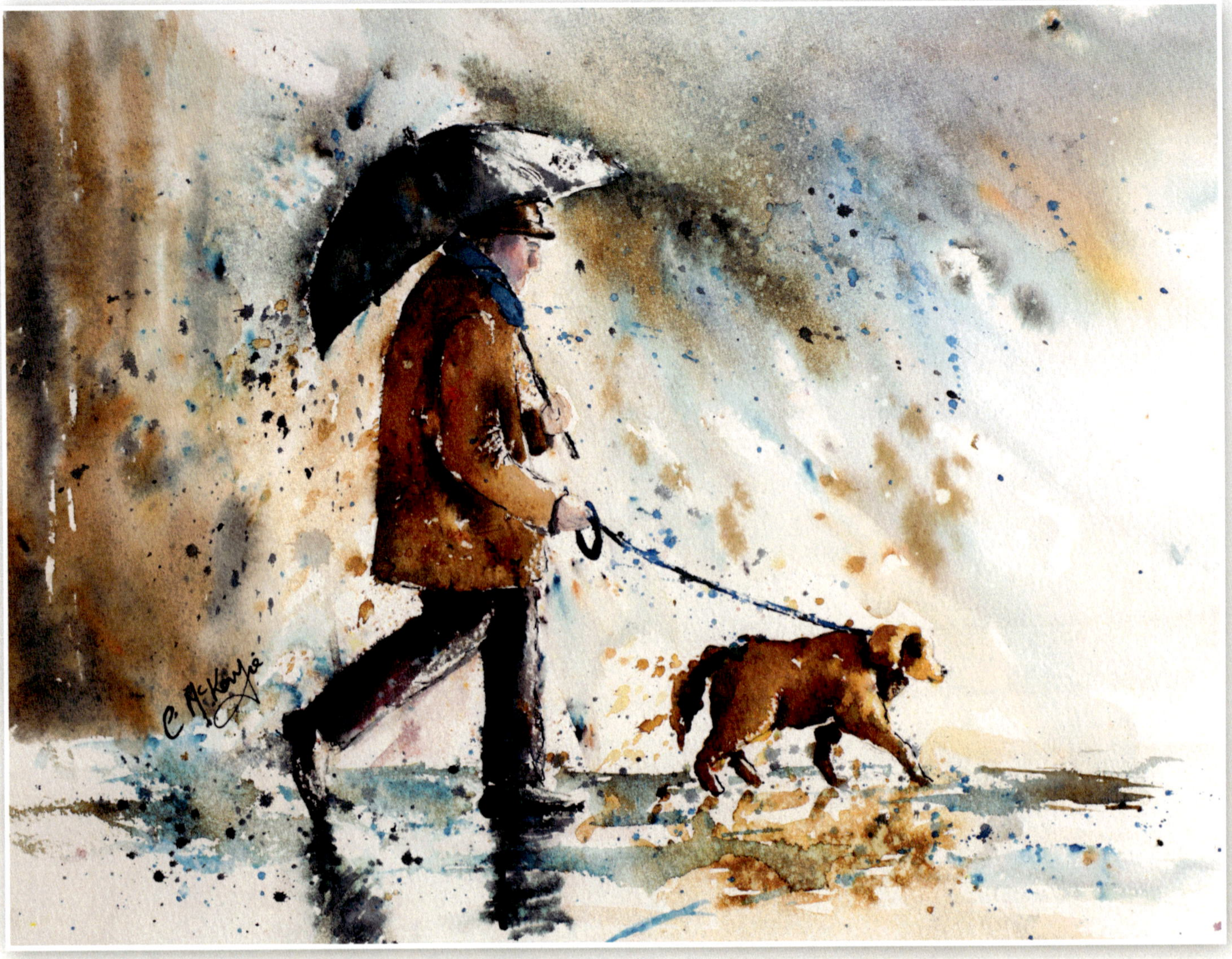

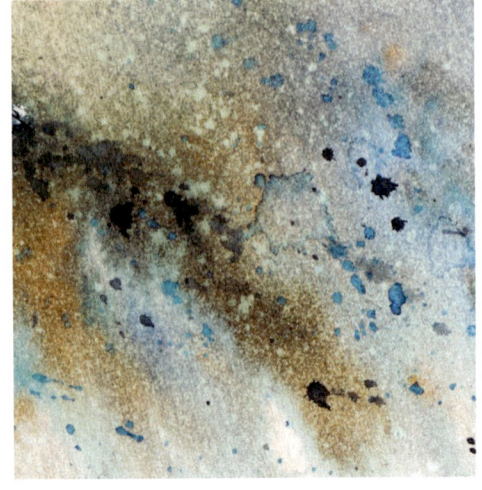

*Detail of sprayed
bleach effect*

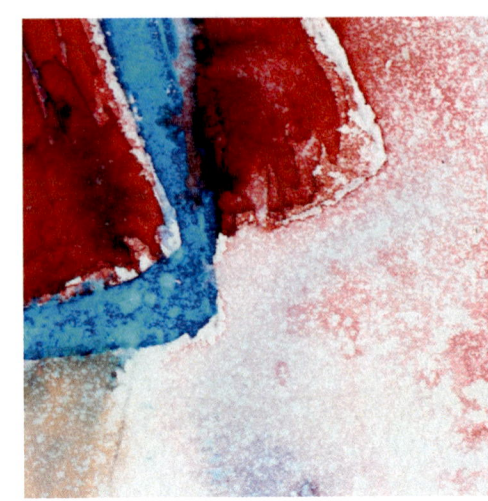

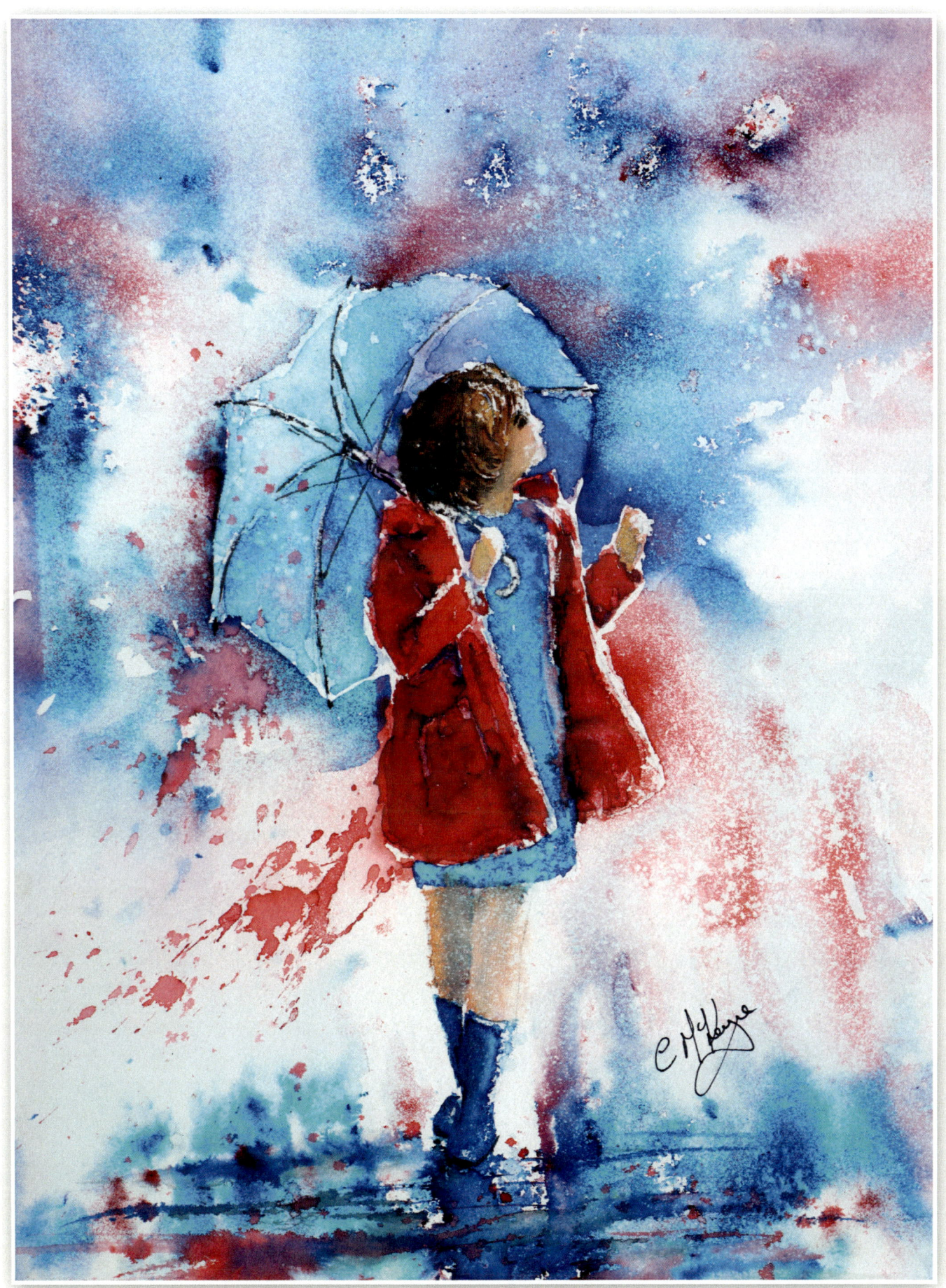

7 : FUN WITH ABSTRACTS

It can be great fun to try using Brusho with different kinds of materials. I suggest you set aside a couple of hours to just experiment and create unusual abstract effects without worrying too much about creating a masterpiece.

I find it best to leave these experiments for a few days then have a fresh look at them to see what you could turn them into.

There is no reason why you need to limit these techniques to abstract painting; you can incorporate them into all your other styles of painting. This can, of course, be frustrating or liberating depending on the result!

Here are a few ideas that you might like to try out. I'm sure you'll come up with lots more yourself — the possibilities are endless!

Brusho on starch

Spraying starch on your paper, before sprinkling with brusho, tends to produce a soft, feathery effect.

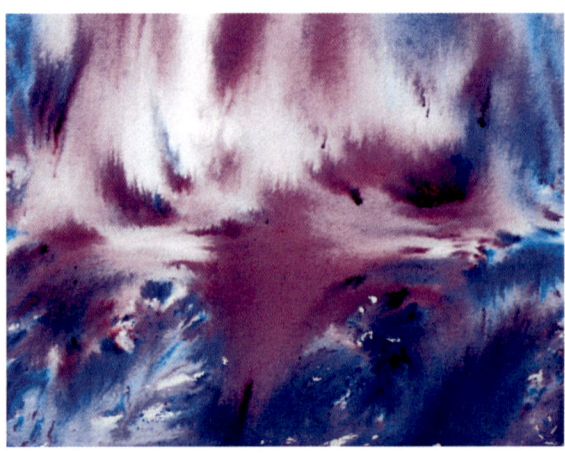

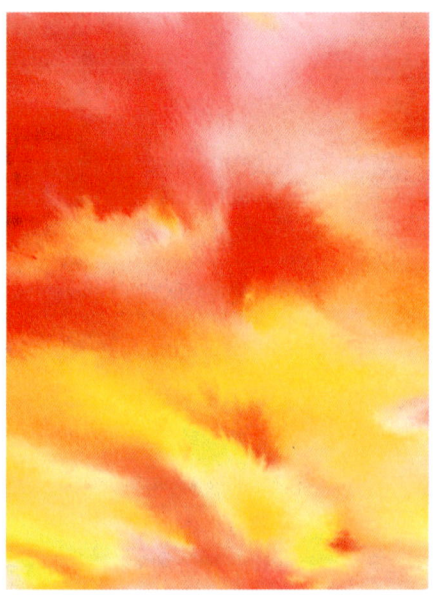

In the example below, I wanted to create a soft feathery effect to represent the beautiful spreading feathers of a peacock. I sprayed the paper with starch first, then sprinkled some Yellow, Leaf Green and Ultramarine at the right hand side and left the colours

to merge gently together. When the paper had dried, I completed the rest of the peacock with a brush, using the same colours along with some Turquoise.

I sprinkled all the colours on the foreground and spritzed lightly to create the grassy texture.

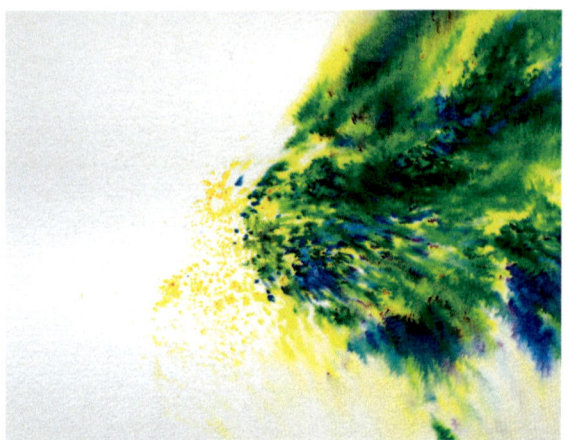

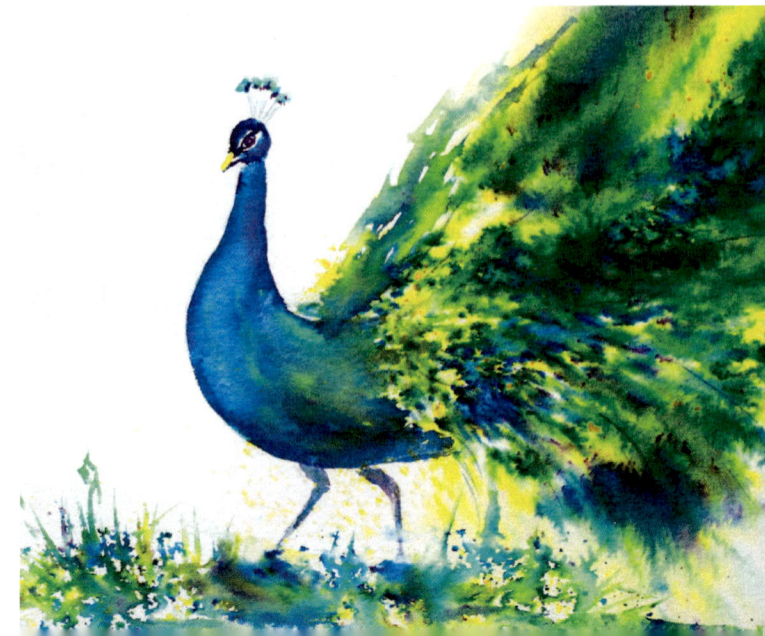

Brusho on Yupo

Yupo paper is actually not a paper at all; it is a synthetic plastic made for the printing industry. Yupo is waterproof; one of its key features is that it repels water so you get some wonderful effects when the wet paint is drying.

Often, I let the colours just run together and do their own thing. You can wipe colour off with a paper towel, q-tip, sponge or wet brush to create interesting images and textures. You can also scoop and scrape into it to remove colour and get back the white paper underneath. Tilting the paper and allowing the colours to flow and mingle can create lovely abstract patterns and translucent colours. Dabbing a crumpled tissue into your paint before it completely dries or covering with plastic wrap also makes interesting abstract patterns appear.

You can't hurry the drying time by using a hair dryer as the paper is quite flimsy and tends to buckle if it gets too hot.

It doesn't behave like normal watercolour paper – when you leave a piece to dry and come back to it you will find it has done surprising things.

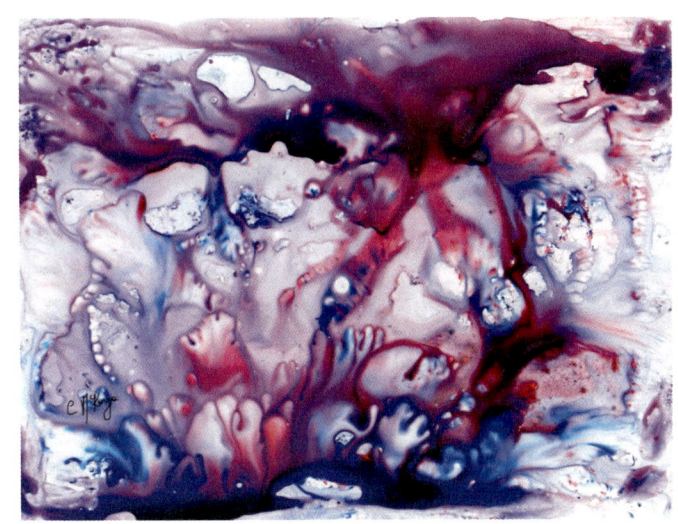

In the example below, I dribbled on some PVA glue in a haphazard fashion. I then sprinkled and spritzed on some Brilliant Red Brusho, which the glue absorbed. When it was dry, I painted in-between the glue shapes with Ultramarine Blue.

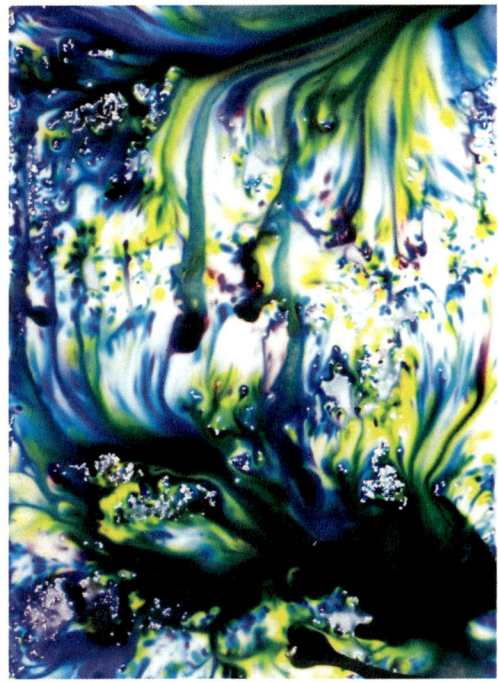

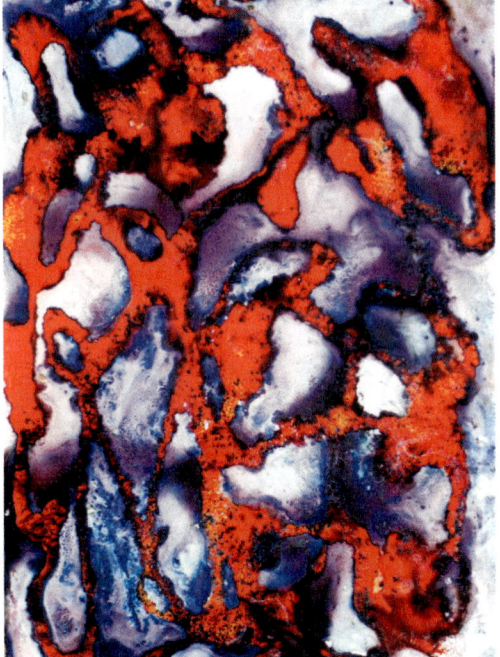

In the example opposite, I dribbled some PVA glue around the Yupo paper, and then sprinkled and spritzed a few different Brusho colours over the whole paper before the glue dried so that the glue lines were multi-coloured as well as the paper.

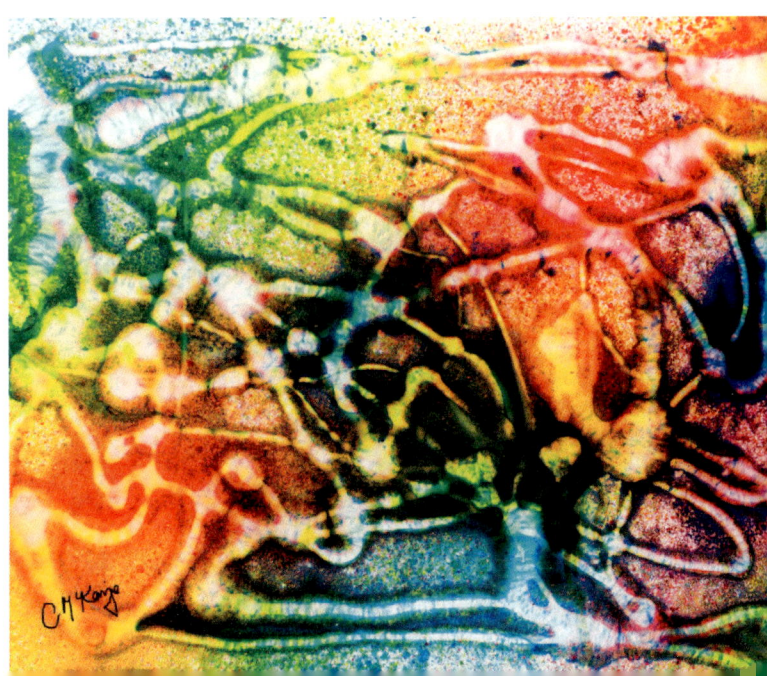

THE GOOD EARTH

This 'happy accident' abstract was the result of experimenting with Brusho on yupo paper in a slightly more controlled manner. I deliberately tried to divide the paper into one-third sky and two-thirds land. I used some Brusho earth colours – ochre, moss, olive and dark brown. When it dried the land area reminded me of tree roots growing down into the earth's strata, so I spritzed and dabbed a few tree shapes along the landline

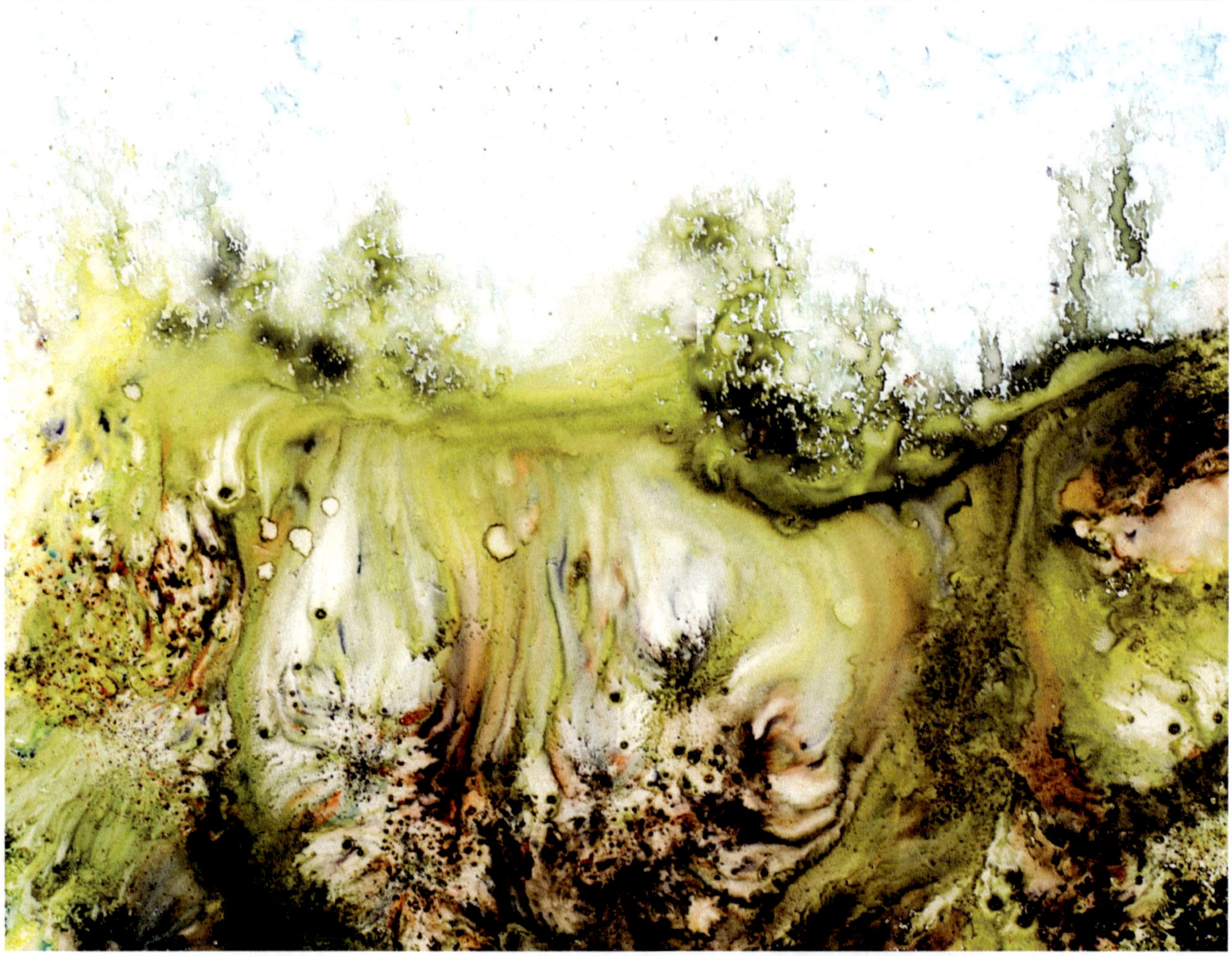

DRAGONFLY DREAM

Here, I created the background first by sprinkling and spritzing some cobalt blue, turquoise, violet and purple over a piece of yupo paper. When this was dry, I picked out the shape of the dragonfly with a mixture of positive and negative painting.

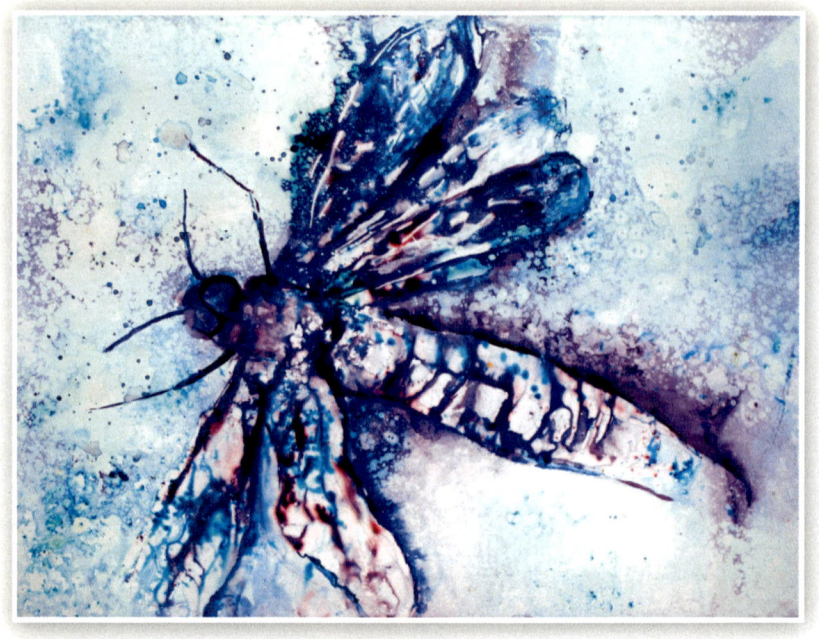

Brusho on Gesso

Gesso is great for creating texture with all sorts of painting mediums and Brusho is no exception. The Gesso tends to repel paint and water, which allows you to get some interesting effects when you paint over it. It's also easier to wipe colour off dried gesso than paper.

For the painting below, I smeared some gesso onto the sheep's woolly body and dabbed it in various places along the foreground where there would be rocks and grasses.

I painted the bold turquoise and violet sky, wet-into-wet, with a brush. When the sky was dry, I skimmed some clear wax across the raised gesso on the sheep's body to retain some white highlights, then I sprinkled and spritzed the same Brusho colours sparingly over the sheep's body, dabbing it with a brush here and there to vary the tone. Finally, I sprinkled and spritzed some green, yellow and turquoise over the foreground, flicking up some grasses with a brush while the paint was still wet.

When the foreground was dry, I used some damp paper towel to rub some of the paint off the gesso and reveal a few lighter coloured grasses.

FROSTY MORNING

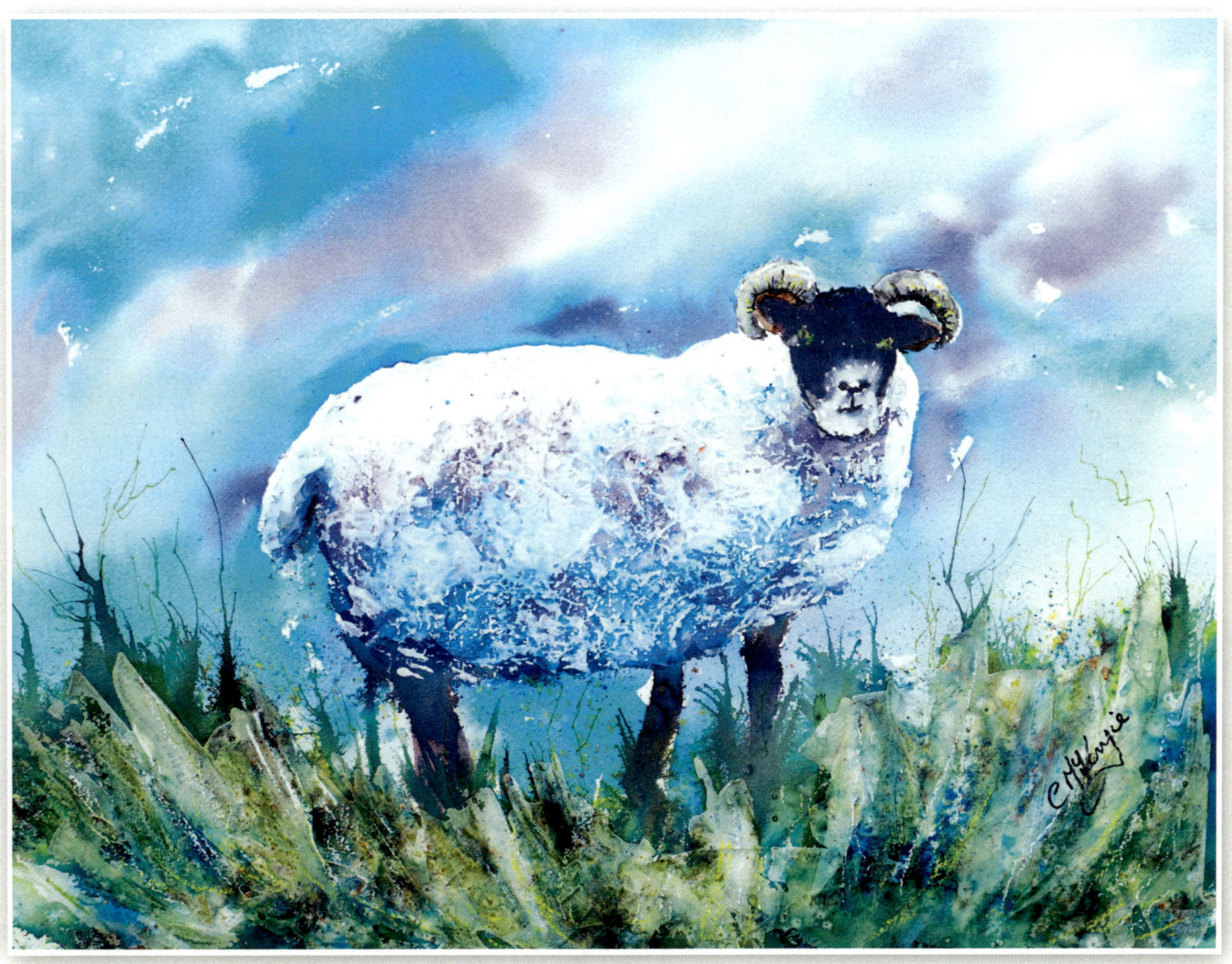

Brusho with soap bubbles

Here's something really different to try, especially when you have a moment of 'painter's block' and just need to let loose and doodle!

1 Lather up some soap bubbles in a washing up bowl – you can use washing up liquid or shampoo.

Scoop the bubbles (avoiding the water) and gently spread roughly a 2" layer of bubbles over a piece of watercolour paper.

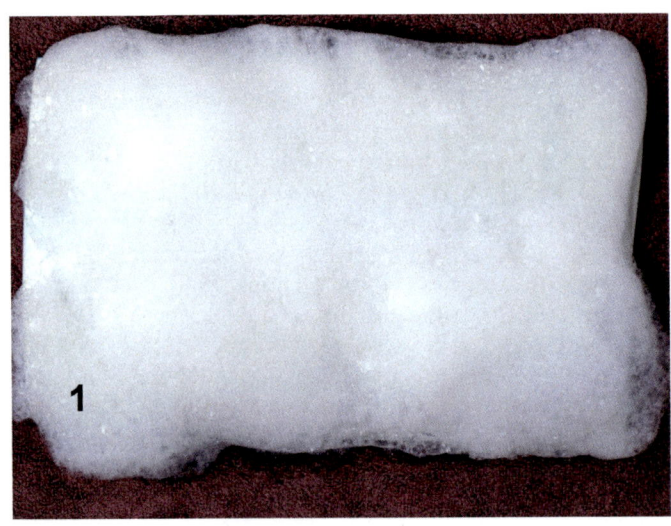

2 Sprinkle a few brusho colours sparingly on top of the bubbles – here I've used Yellow, Turquoise, Emerald and a little Ultramarine. Don't overdo the amount of colour or you will lose the effect.

3 It takes a while to dry naturally, so it's probably best to leave it overnight. When you next look at the result you'll be amazed at the beautiful bubble patterns that have emerged in the drying process.

Here are a couple of examples to two experiments that I came up with. If yours don't have enough colour you can always repeat the process again.

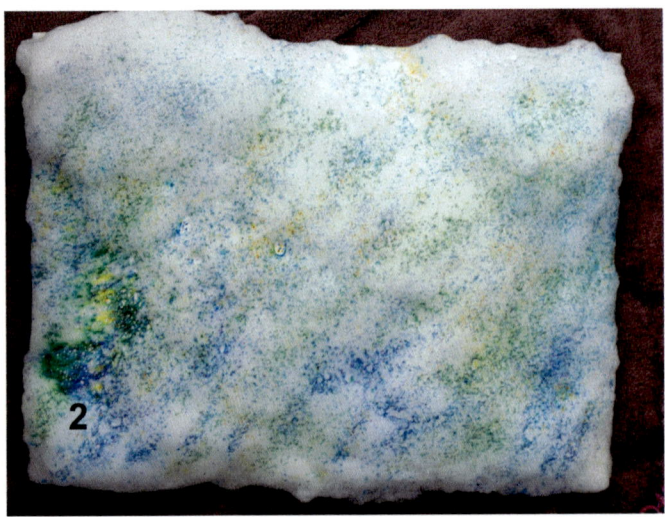

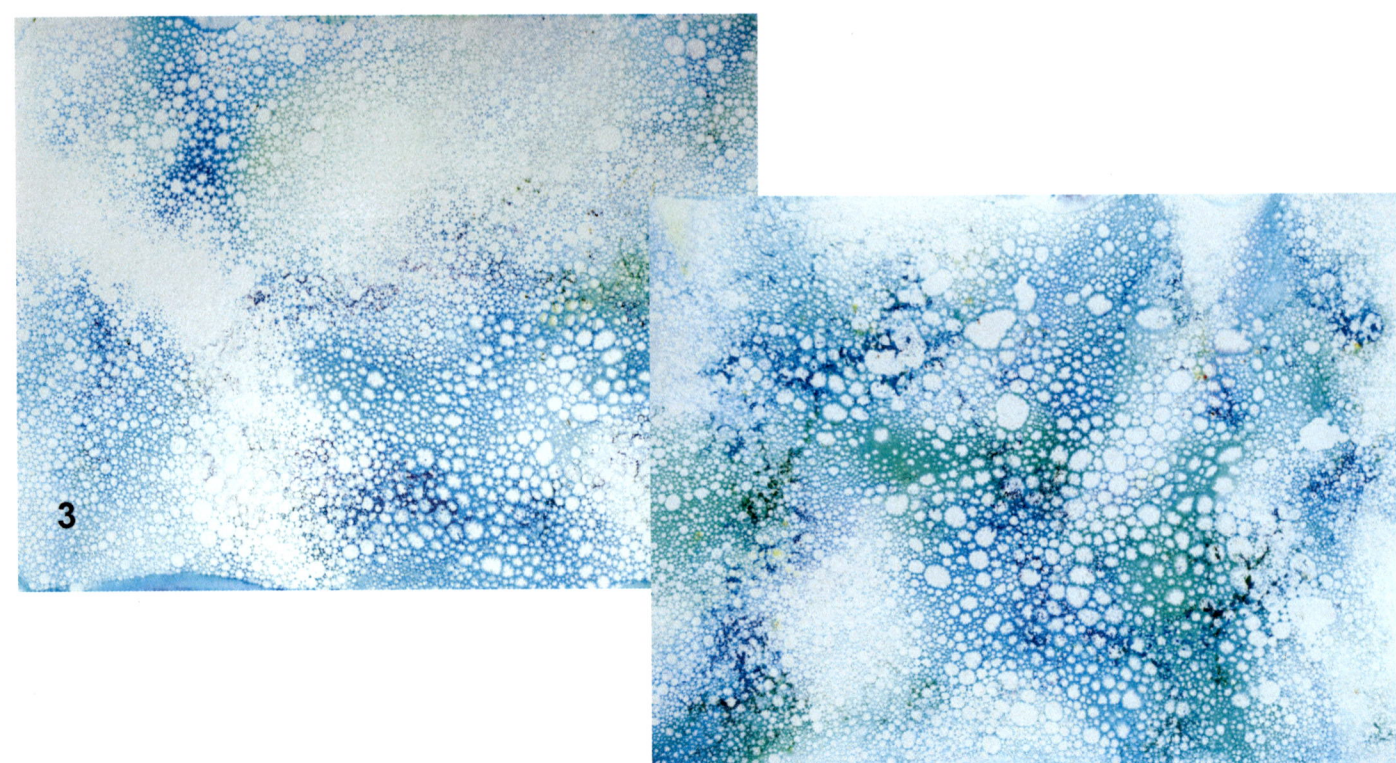

90

I decided to use my bubble backgrounds to paint some underwater scenes. I sprinkled and spritzed some more colours along the bottom of the paper to represent plant life and coral growing on the seabed. Using the shapes that I could see amongst the bubbles, along with my imagination, I then used a brush in the traditional way to paint the seaweed, rocks and fish. It doesn't matter if you don't always create a masterpiece, sometimes it's nice just to play with your paints and have a bit of fun!

LITTLE
FISHIES

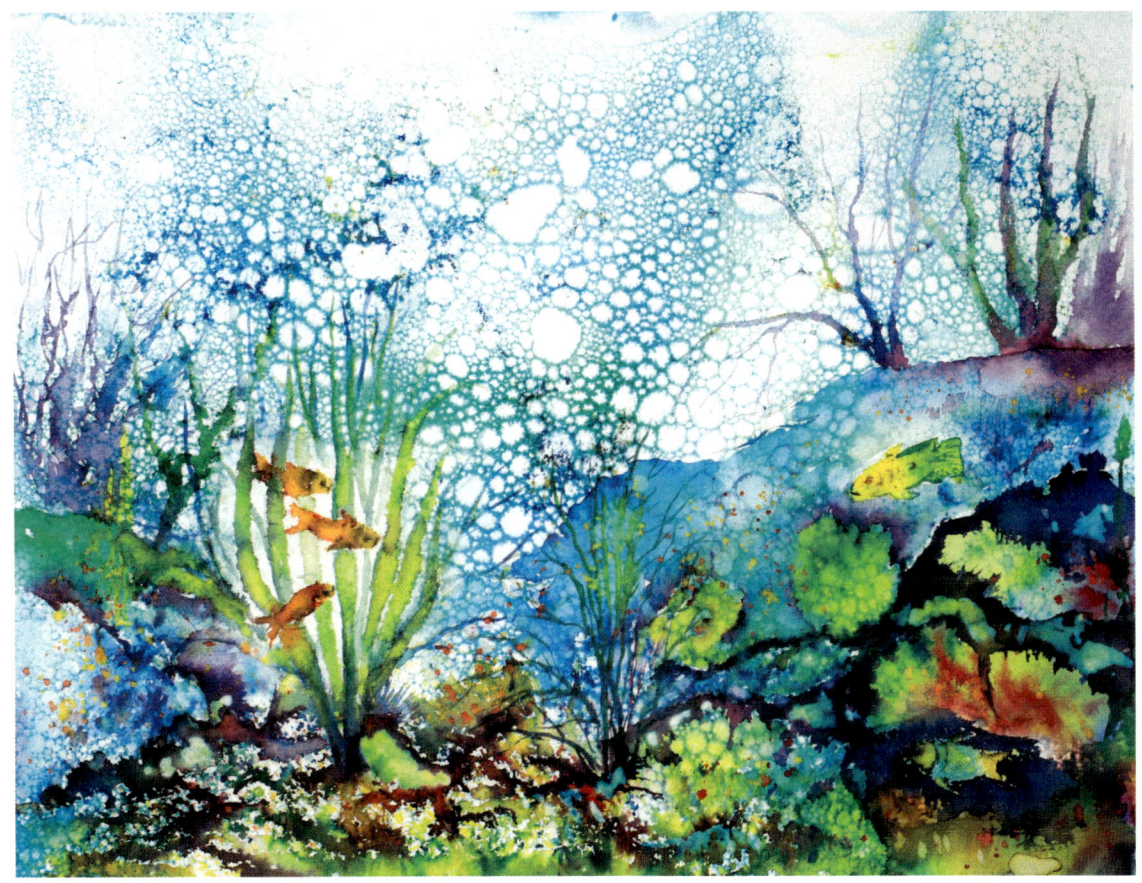

BENEATH
THE
WAVES

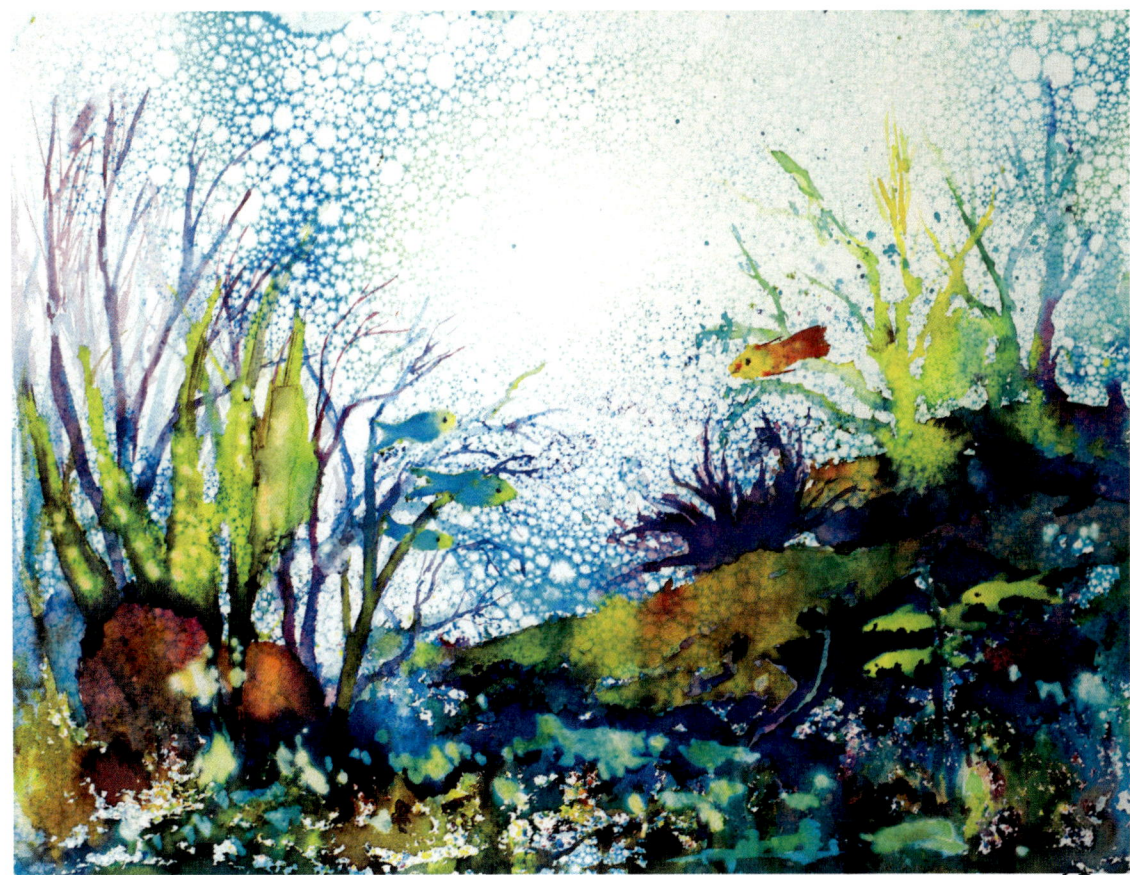

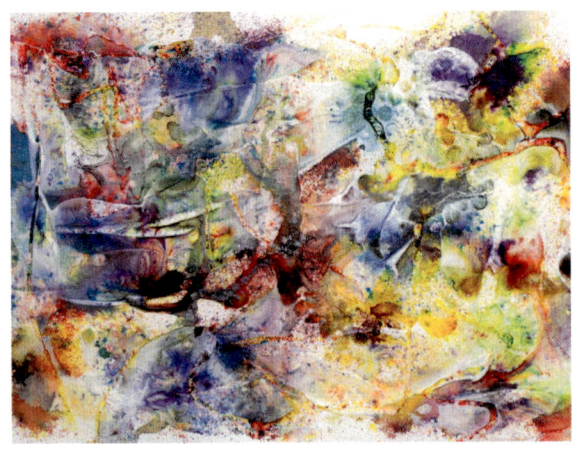

For this abstract painting, I mixed up a whole lot of abstract effects and was quite pleased with the result.

I scraped some random patches of gesso across a piece of watercolour paper, squirted some trails of pva glue across it and left it to dry.

Then I sprinkled and spritzed some different Brusho colours over the whole paper, letting the water blend the colours in places but leaving texture in others. Whilst the paint was still wet, I drizzled some granulation medium and acrylic ink in various places. I also pressed a few scraps of bubble wrap into some of the wet parts to create marks.

When all this was completely dried, I removed the bits of bubble wrap. I used a couple of water-soluble crayons to add some darks, and finally flicked on some white acrylic ink highlights.

DREAMSCAPE

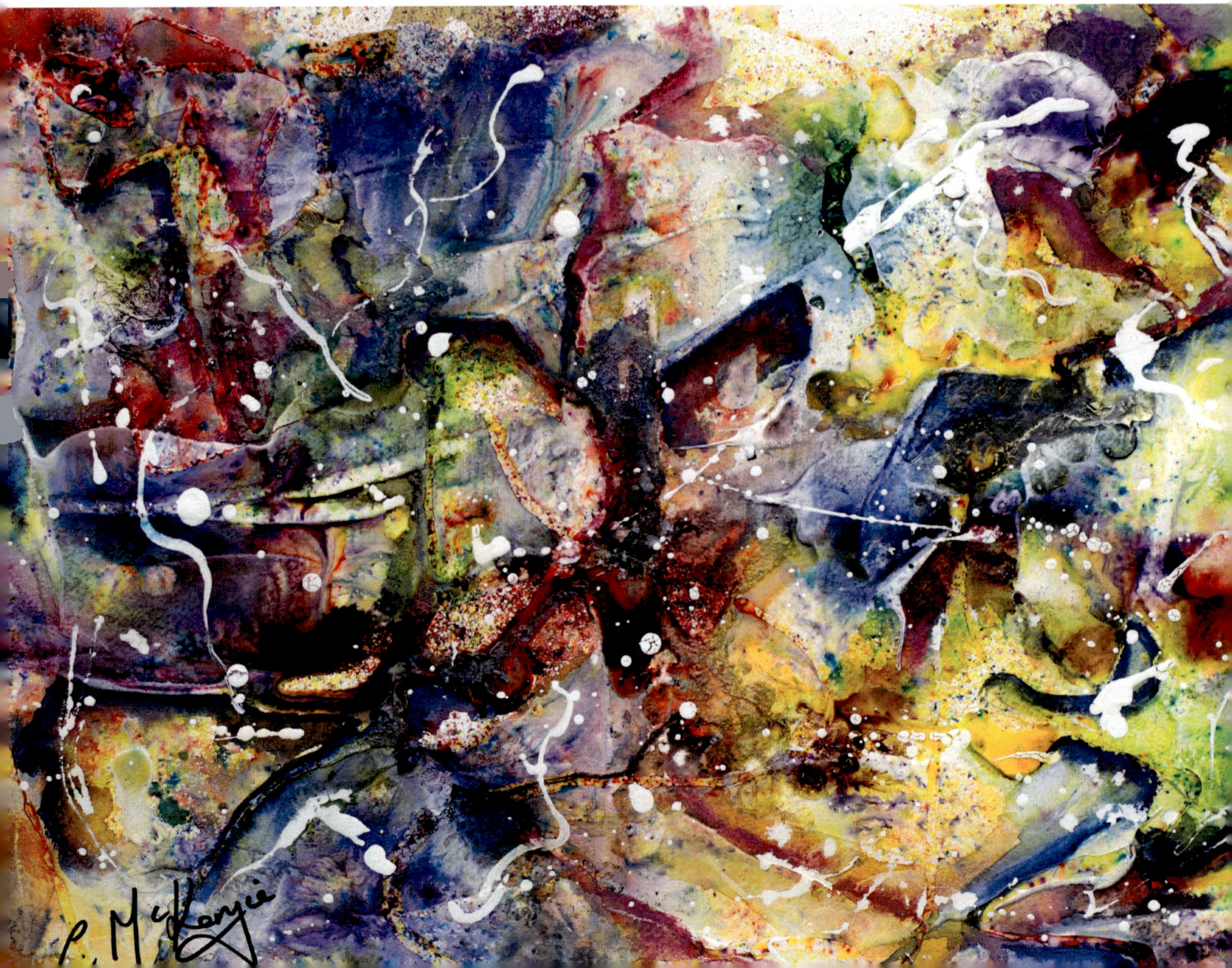

8 : ADDITIONAL PROJECTS

I hope you have enjoyed working through the different techniques and demonstrations throughout this book. I also hope what you have learned has enthused you to use Brusho for some of your own paintings, either as a sole medium in its own right, or as a component of other mixed media.

To conclude this book, I have included a few extra demonstration exercises that encompass some of the Brusho techniques already learned, and also to provide you with further inspiration for what can be achieved with these rather magical little pots of crystal colour.

The Enchanted Wood demonstration will appeal to all those people who love Brusho for it's vibrant bursts of rainbow colour.

Alternatively, why not try painting the same scene with some of the earth colours instead; Moss Green, Olive Green, Yellow Ochre, Burnt Sienna and perhaps a touch of Rose or Violet here and there.

The Two's Company demonstration uses a more subdued and limited palette of colour. But again, you could work through the demonstration using your own favourite colours.

The choice is yours — Beautiful Brilliant Brusho!

THE ENCHANTED WOOD

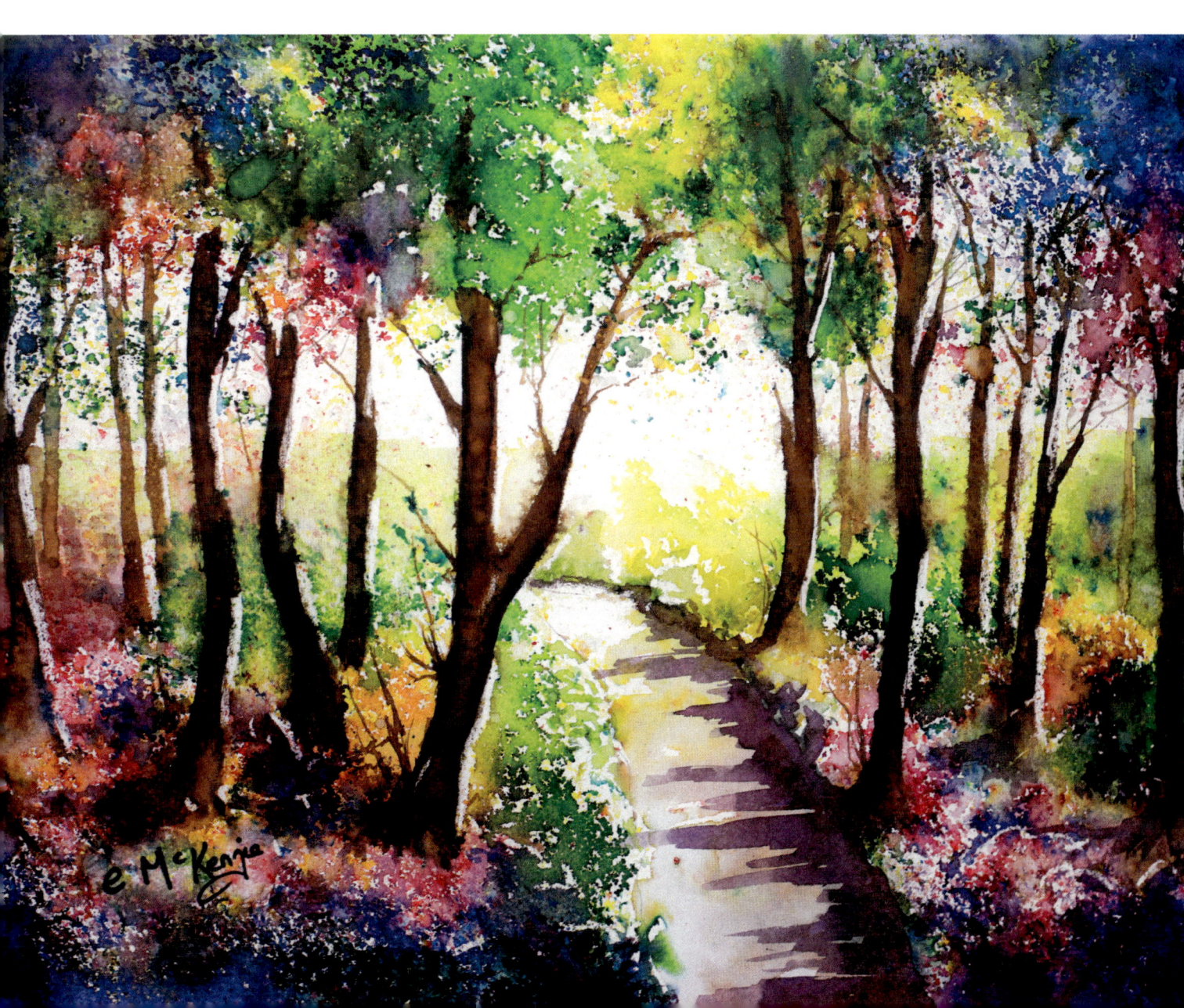

Demonstration

THE ENCHANTED WOOD

Busting the concept of the limited palette, this painting is an explosion of Brusho colour and fantasy. However, it's your painting, so feel free to be selective with your choice of colours – choose earthier ones if you prefer a more natural or subdued effect.

MATERIALS
Yellow
Orange
Dark Brown
Purple
Brilliant Red
Ultramarine
Leaf Green

1 Draw the basic outline of some trees in a forest glade – vary the shapes, sizes, and spaces between. You don't need to put in much detail, just their positions.
Draw a winding path that vanishes behind one of the trees.

Use a piece of wax to add in a few highlights on the right side of some of the tree trunks to show where the light is coming from – this will also help you to see where the trees are later.

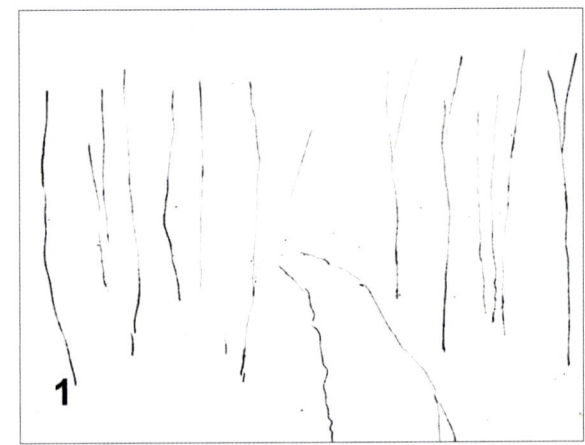

2 Mix some watery Yellow and Leaf Green in your palette. Starting just above the middle of the paper, paint a two-inch band of these colours to represent the distant foliage. Keep it light in tone, particularly just off centre.

Sprinkle some different colours across the foreground, missing out the path. It doesn't matter if a few stray speckles land on the path, but if you get too many, use a soft brush to brush them off.

Spritz lightly to retain texture.

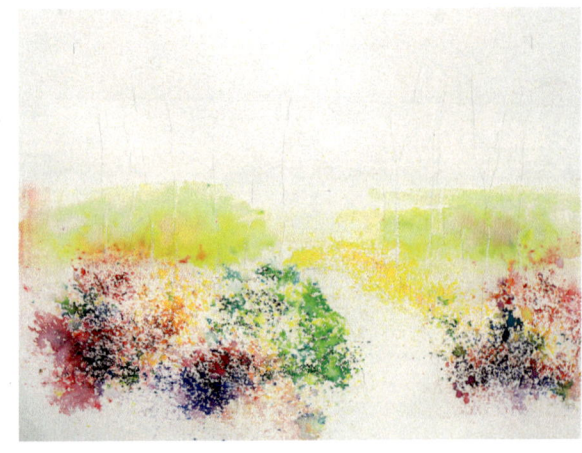

3 Sprinkle the same colours you used for the foreground across the treetops. Use darker colours for the undersides of the tree canopies and at the far left and right of the paper. Keep the central area lighter. (Don't worry about going over the tree trunks as these are going to be painted in a darker colour in the next step.)

Spritz lightly to retain texture.
Leave everything to dry.

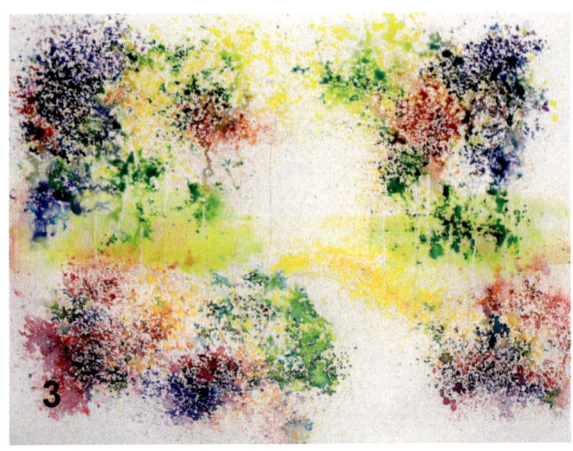

4 Using your pencil lines, as a guide paint the tree trunks and some of the larger branches with Dark Brown. While the paint is still wet add a mix of Ultramarine and Purple to the left side of the tree trunks and let this blend with the brown to give them form.

Use a rigger brush to paint in some of the smaller branches appearing in between the leaves.

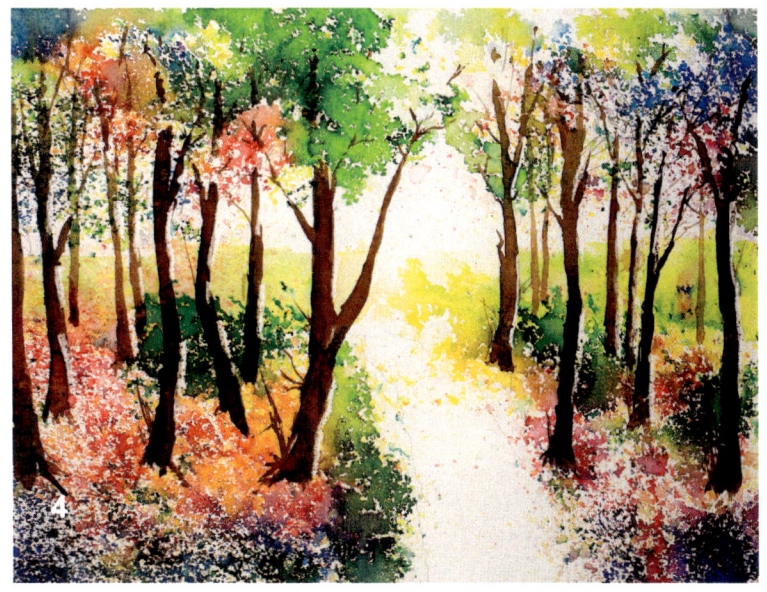

5 Using a wet brush gently wet the path area with horizontal strokes. The stray speckles that landed on it earlier should now reactivate and provide some colour. If not, mix some in your palette and paint it on. Keep the colour light in tone on the left side of the path, medium tone in the middle and darker at the right side.

Touch in a little darker colour along the right side of the path, letting this mingle into the foliage that runs alongside.

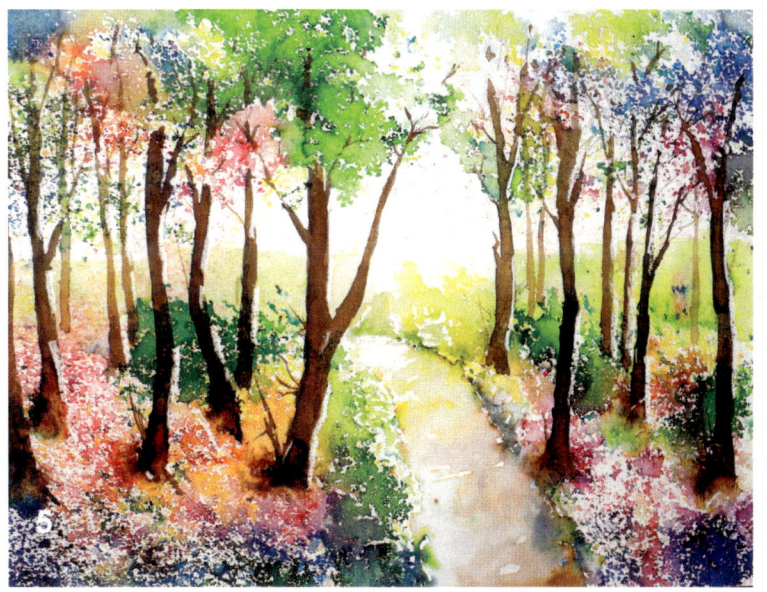

6 To complete the painting, mix some stronger tones of the same colours in your palette, then use the tip of your brush to add these colours to the tree shapes (to increase depth and contrast). Be careful not to lose all the texture you created earlier.

If there are any gaps in your tree canopies, you can always sprinkle on a little more Brusho and spritz lightly again. You can tell that I did exactly this because some of the tree trunks have gone a little 'fuzzy' when I spritzed again – I rather liked this effect – a good example of a 'happy accident'!

Do the same thing for the foliage in the foreground, particularly darkening the places where the tree trunks meet the ground so the trees look 'rooted'.

Leave to dry.

Finally mix some Ultramarine and Purple to make a dark bluey-purple for the shadows on the path. The light is coming from the right, so the tree shadows need to start at the bottom of the tree trunks on the right side of the path. Continue the shadows across the path, varying the spacing and tone.

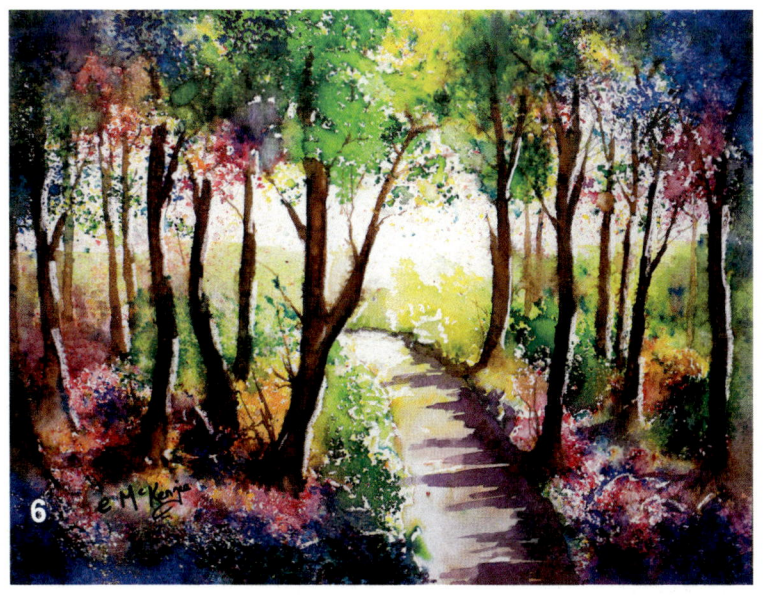

Demonstration
PRICKLE & SPIKE

This project Is a variation on one of my Gallery paintings in Chapter 2, Mrs Hedgehog and Quilliam, which I tackled in exactly the same way. I do enjoy painting these little chaps.

Reference photo

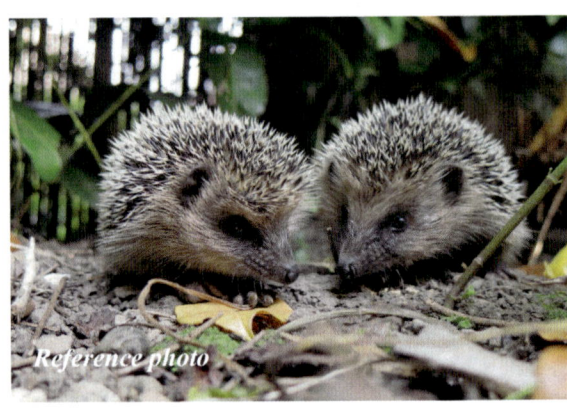

1 Draw the outline of the hedgehogs. I didn't mask the eyes, but now is the time to do it if you feel safer protecting them for later. There is no need to draw all the foreground detail as we are going to simplify it.

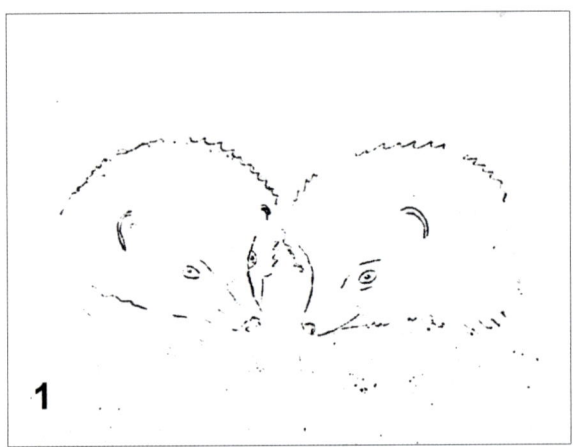

2 Mask the hedgehogs' faces with some paper towel to protect them. Sprinkle Yellow, Scarlet and a touch of Dark Brown on the bodies of the hedgehogs.
   Spritz lightly. Leave to dry.

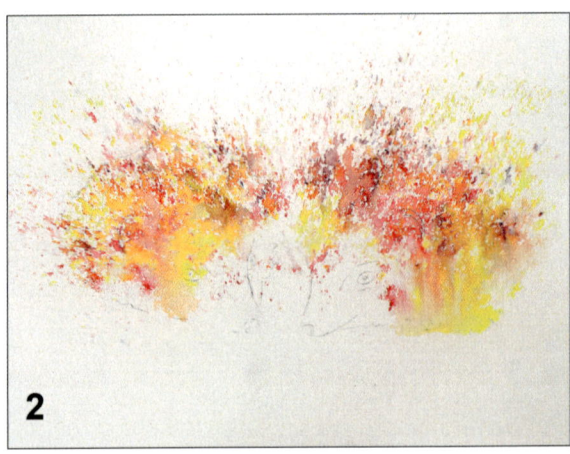

3 Use clear wax to preserve the outer ear shapes that are poking through the spikes.
   Sprinkle a little Dark Brown here and there and spritz again lightly. Use a rigger brush to flick some of the brown droplets so they resemble spikes.
   Mix some Dark Brown, and also a darker mix of Dark Brown with Ultramarine, in separate wells of your palette.
   Still using your rigger brush, and alternating the two brown colours you have just mixed, add more spikes to the bodies of the hedgehogs, softening these in at the base here and there.
   Also darken just behind the ears to make them more visible. Leave to dry.

4 Paint the faces of the hedgehogs with the same colours you used for their bodies, but dilute the pigment to lighten the tone especially around the snout area. Leave to dry.

Gently rub off the masking fluid from the eyes if you applied it earlier. Use a small brush to paint the eyes with Black, leaving tiny flecks of white paper for the catch lights.

Use black for the tip of the snout, blending this a little with a damp brush where it joins the snout so it doesn't look bolted on. Leave to dry

5 Protect the hedgehogs with some paper towel. Sprinkle Yellow, Scarlet and Dark Brown across the foreground area. Spritz lightly to retain a grassy, earthy texture.

6 Use the tip of a damp brush to join up some of the coloured droplets but be careful not to lose all of the lovely texture you have just created.

Add some shadow beneath the hedgehog bodies with a mix of Dark Brown and Purple.

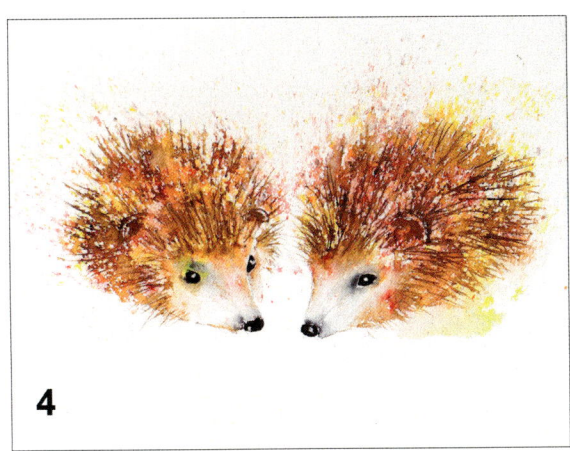

4

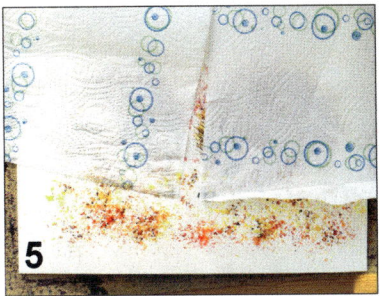

5

PRICKLE AND SPIKE

E McKenzie

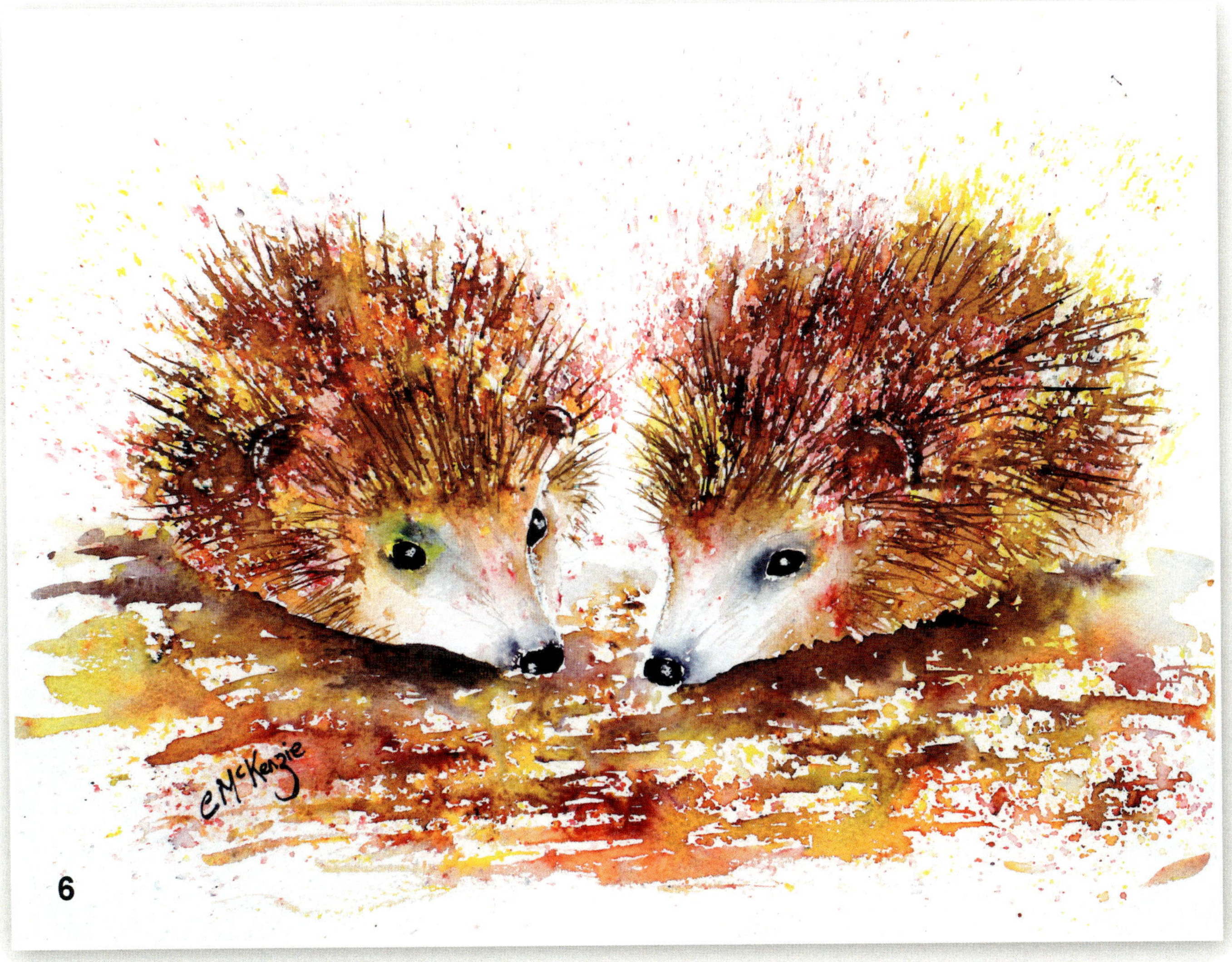

6

Demonstration

TWO'S COMPANY

Despite using a limited number of colours, this project puts vibrant colour into a rainy day painting. In fact, you can see that it wasn't actually raining at all on the reference photo that I took, but I thought the subject leant itself well to an umbrella scene and have used artistic licence to make it so.

MATERIALS
Black
Dark Brown
Ultramarine
Cobalt Blue or
Turquoise

Masking fluid
and/or clear wax

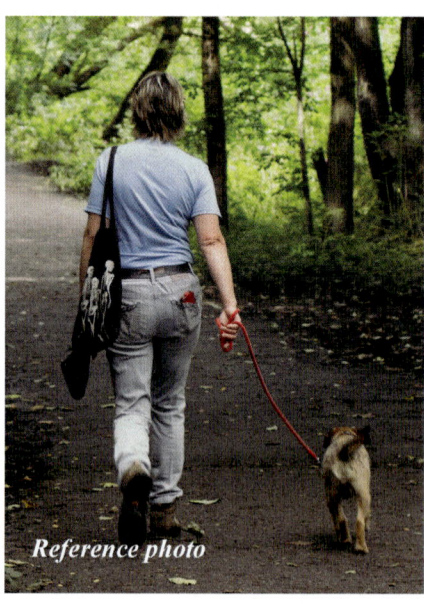

Reference photo

1

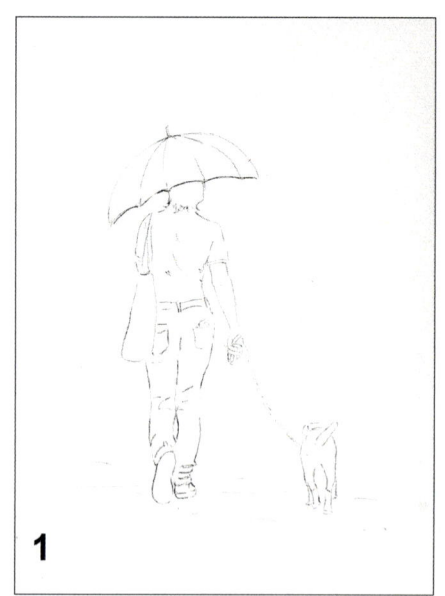

2

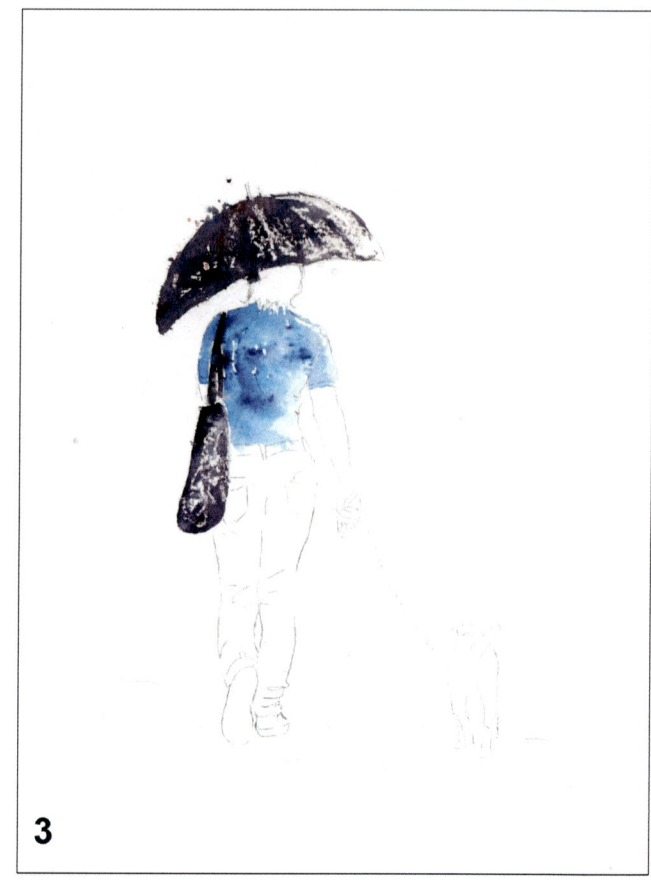

3

1 Draw the outline shapes of the woman and dog without going into too much detail. Use masking fluid to preserve white paper for the mobile phone in the woman's back jean's pocket, and also the dog's lead. (I forgot to do this and had to bleach out a small patch on the pocket later before I could re-paint the phone – this is one of Brusho's most useful features!). Use clear wax to scribble an abstract pattern on the woman's shoulder bag. The light is coming from the right, so also retain some white paper highlights on the right side of the umbrella, woman and dog.

2 Sprinkle some Black on the left side of the umbrella and spritz lightly. Use a damp brush to spread the paint in between the umbrella spokes. Mix some Black in your palette and paint the shoulder bag – the wax you scribbled on earlier will emerge now as a white pattern.

3 Sprinkle some Turquoise on the left side of the woman's t-shirt and use a damp brush to spread the paint across the t-shirt, adding more water at the right side to lighten the tone where the light is coming from. Try using the side of your brush as well as the tip to create interesting body shapes and suggest folds in the fabric.

4 Sprinkle and spritz some Ultramarine on the jeans, spread the paint as you did before with a damp brush, adding more water at the right side of each leg to lighten the tone. Change the angle of your brush marks to indicate creases in the fabric. Don't worry if you get some stray speckles of paint on other areas of the paper, it helps to create some unity in the painting and give a looser look. A few wonky lines here and there add to the liveliness of the finished painting – you don't want it to look as if you've coloured in the lines of a child's drawing book

5 Paint the little dog with Dark Brown, again keeping the tone lighter towards the right and angling your brush to create the shapes and texture.   Add a little brown splatter to make it appear as if the dog is shaking some rain out of its fur. Use a watery mix of Dark Brown to paint the hair and the boots, when this is nearly dry use the point of your brush to add some lines and texture to the hair in a stronger brown mix. Also add some Dark Brown mixed with a touch of Black to the undersides of the boots and at the top where they meet the jeans.

6 Mix some Red, Yellow and a little Blue in your palette to paint the skin tones on the arm. Add some more creases and folds on the t-shirt and jeans with the same colours you used to paint them before.

Mask the woman and the dog with some paper towel to protect them from the next step. Sprinkle all the colours you've used so far across your sky area but don't use too much Dark Brown or Black. Keep the Black mainly around the right side of the umbrella so that the light highlights stand out.

Use your water sprayer to blend some of the colours, and tilt the paper diagonally to move the colour across the sky - try to keep the central area light. Drop in more colour with your brush if you need to emphasise any particular areas, such as around the umbrella. Leave this to dry.

Paint the reflections of the woman and the dog in the foreground. Reflections are darker where they begin and fade away the further they get from their subject. In order to make the reflections look watery, use a damp brush to soften the edges of the reflections so they bleed away into the white paper.

When the reflections are dry, repeat what you did for the sky to the foreground but this time tilt the paper horizontally to create linear marks – you can also use the point of your brush to drag some stronger linear marks if you need to. Use your brush to paint in a couple of abstract shapes in the distance to give the painting some depth. Leave to dry.

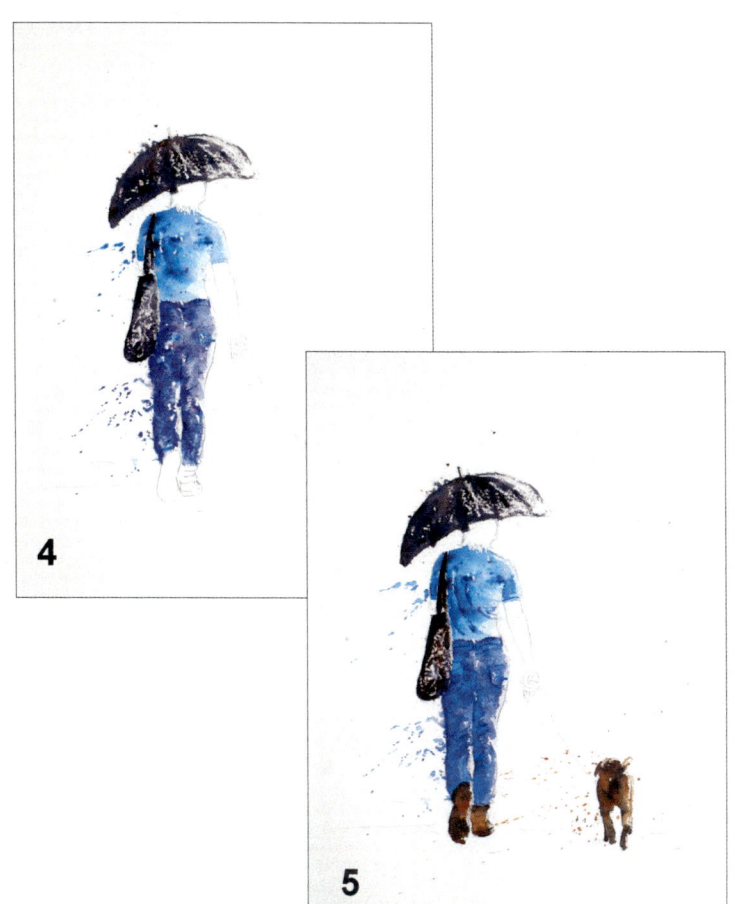

4

5

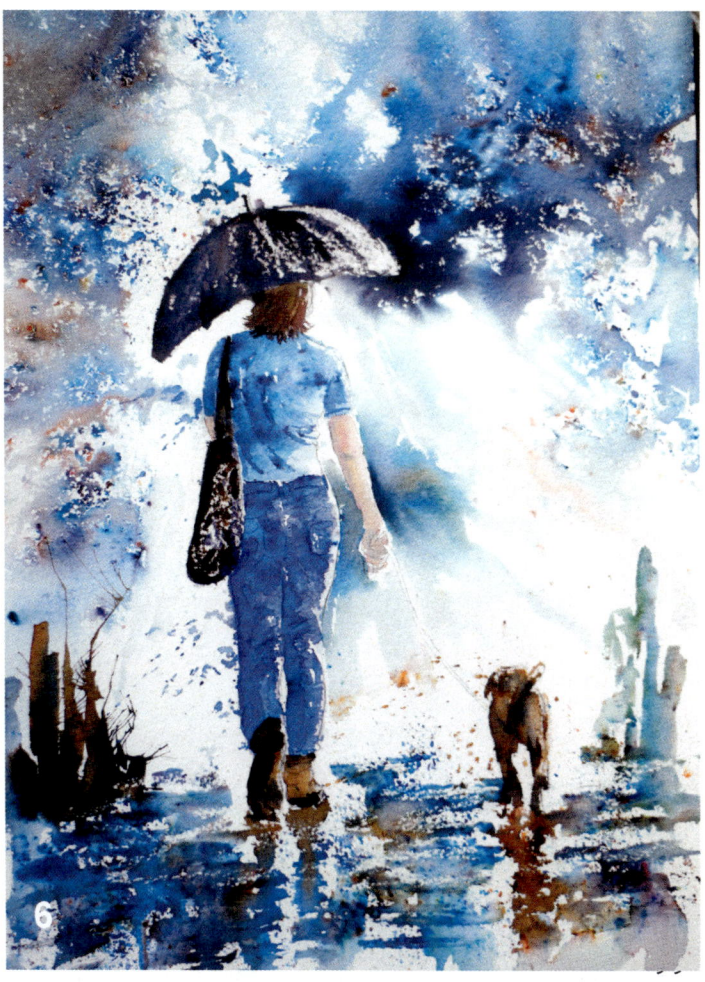

6

7 Remove the masking fluid from the mobile phone and dog lead. Use Brilliant Red to paint the mobile phone and the dog lead, adding a few splatters for raindrops. (I had forgotten to protect these with masking fluid earlier, so had to bleach out the phone area and let it dry before painting over with red.) Finally, paint the reflection of the red lead in the foreground.

TWO'S COMPANY

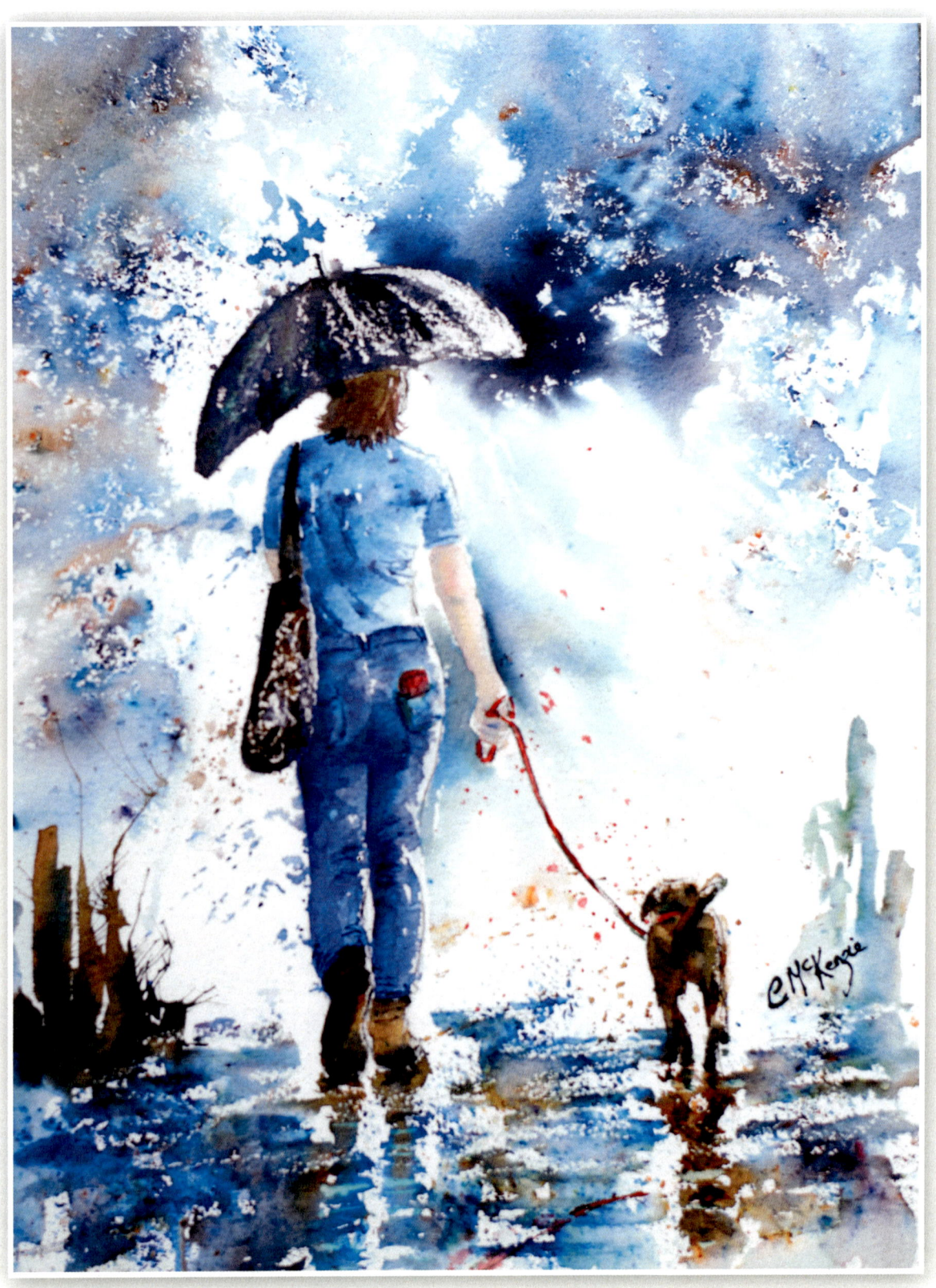

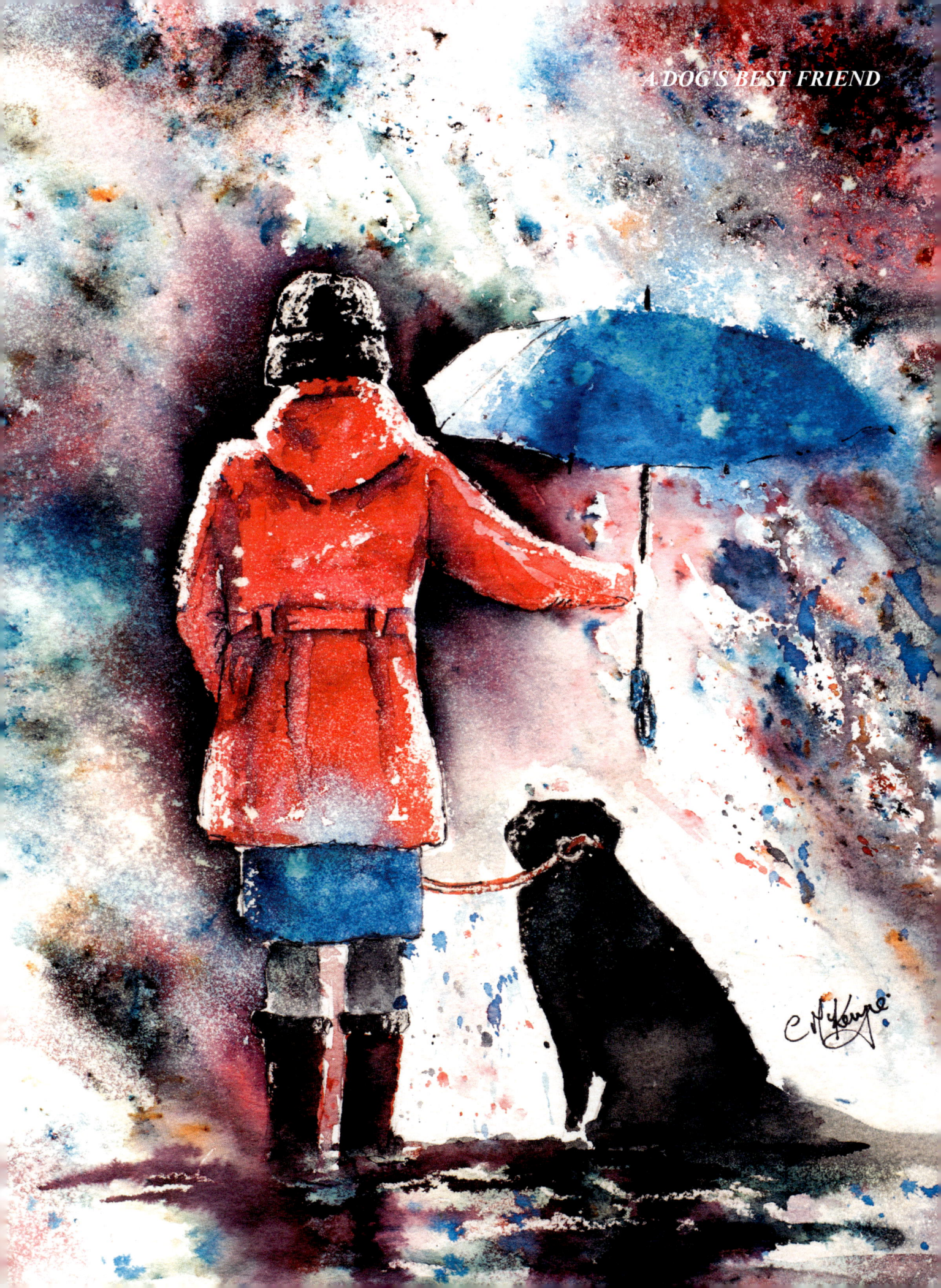

A DOG'S BEST FRIEND

ABOUT THE AUTHOR

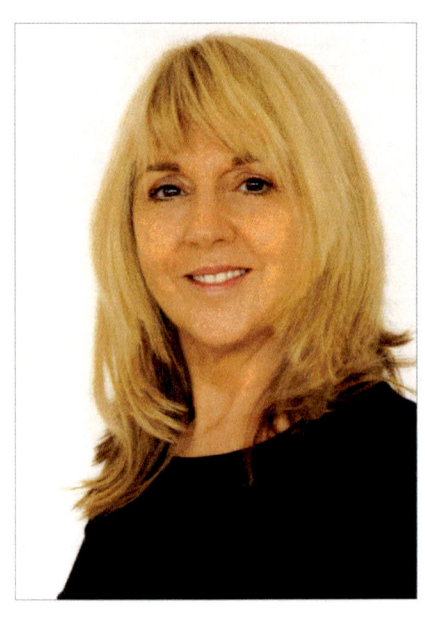

Born and raised in West Yorkshire, England, Carrie McKenzie lives with her family in Halifax. Her home was extended to include her beloved art studio in which she works as a freelance artist.

Carrie has trained with some of the leading national and internationally acclaimed artists, who have influenced the development of her own personal style. "I believe it is important for an artist to keep learning and refreshing ideas – it's an exciting journey!" She paints in oils, acrylics, pen and ink, and mixed media but leans toward water-based mediums of Watercolour and Brusho for the magical effects they produce when paint and water mingle on the paper to shape the image in exquisite ways.

Fascinated at the play of light and colour that completely changes the appearance of the environment, its people and wildlife, she believes this to be one of the most transformational aspects of any painting, whether it be landscapes, people, nature or still life.

Carrie is constantly striving to reflect the impact of light and colour into her own work. She is keen to experiment with all sorts of art mediums and tools, but feels her biggest inspiration comes from the beautiful and fascinating world around us.

Her artwork hovers towards illustrative and contemporary, rather than photo-realism, as she continues to explore expressionistic loose styles, which bring out the colour, light and atmosphere or mood of her subjects.

"We often see things differently in our mind's eye than with our real eye. It is the uniqueness of the image in every person's mind eye that creates such a wonderful array of individual and distinctive art."

In addition to original works of art, she offers premium prints and greeting cards. Her paintings are exhibited regularly at a number of galleries and venues across West Yorkshire and her artwork has been selected for collections in UK, Europe, USA, Australia and New Zealand.

A showcase of Carrie's work can be viewed on her Website: www.carriemckenzieart.co.uk or her Facebook page: www.facebook.com/Carrie.McKenzie.Art

Beautiful Brilliant Brusho!

INDEX

Brusho® is manufactured by Colourcraft (C&A) Ltd, Unit 5, 555 Carlisle St E, Sheffield S4 8DT
https://www.colourcraftltd.com

Made in the USA
Monee, IL
03 October 2022